PRAISE FOR

A PITCHER'S STORY

SELECTED AS ONE OF THE TOP TEN
SPORTS BOOKS OF THE YEAR BY *BOOKLIST*

"[A PITCHER'S STORY] is further proof that Roger Angell is the best baseball writer of our time—maybe ever. And Angell's graceful prose and passionate fandom coupled with Cone's brooding insight into his own miseries has produced one of the most memorable baseball volumes ever. . . . This book has the texture of a great novel as Cone endures more and more pain, physical and psychic, in the increasingly faint hope that he might coax just a little more out of his tattered shoulder."

—Newsweek

"Angell uses plain, graceful prose to tell the complex tale of Cone's season without ever falling into glib psychobabble or wormy sentimentality. The warts in the portrait are given their proper place. But David Cone is always firmly at the heart of Angell's tale. And reality allows both men one final moment of sheer redemptive magic."

—Pete Hamill, *New York Times Book Review*

"Unlike so many baseball biographies that are painted with a broad stroke—whole seasons dismissed with a Pollock-like flourish—A PITCHER'S STORY illustrates that Angell is a pointillist. It's his tiny, telling observations that make this book work."

—Washington Post Book World

"What had been planned as a book about baseball mastery turned into a book about baseball's difficulty. It's a better story, and shows off the talents of these formidable batterymates: Cone's focus and determination, Angell's ability to evoke the way that, sooner or later, the game breaks your heart."

—The New Yorker

"You could not ask for a better pairing, and Angell delivers the goods. . . . A PITCHER'S STORY can't help but make anyone who reads it an admirer of Roger Angell and David Cone. It's one of the best baseball books of this and many seasons."

—*Boston Magazine*

"There's lots of inside baseball. . . . A terrific book."

—*Tampa Tribune-Times*

"A brilliant book about baseball and about pitching. . . . Angell, perhaps the best baseball writer of our time and one of the best writers period, uses every tool at his command to tell Cone's story; it is beautifully constructed, carefully thought out, and elegantly composed. Sobering and enlightening and funny and real, Angell's account makes us understand why Cone went to Boston, and we hope that will work for him."

—*Booklist* (starred review)

"Angell not only details Cone's highs and lows on and off the playing field, but does a superb job in recording Cone's anxieties and frustrations as the two men move through the disappointing 2000 season. The combination of Angell's love and knowledge of baseball and his truly fascinating subject makes for another win in Angell's long list of hits about the American pastime."

—*Publishers Weekly*

A
PITCHER'S
STORY

Innings with David Cone

Roger Angell

WARNER BOOKS

An AOL Time Warner Company

Copyright © 2001 by Roger Angell
All rights reserved.

Warner Books, Inc., 1271 Avenue of the Americas, New York, NY 10020
Visit our Web site at www.twbookmark.com.

Ⓦ An AOL Time Warner Company

Printed in the United States of America
Originally printed in hardcover by Warner Books, Inc.

First Trade Printing: April 2002
10 9 8 7 6 5 4 3 2 1

ISBN: 0-446-52768-8 (hardcover)
Library of Congress Control Number: 2001087327
ISBN: 0-446-67846-5 (pbk.)

Text design by Stanley S. Drate/Folio Graphics Co. Inc.
Cover design by Flag
Front cover photograph by Peter Griffith / Masterfile
Author photograph by Joanne Savio

Contents

A
PITCHER'S
STORY

Perfection

The shortstop, Orlando Cabrera, up at bat for the third time, swings and lifts a little foul fly off to the left of the infield. The pitcher, hurrying off the mound, watches the ball anxiously, pointing up at it, and shoots a glance over at his third baseman. Yes, this ball will be caught—it's the last out—and when the pitcher, David Cone, takes in the moment he sinks to his knees with his head flung back and his hands up above his ears. It's over. In an instant he will be rushed and ganged by his team-mates, converging from the field and flooding across from the dugout, but the scene—the ball in the air and the pitcher unex-pectedly falling into an attitude of worship—is already fixed in baseball time, there with Carlton Fisk dancing up the first-base line and gesturing wildly to keep his shot fair; Willie Mays with his back to us, looking up over his head to gather Vic Wertz's drive at the Polo Grounds center-field wall; or, for that matter, Don Larsen pitching to Dale Mitchell here at Yankee Stadium (the old Stadium then), with the numbers, all zeroes, enormous on the black scoreboard behind him. Larsen is back today, as it happens; so is his catcher in that game, Yogi Berra. This stuff can't be happening.

Cabrera, the ninth batter in the order for the Montreal Ex-

pos, who have just been beaten by the Yankees, 6–0, in this perfect game—no hits, no runs, nobody on base—has foreseen his
role in this freeze-frame as far back as the sixth inning, when,
looking at the man on the mound and then counting the deplet-
ing outs and innings ahead, he sensed that he could be the final
batter of the day. And Cone, for his part, will come to believe
that he unconsciously picked up that ecstatic, down-on-his-
knees-and-head-to-heaven victory posture from watching some
center-court Wimbledon winner on television, long ago, and
tucking the picture away in his mind. "You always wonder how
you'll look when the time comes," he says. "Players talk about
stuff like this among themselves, believe it or not. You want to
be ready." He can't decide whether his model is John McEnroe
or an earlier, lesser-known Spanish star, Manuel Santana, whom
he would have seen winning Wimbledon.

Cone, one could say, was ready and then some. His coup,
which he pitched at the Stadium on July 18, 1999, is only the six-
teenth perfect game in a century of major-league ball, but was
also his own first no-hitter of any description. On three occa-
sions in his fourteen-year career in the majors, he had carried a
no-hitter into the eighth inning, only to be foiled. He remembers
those scenes, too—in particular a wrong-field dribbler cued toward third with one out in the eighth by a Houston batter named
DiStefano in 1992, when Cone was pitching for the Mets; the ball
died just in front of Dave Magadan's frantic late charge from
third. A Mets teammate of Cone's, the great reliever John Franco,
thinks back to that injustice—and to DiStefano's lifetime .228
batting record—every time Cone's name comes up in conversation. "I was even in school with the guy," he says disgustedly.
"Benny DiStefano, behind me at Lafayette High in Brooklyn, and
he kills Coney that way." He could be talking about Lee Harvey
Oswald. The real enemy here—for Franco and every pitcher—is
luck, which stalks the field in every low-scoring game, guiding
this rocketed line drive into the third baseman's mitt or nudging
that bloop into an unreachable few inches of terrain, but which
perversely must be given a secret save in every no-hitter.

The ache of the ancient DiStefano wound comes also from Franco's admiration for Cone's heart and stuff. "He's a Picasso out there," he once said to me. Now John can wipe the crime from his recollection. Hearing about Cone's perfect game down in Baltimore, where the Mets are playing the Baltimore Orioles, he asks team public-relations director Jay Horwitz to have a bottle of Dom Perignon rushed to his friend.

Another pal and former pitching teammate, David Wells, who had thrown a perfect game for the Yankees at the Stadium a bit more than a year before—his and Larsen's, which came in the World Series of 1956, are the Yankees' only previous perfectos—gets the news at the SkyDome in Toronto, where he watches the final outs on the tube and manages to reach Cone by telephone in the Yankee clubhouse. Traded away to the Blue Jays over the winter, the Boomer is as happy about the feat as anyone in New York. "My goose bumps are bigger than yours," he says to Cone. "Welcome to the club." He promises to fly down that night, to celebrate with David. Maybe they'll drink Franco's champagne.

No-hitters are spare by nature because of what doesn't happen, and a perfect game almost Puritan, so the sense of release and jubilation over Cone's accomplishment extended everywhere in baseball that day. Waking up the next morning, I pictured how it would be talked about in the clubhouses around the leagues, with Cone's fellow-professionals arriving for work and telling each other how he had looked on the late news, down on his knees that way, and then turning his face toward the fans. Baseball's ceaselessly woven network of circumstances and conditions can be stopped at a moment's notice, frozen, as it were, and turned into lore—where the ball came down, what the count was, what the weather was, what the standings were, who was in the on-deck circle, where we were sitting in the stands, or how we got the news watching at home. I have been following the game for more than seventy years and writing about it for almost forty, and I have my own little store of where and when. Mention Bobby Thomson's homer in 1951,

Bucky Dent's deadly little flyer into the screen at the shadow-struck Fenway Park in 1978, or how New York sounded—that vast murmur across the parks and streets—at the moment when the Mets beat the Astros, down in Houston, after sixteen innings, to win the league championship in 1986, and I'll tell you how I felt at the instant, who was near me, and how we hugged or groaned or yelled. Cone's game fits in here nicely, with the kick this time coming not from significance—the game meant nothing in the standings to either team just then—but from what I already knew about him as a pitcher and a man on that broiling Sunday.

There is also the matter of perfection, which baseball offers as a possibility in every game but at such odds that it's never mentioned. It doesn't cross your mind if you're a fan or a writer pencilling the lineups into your scorecard, even though those empty white boxes on the page sometimes whisper about an elusive little clarity that might lie out there beyond the accumulation of pitches and outs, grounders and base runners that will tell a game's story when it's done. *Could be*—but the thought flies out of your head because it's so crazy. "Nothing went through my mind until the seventh inning," Yogi Berra said this time, afterward. Not another Yogi gem but close enough, and, as always, you knew what he meant.

Nothing was going through my mind that Sunday except the weather. I didn't have tickets, but the idea of seeing Yogi back—it was going to be his Day at Yankee Stadium, with plaques and platitudes celebrating the official termination of a fourteen-year falling-out between the great Yankee catcher and his bygone boss, George Steinbrenner—had once tempted me. But forget baseball, I decided, it's too hot. This would be another beast of a day, the third or fourth in a row with the temperature in the upper nineties and the humidity nearing a hundred per cent—the same sweaty blanketing we'd gone through in New York for a week at the beginning of the month, when there had been power blackouts and more news stories and sombre television panels about global warming. Now another dark cloud had come down. Two days before, the small plane in which young John F. Kennedy, Jr., and his wife, Carolyn Bessette Kennedy, and her sister were flying to Martha's Vineyard had disappeared into the night waters near Gay Head, and this morning's *Times* said that debris from the plane had washed ashore. As it happened, I had seen him up at the Stadium at a game a couple of days earlier—and so had Cone—which made this story even harder to take in. A young prince of the city gone. This felt like the sixties—something was broken, and not just the weather. In the middle of the night, the expression *worse luck* had stuck itself in my mind.

I said goodbye to my wife, Carol, after breakfast and took myself down to my office, on Forty-third Street, where it would be cool if nothing else. I was packing up there—*The New Yorker*, where I work, was about to move quarters to the new Condé Nast Building, over in Times Square. I hated the whole idea, but an empty Sunday given to file drawers and reading and throwing away ancient letters suited my self-pity. By the time I made it back home again, in midafternoon, there had been showers, but the doorways and store windows and side-walks in my neighborhood threw off an implacable glaze of heat. At least the power hadn't gone out in our building this time.

As I let myself into the cool bedroom, I heard Carol say, "You're not going to *believe* this!" She gestured at the television screen, where I saw David Cone oddly propped in the back of the Yankee dugout, with a towel in one hand. His face was flushed and his eyes in some other galaxy. He had just gone through the sixth inning, retiring the last three young Montreal batters in five pitches. He was working on a perfect game. There had been only one close play so far, Carol said—a running, rolling catch by Paul O'Neill in right field, early on. There had been a rain delay—the station had put on a rerun of "The Simp-sons"—and Cone had kept loose tossing with a ballboy in front of the stands. I sat down on the foot of the bed.

I'm not sure I moved from there for the hour or so that it took to get the job done. Cone, hunched with a ferocious intent, worked quickly, delivering the strikes to the outer corners and striding backward up the mound as he took the return peg from his catcher, Joe Girardi. You could almost see his mind seizing and shaping the next pitch and the one after that. "He knows it! He knows it!" said the telecaster, Tim McCarver. "A no-hitter on Yogi Berra Day—c'mon, no way!"

He and his sidekick Bobby Murcer were not giving in to the superstition that forbids mention of a no-hitter when it is in progress—a great step forward, as far as I was concerned—but the day and the setting had taken on an eerie quality. None of these Montreal batters (who had arrived by bus from Baltimore, late the night before) had ever seen David Cone before, much less batted against him. This two-game interdivisional series had opened on a Sunday afternoon: unheard of. The fans, squinting in the heat, were in a gabble of anxiety, and there were glimpses of Larsen, tucked away in the back of a box, looking down at the field with an expression I couldn't read. We were in the seventh, then quickly out of it. Cone, with one eye just visible under the brim of his cap, exuded malice as he peered in at a pinch-hitter, James Mouton. Then he struck him out, swinging, with a slider way away. Fans marking up the K's put up another image of Yogi Bear on the facing below them. *Yogi Bear?* —they'd lost their minds. Oh, yes, for Yogi Day. I was losing my mind, more likely. "C'mon, c'mon," I whispered to myself when the Yankees came up to bat. Come on and make an out, get this thing over.

Into the eighth now, and Carol and I let out a "Yes!" or "Wow!"—maybe we jumped up and high-fived, too—when Yankee second baseman Chuck Knoblauch darted to his right to grab a ground ball smoked up the middle by Jose Vidro (who *were* these guys?) and threw him out at first. This last part, the peg, was what mattered, since Knoblauch had been tortured even by his routine throws to first in recent weeks, producing off-line bounced throws or halfhearted lobs while he battled to unknot this kink in his unconscious. This time, he took four quick braking steps, got his feet right as he turned, and fired the bullet.

The rest was impressionistic: a last in-running sprint and half-bobble by Ricky Ledee in the ninth as he held on to Ryan McGuire's pop fly to left, for the twenty-sixth out, and then Cabrera and glory. David Cone, carried off toward the dugout in ritual fashion, was put down at last and shared a long embrace with Girardi. Interviews and recaps and reruns followed. Cone had required only eighty-eight pitches, it came out, and never went to ball three against a batter. I couldn't stop smiling, and neither could Murcer and McCarver, together in their shirt-sleeves again before the sign-off. "I don't know about you," Bobby said, "but I'm not ready to go off the air yet."

"I'm not leaving," Tim said. "We'll just stay here."

Something had changed the weather. Who better than Cone?

Early February in Tampa, and I am tailing a gray Porsche Carrera in a middle lane on North Dale Mabry when a white Mustang convertible comes rocketing up on my left at a red light, brakes sharply, and stations itself next to the Porsche, but a foot or two astern, in full view of its left rearview mirror. The Mustang driver slips out of gear and guns his engine invitingly— *racka-trooom!* Hey, Mister Important Wheels, let's get it on! When the light goes green, the Porsche eases forward gently, at the same pace as the traffic in the other lanes, and the driver of the Mustang—a kid, by the look of him—now shoots up level with the Porsche and aims a disdainful look at the guy behind the wheel. Then he looks again, a double take, and changes his mind. He drops back, easing off until he's behind me, and becomes part of the traffic. The man driving the Porsche has been staring straight ahead all this time, but the kid has taken in the pale, calm face under the curved cap brim, a downturned mouth, and an angle of chin and shoulders that brings a click of recognition. This backing off, the instant-grownup effect, isn't about the comparative prices or r.p.m.s of the two sports cars; it's that the young driver has seen some established will power sitting over there and has drawn the proper conclusion: David Cone isn't here to play.

I am here watching highway psychodramas in my red Hertz midsize, because David Cone has been leading the way to a Cuban lunch shop, where the two of us will have a bite to eat, and because tailing him is going to be more or less my plan for the next eight months. I have been watching Cone pitch, off and on, for fourteen years now—the first writing of mine about him I can find was when he smacked a double for the New York Mets, in an early-season game against the Pirates in 1987, and was out at third base, stretching—and have lately decided to pay more attention. Success is one of the reasons, to be sure: I'm just another writer chasing another winner. Cone's hundred and eighty lifetime victories put him sixth among active pitchers, while his 2,420 strikeouts make him the third among all current practitioners, and his lifetime earned-run average of 3.21 ties him for fourth place (with the Braves' Tom Glavine) among all pitchers who worked in the nineteen-nineties, behind Greg Maddux, his Yankee teammate Roger Clemens, and Randy Johnson. In 1991, he struck out nineteen batters in a game against the Phillies, tying a league record held by Steve Carlton and Tom Seaver. He has racked up two twenty-victory seasons, and he captured the Cy Young Award as the best pitcher in his league in 1994. He has been a significant starter with four different major-league clubs—the Mets, the Toronto Blue Jays, the Kansas City Royals, and the Yankees (with two separate tenures at K.C. and Toronto)—and has performed obdurately and sometimes brilliantly in nineteen post-season games, including the World Series, in which he is 2–0 in five starts and twenty-nine and a third innings, with an earned-run average of 2.15. His team has won every World Series game in which he pitched.

Cone's record, I have noticed, escapes the faint tedium that can attend the numbers put up by implacably triumphant pitchers, since it includes so many entertaining oddities and spectacular disappointments and crashes. When he dropped games to Toronto and then Baltimore in September, 1998, he ended a string of ninety-six consecutive starts without back-to-back losses. He is tied for second in this semi-obscure category, four shy of the one hundred established by Firpo Marberry, a durable right-hander who toiled in the American League in the twenties and thirties, mostly for the Senators. I saw Marberry pitch a couple of times when I was a kid. And Cone's 20–7 pitching record in 1998, coming a full decade after his 20–3 for the Mets, marked the longest stretch between twenty-game seasons for any pitcher in major-league history. The previous holder of this title, Jim Kaat, now an esteemed broadcaster with the Yankees, had gone seven summers between his 25–13 in 1966 and 21–13 in '74, and when he came over to congratulate Cone for his feat (if that's what it was) he said, "Listen, I've always wondered about this. Was this a record or was I just horseshit all that time?"

I hadn't thought about Marberry for years, until he resurfaced in the Cone annals. Now I'm thinking of giving the name to the next cat or kitten to come into our house—"Here, kitty. Here, Firpo." My lately deceased smooth fox terrier, Willie, was named after Willie Stargell, the great Pirate slugger, and he lasted for sixteen years. The dog, I mean, not the Pirate. Stargell played for twenty-one years and went into the Hall of Fame. Where is the Dog Hall of Fame, I sometimes wonder. How many cats or dogs get named for major-league players nowadays? I know a serious Red Sox fan who tried to name a new family dog Yaz, for Carl Yastrzemski, after failing to persuade his wife to bestow the honor on their firstborn son. She nixed the pooch, too. But I do recall two or three cats named Mookie, back in the eighties, when the Mookster was at his peak with the Mets. End of digression—except that there *are* no digressions in baseball, where everything connects to everything else.

Back in May of '99, I wrote out a little time line I'd been putting together in my head and gave it to David Cone in the clubhouse:

Six Degrees of Separation

David Cone (1986–) pitched against
Nolan Ryan (1966–93), who was a teammate of
Frank Robinson (1956–76), who played against
Stan Musial (1941–63), who played against
Mel Ott (1926–47), who played with
Rogers Hornsby (1915–37), who batted against
Christy Mathewson (1900–1916)

Cone glanced at it and said, "Hey!," then folded it and tucked it away in the top shelf of his locker. The next day, he thanked me and said that he'd never thought of his time in the show in those terms. But Cone is a computer hacker as well as a polite guy, and I doubt that I'd surprised him. Players who last for a few seasons come to understand that even a single major-league batter faced or a lone at-bat in the majors connects them to something fixed and orderly; they're in the annals, and can now be found in the next edition of *The Baseball Encyclopedia* or punched up at TotalBaseball.com, or at Cooperstown.

At the same time I gave Cone his slip, I handed a slightly different one to Roger Clemens. It also took him back in six steps to Mathewson, the ur-hurler, but with Robin Yount, Red Schoendienst, and Grover Cleveland Alexander replacing some of the stepping stones in the Cone saga. The Rocket never responded, but I persist in a belief that connection is one of the prime sensuous attractions of baseball. You first notice this as a kid, on the day when a glimmering perception of the interconnectedness of today's names and batting averages and line scores and box scores—and all yesterday's, too, and others five years or five decades gone—suddenly sweeps over you in a rush, like the dawning of sex. And if you've stayed on as a fan you feel it on mornings when you wake up and discover that without trying you've seen McGwire and Brett and Ott, Koufax and Yaz, Mickey Lolich and Mickey Cochrane, Willie Mays and Carl Hubbell and the Babe, not to mention, oh . . . Ray Oyler and Oil Can Boyd.

Baseball shrinks time and makes it handier, and gives you a little clap on the back along the way.

Cone has agreed, for his own reasons, to let me hang around with him during the coming season, and, for my part, I'm happy to be watching and talking with someone at his stage of a great career as he sets about winning again—winning when it's work, with hard days and nights to get through, and times when the fastball is snoozing and the slider has gone off to the dentist or to the races. Cone and I aren't too different in some ways. Neither of us knows how this will work. "Here's the deal—I just figured it out," I said to David a day or two ago. "My brain and your arm are the same age. Let's do it."

He laughed, a little. David likes to control the situation—it's his primary trait—and he doesn't make a conclusion or even agree to a joke until he's worked it over in his mind. This is evasive but tough. He is hard on himself and scouts old ground, particularly his losses, with unpitying zeal. He wants a better result next time.

Cone's most bruising career setback to date remains the five runs he gave up to the Dodgers in the first two innings of the second game of the 1988 National League Championship Series, in an eventual loss that led, in time, to the Mets' shocking dismissal by a team they were expected to dominate. Cone also walked in the tying run in the eighth inning of the fifth and final divisional playoff game between the Yankees and the Mariners, at the Kingdome in 1995 (his first year with the Yankees), permitting the Seattles to draw even in the series in which they had trailed from the outset; no one was entirely surprised when they scored two runs in the eleventh and eliminated the Yankees.

Defeat is a form of silence—we don't like to linger over it—but again in Cone's case the bad news often has an added twist or flair that gets your attention. As the young ace of the overpowering 1988 Mets team—he was 20–3 that year—he had agreed to have his byline appear over an unfortunate ghosted column in the *News* that taunted the Dodgers before that second playoff game and sparked their uprising. (More about this is to be told here.) Even the base on balls in Seattle didn't go away quickly, because Cone had chosen to throw a split-finger pitch to an innocuous pinch-hitter, Doug Strange, on a full count, instead of the expected and safer fastball—a choice he will defend to this day—but lost the gamble. Never mind that Seattle then went on to lose to the Indians in the American League Championships. The Mariners' sudden glory in this, their first post-season effort after nineteen years of relentless mediocrity, was a populist triumph that kept the Seattle franchise in town. It was also a huge boost for the new and widely disparaged extra tier of playoff games (which had allowed the Yankees and Mariners to meet in the first place), and a television godsend for baseball itself at the end of two unhappy, strike-shortened seasons. All this, one could say, from a base on balls.

Just the other day, I told Cone that I'd been thinking back to 1995, too, and that ball four to Doug Strange. Murray Chass, the *Times* baseball pundit, had said to me recently that he'd run into David at a Players Association executive-board meeting in Florida, nearly two months after the game, and found that David was still brooding about the pitch.

"It took me forever to get over that," David said. "I couldn't sleep. I almost didn't go out of my house for a couple of weeks after. I'd thrown a hundred and forty-six pitches in the game up to that point, and I had nothing left, but I was still sure that was the right call. I just didn't execute. Maybe I'm stubborn, but I have this conviction that I should be able to deliver any pitch in any situation."

He looked stricken, even now. "I'll never forget that flight home," he said. "My catcher, Mike Stanley, kept telling me it was his fault for calling the pitch, but I wouldn't let him get away with it. Buck Showalter, the manager, must have known that he was finished with the Yankees after the loss, and Donnie Mattingly is somewhere else in the plane, going home for good and knowing that he's never going to play in a World Series. I'd let them all down."

There's always a game or a series that needs to be pitched over again, I remind myself now. Look at 1999. Cone, seemingly at the pinnacle of his career after the perfect game, runs into unexpected setbacks for the remainder of the year: he gives up six runs in four innings to the Indians, including a grand slam, in his next start, and is later driven to cover in a game against the Rangers, coughing up six runs in an inning and two-thirds. He goes without a win for more than three weeks, and picks up only two over the remainder of the season. Suspecting that Cone's age has begun to show in his work—he is thirty-six, and has thrown close to twenty-six hundred innings at this point, and, counting warmups and side sessions, more than a hundred thousand major-league pitches—Yankee manager Joe Torre and pitching coach Mel Stottlemyre reluctantly begin to space him out a bit, adding a fifth day between his starts, when possible. Cone resents the move and its implication, but says little. Starting the second game of the American League Championship Series (he didn't get a call in the Bombers' three-game sweep of the Rangers in the divisional series), he spins a devastating win against the ambitious Red Sox, surrendering two runs over seven innings and fanning nine. In the World Series, he shuts out the Atlanta Braves in another seven-inning stint, giving up a lone hit, and the Yankees cruise to their third World Championship in the five years he has been with the club. Which is the real Cone?

Cone's Porsche is flashing a right turn, and I slide over a lane. There's the Havana Sandwich Shop up ahead, just this side of Kennedy Boulevard.

So where does Cone fit in, I'm asking myself. Pedro Martinez, who's gone 42–11 with 564 strikeouts in his first two seasons with the Red Sox, is the best pitcher in baseball right now, no two ways. His preternaturally long fingers and absolute dominance over the hitters with that darting, down-moving stuff bring Sandy Koufax to mind. Pedro will breeze into the Hall of Fame at this rate, and so will the Big Unit, Randy Johnson, whose hair and height—he's six-ten, and *flying*—and ground-devouring stride down the mound make you laugh nervously with every pitch, so happy you are that you're not the batter. Greg Maddux, the whey-faced Atlanta grandmaster, won four consecutive Cy Young Awards in the mid-nineties, and on a good day his pitches still gnaw relentlessly around and under the edges of the strike zone, silently eating up outs. The three stand apart, but Cone holds the warmer place in my regard.

Never mind his pitching style—we'll get to that—it's the man's contradictions that grab me. Back in the late eighties and early nineties, when he was a baby-faced starter with the brilliant and notorious Mets, he quickly became known as another hard-party nighthawk, with a penchant for sexual misadventures that repeatedly made the tabloids (". . . despite the choirboy looks" became a favorite tag). Champions in 1986, before Cone's arrival, those Lenny Dykstra, Gary Carter, Keith Hernandez, Doc, and Straw Mets were a celebrity force majeure in the big city, but high salaries and a penchant for second place began to wear out their welcome over the next few seasons. Dykstra was traded off to the Phillies, and others followed him out the door, as the team was dismantled, star by star, with manager Davey Johnson joining the exiles in 1990. Cone's best friends on the club, Bobby Ojeda and Ron Darling, went next, but when he himself was shuffled off to Toronto, in 1992, the move came as a shock. "We underachieved," Cone once said of his old club, "but that team was broken up too soon. New York belonged to the Mets then, and we were all proud of that. Part of me will always be a Met."

Cone performed strongly for the Blue Jays that year, helping them to a World Championship in October, but over the winter he moved along as a free agent to the Kansas City Royals, the club that had first drafted him, years before. A Cy Young Award rewarded Cone's 16–5 record with the Royals in 1994, but the players' strike that August amputated the season, costing his Royals a shot at a championship. When peace was restored and play resumed the next spring, he was summarily dealt back to the Blue Jays, then soon sent along to the Yankees. All these teams and all that money—by now, he was a $6-million-a-year pitcher—subjected Cone to the "hired gun" obloquy that disgruntled fans (and some sports columnists as well) were aiming at the players in the wake of the unpopular strike, but again he defied categorizing. One day back then when I asked him about the high pay and low public regard that the players seemed to have won for themselves, he said, "We'd be more popular if we'd won a lottery, instead of being someone who's tried to perfect his craft and tried to put himself in a position to earn an exorbitant amount of money."

This new David Cone, poised and articulate, and a distance removed from the party boy of a half decade before, had been chosen by his peers in the Players Association to represent the American League at the bargaining table during the hardest weeks of the strike, and he turned up again and again in front-page photographs and on the late news during the protracted negotiations. His presence at labor councils in Florida and New York and Washington, and with the group of owners and players that met with the President at the White House, and his suave summaries before the cameras of the latest issues and talking points were surmised, by Cone and everyone else, to be the probable cause of his swift dismissal by the Royals, once the strike was over.

After his first year with the Yankees—by 1996, that is—Cone had assumed a unique and self-invented role with the dynastic and once disputatious old champions as a team spokesman: an anchorman explainer of controversial plays, dugout gossip and player psyches, and the daily run of rumors, anxieties, injuries, and front-office maneuverings that afflict every clubhouse over the long season, never more than in New York. Beat writers and columnists and TV people began to gather in front of his Stadium locker even on days when he hadn't pitched or wasn't about to, and in taking them on he appeared to sense, almost uncannily, how his words and ideas would work for the team and for the avid needs of the media at the same time. Instead of conflicting with Torre's pre-game and post-game press conferences,

he became a resource for the manager, and an extra, more nu-
anced source of news about the players. When pitching coach
Mel Stottlemyre was diagnosed with multiple myeloma just after the beginning of the 2000 season, Cone said, "Every American family has to deal with cancer in one way or another. We're
no different"—a line that flew into every reporter's notebook.

Other teams have produced these media captains—Keith
Hernandez, a genius at game analysis, did it for the hard-line
championship Mets—but none have understood the needs of
his listeners better than Cone. "David is the best since Stengel,"
Jack O'Connell, the national baseball writer for the Hartford
Courant, told me one day. "He understands the whole thing—
who you are, who you're with, and what you've written. He
knows your deadline and he's always there. He'll wait until the
last guy has all he wants. He never looks tired or bored. He's
smart and generous."

We're here—I pull into the dusty little parking row next to the
diner, where Cone is waiting for me, smiling behind his shades.
Off the field, he is non-combative, with a Milquetoast handshake—it's a protective mannerism for his pitching hand—and
an almost indolent backward tilt to his head. He is six-one but
non-hulking, and when we get inside he draws only a scattering
of stares. After we've ordered I ask him if he's talked to the Boss,
George Steinbrenner. We're still ten days away from the official
pitchers-and-catchers opening of spring training.

"No, but he's here," he says. "George takes spring training seriously. A couple of years ago, I gave up a grand slam to Andrés
Galarraga, and he didn't talk to me for three weeks. In a spring
game? George wants to win. Before the infamous Game Five in
Seattle, in '95, he'd given us one of his traditional pep talks in the
clubhouse, and then he comes over to where I'm sitting with
Jack McDowell. He looks Jack up and down and says, 'And you,
you little Stanford fuck, are you going to be ready?'"

Our laughter makes us sound like kids snickering about their
dad.

"Sometimes this stuff works," David says. "But George . . . Before the playoffs in '96, we're all in the players' lounge, where there's a spread of food. George goes over and picks out a strawberry and comes over to Kenny Rogers, who was going to pitch that day. He stands over Kenny and says, 'Do you know what this is? It's a strawberry—and that's where you're going to be, back on your daddy's strawberry farm if you don't do it today.'"

Doing it for Cone nowadays may require some way of saving his middle-aged arm. My recollections of him in a game always involve a heavy accumulation of high counts, fouls, strikeouts, and bases on balls, with a hit batsman or two thrown in as well. Why so many pitches? I ask.

"I'm working on that this year," he says. "It's time for a little conservation." But in the next moment he has brought up a Mets game in 1992, right after the All-Star break, when he beat the Giants at Shea, 1–0, with an insane admixture of prodigality and thrift.

"A hundred and sixty-six pitches and a 1–0 shutout—I don't know if that's been done before," he says. "That was just before I got traded to the Blue Jays. I was averaging about a hundred and forty pitches a game. Maybe they'd thought my arm was going to wear out, but I was pitching great then. When I got traded, there was a Mike Lupica column in the *News* which agreed with the decision to let me go. Standard Lupica—he decides what people are thinking and then goes the other way. I still have it put away somewhere, because it's been a motivation for me. Anything to get that edge out there. The piece asked how many innings I could have left in my arm, after throwing a couple of zillion. That was about fifteen hundred innings ago."

But all the same, I say—a one-hundred-and-sixty-six-pitch shutout?

"It's one of the three or four favorite games of mine, ever," he says defiantly. "John Franco was down with an injury, so they couldn't call on him. We had no pen, and we're trying to stay alive in a pennant race. That game made me so proud—maybe I thought it connected me with the ghosts of the past and the days

when pitchers stayed in forever. Guys I tried to model myself after like Luis Tiant and Juan Marichal and Satchel Paige."

There's a pause while I try to get all this into my notebook.
The table is littered with crumbs from our Cuban sandwiches.
The restaurant is just about empty.

"I wouldn't try it now," David says, more quietly. "I still hate
to come out of games, but I'm trying to get better habits. The
Yankees are like a second marriage for me—they've gotten the
benefit of all the mistakes I made with the Mets. I've become a
good second husband."

2

Tony's Place

February 14th, Tampa:

The next day, driving to Clearwater with David—in his car, this time—I try to clear away some underbrush. He was born in Kansas City on January 2, 1963, and grew up in the working-class Northeast area of the city, the youngest of four children. His father, Edwin (Eddie Mack) Cone, was a night-shift master mechanic in the Swift meat-packing plant. "Blue collar all the way," Cone says. David describes himself as the runty kid always hanging around the fringes of his older brothers' crowd, hoping to get into the action. His father and his brothers, Chris and Danny (a sister, Christal, is the oldest sibling), were sports-mad, and there were constant basketball and touch football and baseball—Wiffle-ball, actually—games in the back yard, with neighborhood kids joining in. David, coached by his father, got into Little League ball, and played it at every level, but he couldn't play baseball at his high school, Rockhurst, a well-known Jesuit academy, because there was no diamond and no team. He made do with the Ban Johnson League, a summer circuit for high-school and younger college-age kids. He showed up at a tryout camp staged by the Royals, and was noticed. In June,

1981, after he turned eighteen, a Royals scout named Carl Blando signed him in the third round of that year's draft: the seventy-third pick, nationally. It took him five years to make it up to the majors—a knee injury disabled him for one entire season—but in the spring of 1987, on the brink of joining the Royals' staff, he was traded to the Mets.

Cone's résumé is an American tale almost perfectly matched to its time and place, and we will return to it for a longer visit. Today, though, David and I will be visiting another baseball family of his, at Tony Ferreira's place, in Clearwater. The Ferreiras' house is low and modest, but beautifully kept up. There are plantings on the risers of the wooden porch steps, and shrubs and planters here and there. Everything is neat and cozy, inside and out. Tony is tall and agreeable, with long arms, piercing dark eyes, and a squared-off mustache. He seems younger than his thirty-eight years. He's wearing a faded Pro-Kids baseball shirt, with long sleeves—the same logo that's on the Pro-Kids baseball cap that David is wearing today. Tony's two-year-old son, Tanner, is running around, and Tony grabs him now and gently puts on his size-1/4 Adidas as we talk. He and David are very tight. When the two of them and Mark Gubicza were just beginning in organized ball together, in October and November of 1981, playing on Rookie League Gold and Blue teams at the Royals' training camp in Sarasota, they shared a room out on tony Siesta Key—"pretty good for eighteen-year-olds just out of high school," as Tony says. Bret Saberhagen showed up with the Royals later on and so did Danny Jackson. Joe Jones, now a minor-league supervisor with K.C., was one of their managers, and Gary Blaylock, recently a scout with the Colorado Rockies, their pitching mentor. The next year, 1982, David was sent to the Charleston Royals, in South Carolina, where he did well; when he was moved up in midseason to play high A-level ball at Fort Myers, Florida, he and Tony were reunited. Several young players shared a rented house there. That year, Tony had met Robin Macintosh, on spring break from Michigan State, and when she went back to school he courted her by mail. He and David shared a bedroom with double bunks, and each night Tony, on the top bunk, would dictate what he wanted David, on the lower, to write to Robin—only better.

"He thought I had a gift of gab, so I'd write the letters," David says. "I always told him to copy them over when I was done, so Robin would think they'd come from him, but he would just sign his name at the end. Actually, she fell in love with me."

The letters worked. Tony and Robin got married in Omaha, where he was pitching, and when she came to spring training with Tony the next year the Three Musketeers had gained a little history, a little lore. This is "Cyrano de Bergerac" all over again—de Bergerac that good little southpaw in the Dordogne League. Robin still has the letters. She is at work this morning—she's a stockbroker with the Raymond James company, in Tampa—and their three older boys are in school. David is god-father to all three.

"We two and Mark Gubicza were always close," Tony says. "Three guys from such different parts of the country—me from Riverside, California"—actually, he spent more time in Maui, Hawaii, where his folks came from—"David from Kansas City, and Mark from Philadelphia. When it was over, we scattered again—David in New York, Mark in California, and me down here."

The Old Boy strain survives in baseball—more and more so in this rootless, free-agent era—and strong feelings emerge when you hear players talking about the guys they came up with. Remembering your beginnings in organized ball may be a way of standing up to the vagaries of baseball fortune, which tear people apart, not just by trades but in the fateful and mer-ciless disposition of their talents. This is the one baseball senti-mentality that doesn't make me wince. Cone takes on a different look whenever he speaks of Sid Fernandez, the baggy-looking, boyish southpaw who was an early roommate of his on the Mets. At their first spring training together, Fernandez emp-tied the contents of a large suitcase into the middle of the living room of their condo, and for the rest of the month simply picked out whatever he needed from the pile, one piece at a time. "Sid was a mama's boy but a sweetheart," Cone said to me.

I think David and Tony will be meeting and talking like this thirty years from now, and non-baseball people will still be envying them the connection. Bill Rigney, my oldest friend in baseball—he played for the Giants in the forties and fifties, and went on to manage the Angels and Giants and Twins—lights up whenever he talks about his early spring-training days in St. Petersburg, more than half a century ago, when he and Alvin Dark and Leo Durocher and Chub Feeney and Lee MacPhail and their wives would get together at somebody's beach rental in the evenings. "You had to bring two things," Rig says. "A glass and a chair."

David is the most celebrated member of the Three Musketeers, but Mark Gubicza, a six-foot-five right-hander, lasted thirteen years as a starter for the Royals, plus four final innings with the Angels, in 1997, just before he retired. "Gubie had a nice career for himself," as David puts it. He went 20–8 in 1988—the same summer that David put together his 20–3 mark at Shea. Tony Ferreira, who for a time was considered the brightest prospect of the three, lost his celebrated fastball after an injury and only made it up for a cup of coffee with the Royals—five and two-thirds innings in 1985—then levelled off a notch lower. In 1986, David's first year with the Royals, Tony pitched the entire season for the Mets' top farm team, in Tidewater. He retired in 1992, but he must still feel close to the majors, in his capacity as Cone's long-distance pitching guru. All season, he watches David intently on television, and takes notes. The Ferreiras have a TV dish, and on nights when they can't bring in the Yankees' signal he and Robin go to Damon's Ribs, on West Courtney Campbell Causeway, and watch from there. Later that night, or the next day, he and David will consult by telephone. "How did you hold that pitch to Ramirez?" Tony will ask. "Why did your shoulder open up that way?"

Telling me about this now, Tony says, "Dave tries to throw the ball at all these different angles. He has to fool them now."

"Yeah, right," Cone says, smiling. He's being kidded again.

A car rolls up and parks outside, and yields another friend and pitcher, Terry Leach, the sidearmer who won ten straight games for the Mets in 1987, filling in during a season when five separate starters went down with injuries (including Cone, who fractured the little finger on his pitching hand while bunting against the Giants' Atlee Hammaker on May 27th, and missed eleven midseason weeks on the D.L.). Leach had eleven years in the majors, collecting a Series ring with the Minnesota Twins in '91. He is midsized, with a round head and a gray-streaked mustache; when we shake hands I have a little flashback to his strong shoulders and tough chin out on the mound at Shea, from which he delivered a stream of biting sidearm pitches that made right-handed batters bend and weave like matadors.

Leach and Ferreira are partners in Pro-Kids Baseball, a network of day camps, founded by Tony, that teach pitching and batting and fielding to boys whose parents want something better than Little League coaching for their junior jocks. The programs, which began in 1992 and are scattered across ten states, now draw four thousand boys and girls a year, often bringing them back for more advanced work; some of the regulars have become prospects who are getting calls from college coaches. David has a financial interest in Pro-Kids, and appears at some of the recruiting sessions when he's around in the spring. I've seen a Pro-Kids video in which he is working with a thirteen-year-old girl with a pigtail and a great arm. Other Pro-Kids counsellors (the great majority have come out of organized ball) are helping juniors with their S.A.T.s, and a Fall Ball program enrolls parents in clinics, moms as well as dads, and teaches *them* how to stand up at the plate or keep that front shoulder in on the mound. "You can't just tell kids stuff, you know," Leach explains to me. "You gotta show them before they'll listen." Everyone benefits, it seems, including the faculty. "This has turned into a super venue for old ballplayers who don't want the travel that comes with big-league or minor-league coaching," Leach says. "Players like me, I mean."

David and Tony have gone outside to play catch—oddly, they are tossing a football back and forth out there in the yard—but Leach is anxious to tell me about a much younger David Cone peering over his shoulder at Shea Stadium one day in 1987, while Terry was opening his Mets paycheck. "Man, that's makin' *money!*" the youngster cried. Leach explained to me that he was earning ninety-five thousand dollars a year just then, so David's awe was relative. "Now . . ." he says, smiling, and he spreads his hands. He means that David's new one-year contract with the Yankees is for twelve million dollars.

"What David brought to the Mets was a load of personality," Leach goes on. "He had great stuff and he locked in the minute he got there, but he looked like he knew that in New York you could be a little different. He was never too serious—not a guy who'd bring out his stat book. We had a good group—Sid Fernandez and Rick Aguilera, Dwight and Roger McDowell and Jesse Orosco—and Dave connected right away."

When David Cone won his first major-league game, beating the Reds, 6–2, at Riverfront Stadium on a four-hitter, in 1987, Terry Leach took him out to dinner. The first Cone shutout came at Shea a year later, an 8–0 win over the Braves, and when it was over Leach invited David to go downtown with him to celebrate. "It was late and we were driving around Manhattan in my car," Leach said, "but we had no idea where to go. We kept slowing down and peeking out at these lit-up bars and places, and then we'd drive on." They ended up at a spot called the Milk Bar— Leach thinks it was in the East Village—and not until the two got inside and noticed that the customers were wearing Nazi caps and spiked neck chains did they realize that they'd joined leather. "We had beers at the bar and no one bothered us," Terry says, "but we were real quiet about it."

When we go outside to join the others, David and Tony have put the football away and are long-tossing in the yard. The ball

goes back and forth in easy, flattened parabolas and is taken
with casual grabs that start the return motion. This yard is spa-
cious, with some nice shade trees at the back. There's a Dump-
ster just up the little drive from the Ferreiras' place, and the
scruffy street is littered with those narrow grayish leaves that
you see year-round in Florida. This is suburban ball, a scene you
could fit in anywhere in America, and whatever it is that feels so
pleasing now doesn't come just from the familiar shoulder turn
of the man up closer to me at this end, or the realization that this
is another day closer to pitchers-and-catchers at Legends Field,
the Yankees' spring complex, across the Bay. David, with his
shades hooked into the neck of his hooded sweatshirt, has a
sleepy, easeful expression, and Tony now and then gives a goofy
little El Duque crook to his right leg before he lets the next
throw go. What's warming us all, I think, is the flight of the ball,
back and forth—its movement and mild rotation in the air, and
the gleam of light along its top surface in the sunshine. The
painter Jack Levine once described baseball as "an aerial game,"
and it is this prolonged sustainment—the ball in flight again and
again, never touching the ground—that makes playing catch
feel special. Anybody who's learned to throw can remember the
Kitty Hawk day when this began for him, when the ball took
wing—sailed back and forth all the time, or most of the time, instead of having to be stupidly chased down again and retrieved
beside the porch or from under the Chevy. It was the day when
you threw at last without anxiety, sure that the white, interestingly sutured pill would take itself safely over to your dad or
your brother again, and then back into your mitt, *shlup*, as you
lifted your elbow a fraction this time and styled the moment.
Watch a couple of big leaguers warming up in front of the
dugout before another game and you'll see the very same thing,
even in August. Playing catch is a treat.

Cone, to be sure, is working. He'll repeat this routine with
Tony every day, until he begins to throw off a mound over at the
minor-league complex next week. "I'm just trying to find an arm
slot while I build up my strength, and the only way to do it is

throwing," he says now. "It's fun, it's hanging with friends. I do off-season work in a pool or riding a bike but there's no substitute for throwing."

Terry Leach has been tossing with young Tanner Ferreira—actually, trying to help him hold the ball in one hand instead of two—and Tony comes over to help the process along by persuading Tanner to get rid of his Yankee wristbands, which are as long as his arms. I walk back with Tony down to his end of the battery so I can watch David's pitches coming in, and, sure enough, there's a little sag or semi-swerve on some of them now. The next throw is up, and Tony murmurs, "Throw it, don't guide it."

David, standing motionless, turns his left shoulder a fraction, experimenting with how it feels, and peers down at his glove. He is trying to hide the ball a little more this year and perhaps tighten up his windup in the process.

"Just keep that shoulder down," Tony says. "Keep that hand in close—don't let it go flyin' open." And to me he adds, "With a good pitcher like Dave, you should see that left elbow, the glove side, staying in next to the body. That way, he drives forward naturally—he's all one piece. When the elbow flies open, the pitch is up."

The next pitch arrives with a little ducking inclination at the end, and Tony points at David approvingly. Cone gets the ball back, turns his shoulder again, and redelivers, with the left elbow tucked in and more action on the toss. This is almost the two-seamer—the pitch he throws so effectively to left-handed batters, away, with a ducking little turnover at the end. "*There* you go," Tony says. "When you let it go like that, it's effortless. It moves all by itself. I could never throw that pitch."

Terry is standing near David now, down at that end, and though I can't hear what's being said, he's accompanying himself in pantomime, levelling his arms and shoulders before tilting into motion, gesturing toward his hips while his front shoulder turns, then pointing to his back leg in halted mid-stride. I've seen a thousand pitching coaches enact this dumb show down the years, for pupils going back to Warren Spahn and Whitey Ford, and for rows of long-forgotten, never-to-be rookie hopefuls as well. The lesson never changes and never becomes entirely routine, and Cone, who's been doing it for longer than anyone else here, is still paying attention.

Cone needs arm strength but he must think about saving himself for the season-long run of innings ahead. This is the pitcher's account book, and with Cone the bottom line becomes critical. He throws an inordinate number of pitches and works with such intensity and combative fire that you sense that anything less might bring on disaster. Nothing about him is simple. He is emotional but also extremely intelligent: a power pitcher with an idea. Although his fastball—once reliably in the ninety-one-to-ninety-two-mile-per-hour range—has lost a few ticks of late, it was always secondary to the subtle combinations of pitches he shows the batter: the full range of slider, fastball, curveball (he throws it as a change of pace), and fork ball (the split-finger pitch) that he delivers, in and out, to the corners of the plate, at slightly altered speeds and from higher or lower or farther release points. Sometimes he drops down and goes sidearm to a right-handed batter—the Laredo delivery (it's from down under) that can end an inning with the batter standing spraddle-legged in the box, his bat drooping from his left hand, and the pitcher ambling home from the office.

Cone's aggressive spirit on the mound has been an asset and a hazard for him right along. In "The Worst Team Money Could Buy," a lively book about the Mets of the late eighties and early nineties, the authors, Bob Klapisch and John Harper, talk about the "Marty Feldman look" that would overtake Cone in times of stress: "At the first hint of trouble, he would rush his delivery, overthrow the fastball, choke the slider, bounce the splitter in the dirt. That was the only obstacle between Cone and perennial twenty-win seasons."

But players and managers also admire this spirit in Cone. George Brett, the great Royals Hall of Famer, remembers facing him late in the 1992 season at a time when he was driving hard for his three-thousandth lifetime hit. "I never talk to pitchers," Brett told me, "but he was an old friend of mine and I said, 'Hey, take it easy on me here today, will you? I need hits here,' and he said not to worry, sure he'll give me a break. So I'm up at bat and it's one-and-one or two-and-oh and he throws me this split-finger and all I can do is hit it along the ground. He covers first and makes the out and I say, 'God damn you, you son of a bitch, I thought we were friends!'" He laughed uproariously.

Cone's work is highly visible, which suggests that you can see his thinking as well as his skill and strength, and this, in turn, brings him closer to the fans—to this fan, at least—who secretly believe that they could do this lovely stuff, too, if only. He shares the work with you, and in this he has sometimes reminded me of Juan Marichal, the Giants' Hall of Famer whom many pitchers place in a higher pantheon, and whose high-kicking, down-turning great stuff, delivered from every angle, made him look like a playground pitcher scaring his kid sister. It was nice when David told me that Marichal was one of his pitching idols.

Tony has been counting pitches and when David gets up to-ward fifty he walks in, closing the distance for the last few lobs. He tells me that this yard is where David perfected his split-finger delivery, although David has already told me that he first picked it up from the veteran Diego Segui, down in Puerto Rico, during an early spell of winter ball. But Ferreira learned *his* splitter from Giants manager Roger Craig in the spring of 1988, and claims to have passed it along to David. Whatever. I'm impressed because Craig is the inventor and Johnny Appleseed of the modern-day split-finger, and at one time even wondered whether he couldn't patent the gizmo, instead of teaching it. Now I tell Tony that he should consider putting down a plaque here, marking the site and perhaps the instant of the magical Craig-Ferreira-Cone transfer. "Let's *do* it!" he says cheerfully.

I don't know if David will get any more out of this day than a light workout with some old compadres, but he loves to pitch. His eyes light up when he talks about the work. Only the night before, he said, "I think it's the definitive position. Nothing is more exciting for me than looking for a new pitch or a new grip. Wherever I am, at home or away, I spend a lot of time holding a ball, turning it over and trying to find a way to initiate a new movement, finding a new weapon. I like to think of the world's greatest athlete coming up to bat against me—Tiger Woods, Wayne Gretzky, I don't care who it is—and I'm looking in at him and thinking, *You have no chance.* I never forget that old saying that pitchers aren't athletes. I mean, right, I'm not an athlete—I'm a *pitcher!* I'm very proud to be in the skilled-marksman category."

Hanging around on Tony's porch, drinking Pepsis, we're joined by Tony's next-door neighbor, Kent Henniger, a young landscape gardener with an orange beard. He has been eying David's Carrera—he's a car fancier—and David urges him to take it out for a spin. When Kent comes back, he lets the Porsche thrum for a moment before cutting it off, and steps out grinning. "It still feels small," he says to David. "They haven't messed that up. That steering is so effortless—it pulls you right through." He sounds like a pitching coach.

3

Bluefinger

May 2, 1996, Yankee Stadium:

Out on the mound, away from everything but this next batter, this next slider, David allows his pitching brain to take over. He's been careful at the outset, and no wonder, and it takes a double play to bail him out of trouble in the first inning, but when he drops down for the Laredo against Danny Tartabull and fans him, ending the second, he decides the hell with it, I'm all right now. It's a Thursday game, against the visiting White Sox— too early in the year to be called important but, yes, this matters. Cone, to his dismay, had to pass up his previous turn on the mound while he went through a medical procedure—his first missed start in nine years. Now he's back out there, where he can put aside the distractions. They've cleared him for this game, and he's been taken off the anticoagulant heparin, so he must be O.K. to pitch. He has decided to stay away from the split-finger pitch, just in case, but the game has a little tempo to it now, and here in the fourth he lets go a splitter to Harold Baines—a beauty, a bottom-dropper—and wipes him out, and then does it again to the next man, Robin Ventura. Bye, Robin. He's on a roll now.

Cone pitches a complete game, a 5–1 win—that one run is unearned—and strikes out eight. The victory runs his record to 4–1, with an earned-run average of 2.03, the best in the league, and when he meets the reporters and the television people waiting around his locker he is upbeat. "It's been a long time since I was that free and easy," he says, "I've had a lot of anxiety." He stays on, answering their questions, as is his custom, and only after they've dispersed does he let the worries come flooding back.

Before this, moments after the game ended, he met with Dr. Stuart Hershon, the team physician, who was waiting in the training room, and the two bent over his pitching hand. "The side feels like it's asleep," David said. "All down here, along the bottom. And these two fingers are cold." He held up his ring finger and little finger, and Hershon wrapped a hand around them, to check. The ring finger was pale and purplish, and the fingernail a deep blue.

"It feels like it's ready to fall off," David said. "It feels dead."

Concerned, Dr. Hershon murmured that they might have to go back to the vascular people at Columbia-Presbyterian. One of the doctors there thought he might have seen something, after all, he told David. Maybe another angiogram was needed. But David cups his hand, hiding the affected fingers, when he goes out to meet the media. Anyway, there's nothing wrong with his thumb and the first two fingers, he thinks to himself—look how well I pitched. Maybe it's only a ligament. It was such a good game, how can there be anything wrong?

Every pitcher's arm feels worse after an outing than he ever lets on to the media. Denial comes with the territory, and managers and pitching coaches are on the alert for symptoms of pain or trouble that their expensive starters and relief specialists will brush off or cheerfully lie about. I'd seen Cone often that spring—I was writing a piece about him for *The New Yorker*—and I can remember the relief I felt after the White Sox game and Cone's optimistic press conference. Before this, in Florida, I'd noticed David looking at his hand oddly after a

spring-training game at Baseball City, but he shook off my in-
quiry. He was fine, he said. The same thing happened after his
Opening Day start, against the Indians, on a frigid afternoon in
Cleveland. He'd won that game, 7–1, holding the visitors hitless
in the first five innings, and blamed the chilly conditions for
some difficulties he'd had in getting a grip on the ball.

He went on pitching well, limiting the Rangers to four hits in
each of his next two starts, but his pitching hand felt colder than
the weather could account for. It was clammy and there was
some discoloration of the fingers now. Warming up for his
fourth start, in Milwaukee, he felt a tingling in his hand and
wrist. He pitched poorly, surrendering six runs in five innings,
and took his first loss. The anxiety that hung around him now—
his own and the Yankees'—was becoming exponential, centering not just on his arm but on the club's strategies and
commitments for the years just ahead, and on a multi-team financial drama that had been played out late the year before,
when Cone, still smarting from the Yankees' post-season elimination by the Mariners, had become a free agent after an eventful two and a half months in the Bronx.

By late December, Cone and his agent, Steve Fehr, had almost concluded extensive negotiations with the Yankees over a
contract centering on a base of eighteen million dollars for three
years. When an apparently firm offer was unexpectedly taken
off the table by the Yanks, Cone called Pat Gillick, the general
manager of the Orioles, who had been courting him, and continued talks there, which soon reached the last-detail stages of interest payments on deferred income, and the like. Cone and
Fehr made an offer that, if accepted, would have made him an
Oriole instead of a Yankee, but in a late turnabout George Steinbrenner, weirdly talking from a phone booth in Tampa, put the
full Yankee offer back in play. At eight the next morning, December 21st, David had a last-minute visit from Joe McIlvaine, a
Santa representing the Mets, with an urgent wish to have him
back across town again. Cone admitted that a return to Shea
had always intrigued him, but the Mets' offer was not at the

same level as the others, and later that day the deal with the Yankees was completed and announced: a four-million-dollar salary
with a signing bonus of two million, and two six-million-dollar
years to follow. (There were option-year clauses and buyout
provisions, but these, it turned out, were never invoked.) Cone
was a Yankee again, and a wealthy one.

The Christmas saga resurfaced, of course, in the stories
about Cone's sudden arm debility, and an almost visible aura of
anxiety and apprehension hung over each new pitch and inning
of his strange spring. There was no improvement his next time
out, in Kansas City, where he left the game once again after five
innings, in an eventual 6–2 Yankee win. Joe Torre cited Cone's
old trouble gripping the ball, but Dr. Hershon, increasingly concerned, told the pitcher and the Yankee management that the
problem appeared to be circulatory. He said it was time for an
angiogram—an X-ray procedure in which a tube is inserted into
the groin and guided to the chest, where an injected radio-
opaque dye then outlines the aorta and its major branches to the
head and arms. Perhaps something else was wrong, but this
would look into the most serious possibility of all.

David, instinctively resisting, claimed not to understand why
a problem down in his hand and fingers would require anything
so drastic. He feared the worst, of course—an operation that
would curtail or finish his season. He wanted to brush everything aside and pitch his troubles away, as he'd done so often in
the past. It's possible that a similar desire—a dismissive "Ah, it's
just another sore arm"—may have sifted down from the Yankees' front office, because Dr. Hershon told me that he'd had to
insist on the angiogram. If it wasn't done for this young man, he
said, he'd resign his post as team physician.

David and his wife, Lynn, meanwhile, had gone to another
doctor they knew, Richard Eaton, of St. Luke's-Roosevelt, for an
opinion about angiograms. Eaton, a hand surgeon, had operated
on David back in May, 1987, when he fractured his right little finger attempting to lay down a bunt against Atlee Hammaker. You
can still see the crinkle in Cone's finger, and feel it when you

shake hands with him. "Three-Finger Cone," David sometimes says of himself, and likes to believe that the injury helps with his breaking stuff. Eaton, in any case, told the Cones that an angiogram was appropriate, and on April 26th the test was made.

What the doctors were looking for was an aneurysm—a weakening and ballooning somewhere along the main artery in Cone's pitching arm that could have resulted from the long-repeated traumatic action of his delivery. Aneurysms are not always easy to detect, and tests can lead to differing interpretations, but the news from this one, when it came, was good: angiogram negative.

What did show up were some blood clots on Cone's hand and wrist. "You could see them all over the X-ray," David told me. "The veins there are like a road map and in some places those white lines would stop and go dark. Long stretches of dark that they said were clots. But nobody could tell me where the clots came from." Low-molecular-weight heparin, an anticoagulant, was prescribed, to be injected, and everyone cheered up.

Well, almost everyone. In an article in the *Times* on June 2nd, Dr. Lawrence K. Altman, chief medical correspondent for the paper, revealed that some doctors on the case had not been convinced that the angiogram entirely ruled out the presence of an aneurysm. Dr. Eric Martin, the chief of interventional radiology at Columbia-Presbyterian, hadn't been present when the test was made but on reviewing it later stated that an aneurysm "had to have been there."

Reflections about the test persist to this day, because of the considerable risks Cone could have encountered after he was permitted to pitch that game against the White Sox. Even though the heparin had been stopped the day of the game, to lessen the possibility of bleeding from an unlikely but not impossible game-induced contusion, an undetected aneurysm could have been pushing down more clots, putting David at risk for gangrene and the loss of fingers, or even the loss of his arm.

Dr. Hershon, given the lack of clear evidence for an aneurysm, cleared Cone to pitch and a staff of Columbia-Presbyterian

specialists monitored him between innings. David badly wanted
to get back into action, of course, and he is unreserved in his
praise of Hershon for recommending the angiogram in the first
place, and then going to war for it. "He saved my life," he says.
But the revelation after the game that some unnamed minority-
opinion doctor or doctors believed that an aneurysm was in
there, after all, still nags at him. The doubt has become a central
part of the feelings of privacy and responsibility he holds about
his pitching arm, and his stubborn conviction that it is his property in the end, despite contractual obligations, and that rights to
it must be surrendered only with extreme caution.

Cone now returned to Columbia-Presbyterian, where ultra-
sound and Doppler tests deepened suspicions of an aneurysm,
and these were confirmed at last, on May 7th, by a second angiogram. David remembers the glee of the radiologist—"We
found it! We found it!"—when she brought the angiogram with
the discovered aneurysm to his room: the message that might
mean the end of his career. Don't you grin at me, he thought.
Sure, you're excited because you finally fucking found it, but
there's nothing here that's good news for me. The problem lay in
a passageway of the posterior circumflex humeral and axillary
arteries, which branch off from the larger shoulder artery. Cone,
describing the situation to me, said that the aneurysm, which
was about half an inch long, had been squeezing out clots like
toothpaste from a tube while under stress from his pitching motion. Lying in a hospital bed with a catheter in his groin, he began treatment: a thin tube was inserted and was threaded from
there up into his shoulder and down his right arm, where it
dripped in a clot-dispersing enzyme called urokinase—an inva-
sive and painful thirty-hour regimen.

"I was scared and pissed off," he says. "Even drugged up on
painkillers I knew I was in trouble now."

Major-league pitchers are forever going under the knife.
Advances in sports medicine have diminished the severity of
most such surgical procedures—pitchers can come back from

arthrosopic surgery, even from rotator-cuff repairs, in a matter of a few months—but the number of interventions has gone up, and some are serious indeed. Cone's friend and former team-mate Bret Saberhagen, now of the Red Sox, has persevered after multiple operations that included the reconstruction of a sev-ered ligament capsule on his right shoulder. It is almost typical of Cone, however, that his ailment, an aneurysm, while some-times encountered by kayakers and volleyball players, should be rare to the point of exoticism in baseball. The veteran re-liever Roberto Hernandez, then in the minor leagues, had re-quired extensive surgery on his forearm for a similar condition in 1991, and two minor-league pitchers with the Giants organi-zation, Steve Soderstrom and Kevin Rogers, had gone through uncomplicated aneurysm operations at the Stanford University Hospital, in Palo Alto, in 1994. All of them recovered and pitched again. Hernandez, hearing about Cone's mysterious hand and finger symptoms earlier in the spring, had called David several times and left messages for him to call back: he knew what was going on.

Cone's aneurysm was trickier than theirs, and his doctors— the vascular surgeons George Todd and Alan Benvenisty, of Columbia-Presbyterian, and the orthopedists Hershon and Louis Bigliani—determined that a graft employing a small sec-tion of vein removed from his leg would be required. Other doc-tors were consulted, of course, and a different view, from the specialists at Stanford, cited the extraordinary repeated strains of pitching, and proposed that the grafting replacement should be taken from an artery, rather than a vein—a more demanding procedure, which would leave David recovering from two sur-geries instead of one.

The hours before and after the operation were stressful and exhausting for the Cones. Lynn's father, Frederick DiGioia, a third-stage lung-cancer victim, had just gone into intensive care at St. Raphael's Hospital, in New Haven, where the DiGioias lived, and she had to hurry back and forth between the two bed-sides. Media interest in David's condition and his pitching future had become frenzied, and Dr. Hershon can remember writers and TV reporters shoving and shouting for position before one of the press conferences at the Stadium, where the Yankee front office was trying to keep a lid on things by holding medical speculation to a minimum. David's parents, Ed and Joan, had come in from Kansas City, while David remained catheterized and sedated in the McKeen Pavilion at Columbia-Presbyterian, barely aware of his surroundings.

Lynn took over. Deciding that David himself should be part of any decision involving his arm and his pitching future, she won an admission from Dr. Todd that there was no tremendous hurry about the operation. Everything could be put on hold until the urokinase drip had run its course. The catheter was at last removed, and David, worn out but more himself now, agreed with Lynn and the doctors that a vein graft appeared to be the better course. The operation, a three-hour affair, came on May 10th, when the surgical team, working within a long incision in Cone's armpit, removed the aneurysm and replaced the excised artery section with a one-inch piece of saphenous vein taken from his left thigh—a common source in coronary-bypass resections. The operation went well, but the Columbia-Presbyterian doctors, startled by the crowds and the urgent questionings at the post-op Yankee Stadium interview session, were cautious in their prognosis. No muscles had been cut during the procedure, they said, and a recurrence of an aneurysm was not expected. They would not predict when Cone might be able to go back to work.

David remembers the medical team's extreme concern during the next forty-eight hours, the critical post-surgical period, when the doctors wondered if the vein graft would hold. He woke up often during the next two nights, dopily aware of the bandaged and immobilized bundle of his precious shoulder. "I was on Def-Con-4," he says—an action-movie tag that bullpen pitchers sometimes apply to a tottering enemy starter.

David's physical recovery went well, in fact, but his state of mind had to struggle to catch up with the rush of events. Four

days after the operation, still at the hospital, he and his father
and his friend Andrew Levy listened over the radio—the hospital room had no TV cable hook-up—while Doc Gooden, who
had replaced him in the Yankees rotation, pitched a 2–0 no-
hitter against the Seattle Mariners. Cone's emotions were hard
to contain as the game slowly grew in tension and excitement—
here was his old sidekick from the Mets taking his place out
there, and sending an extraordinary message—and he was close
to tears by the time it was over. "I was still under sedation," he
says now, "and I was pulling for him so hard that it got to me. At
the same time I began to realize how far out of it I was. And I
didn't know yet if I'd get back."

Released from the hospital the next day, David was intent on
joining Lynn at her father's bedside but first he had to get the
media swarm out of the way. He went home and put on a suit
and tie—taking care not to lift his right arm above the horizontal—and was driven back to the Stadium for a quickly convened
press conference. He was all right, he said, and felt sure he'd be
pitching again later in the summer. But he looked pale and thin,
and when he was asked about Doc Gooden he had to struggle
once again to keep from breaking down. He doesn't remember
the rest of the meeting. When it was over he got into a car with
his parents and was driven up the Merritt Parkway to New
Haven.

Time passed slowly that summer. David began his post-operative rehabilitation work at the Columbia-Presbyterian midtown
facility, on East Sixtieth Street—he could walk over there in the
mornings from the Cones' apartment on Fifty-sixth Street—but
the doctors kept the brakes on. He got on well with Vinnie
Perez, the therapist, who tried to keep him upbeat while he went
through his stretching and loosening routines, but weeks went
by before he was allowed to raise his arm over his head. No one
talks or writes much about the desert island of rehab, but players who are going through the dreary process take on a faraway
gaze; not much is within their control, and the game that now

engages them has the slowest clock imaginable. A writer I know, Ray Robinson, was visiting Yankee Stadium in this period while working on a television documentary, and recalls running into David in the Yankee clubhouse. David had his dog with him, a shih tzu named Max, who ran about on the field. Cone was friendly, and optimistic in responding to questions about his shoulder, but Robinson recalls how disconcerting it was to see a famous player out of uniform in midseason, with nothing to do but hang around.

Lynn's father had got a little better and come home, but only for a time. Back in the hospital, he died on July 7th. David was cleared at last for light tossing at about the time of Fred Di-Gioia's funeral, and he remembers throwing a store-bought baseball against a brick wall next to her mother's condo—a brief bright moment. The surgeons and doctors still expressed some concern over what might happen when the time came for him to cut loose—there was no precedent for them to fall back on—but David had put all such anxieties behind him. From the moment he was allowed to pick up a ball again, he thought only about rejoining the Yankees and getting back to being a pitcher.

Stuart Hershon was there on a morning in late July when David turned up at the Stadium, looking for someone to throw to—the team was on a road trip. No one else was around, so Hershon, who is tall and athletic (he was a starting tight end for the Harvard football team for three years) found a catcher's mitt and walked out to the bullpen with his famous patient. "Now, take it easy, David," he said, squatting down. "Anything happens to you here and I'll have to move to Mexico."

The Yankees don't encourage disabled players to use their facilities, but now David and Lynn were allowed to go back to Tampa, where David squeezed in a second spring-training regimen over a two-and-a-half-week span. He was bored and irritable, dying to pitch again, and at last word came down that he could make a limited start with the Yankees' AA team, the Norwich Navigators, in Connecticut. Standing on the mound for the anthem, David felt a rush of feelings about this rough summer.

Fred DiGioia was gone—the two of them had been close—and now here he was, back in Fred's part of the country and ready to get on with his own life again. An overflow crowd had jammed into little Thomas Dodd Stadium, to welcome David back, and for once Tater the Gator, the Navigator mascot, wasn't the main attraction.

"The game was against the Binghamton Mets, and in the first inning their third batter, Brian Daubach, hits a home run against me," David said, bringing it back for me. "Fastball right down the middle, and he takes it deep—I can still see him floating around the bases. Their dugout had a big reaction, but I knew everyone over there was thinking about what this game meant for me, and they were glad that I did well. I went four innings and gave up three or four hits, and I felt great when I came out. No pain and no fear. That was my best game of the whole year. I think I stayed on for more than an hour after it was over, signing autographs."

Not yet restored to the roster, he rejoined his Yankee team-mates at the Stadium for a night and sat on the bench. A couple of days later, he drove back to Norwich and went six more good innings for the Navigators. The news of his start had got out and this time the club set up a table outside the park to accommo-date the autograph seekers, and positioned a couple of cars to il-luminate the scene with their headlights. After an hour of signing, David came down the line of waiting kids and families and told them not to worry, he'd hang on to the end for them to sign programs and souvenirs, and pose for snapshots if they wanted. Lynn, foreseeing a long night, said, "Come *on!* Auto-graphs or photographs but not both, O.K.?" but she knew it was hopeless.

By now his only thought was to get back into the Yankee ro-tation. The club had gone off on a Western swing, and the pitch-ing was in a bad way. Left-handed starter Jimmy Key had been nailed on the elbow by a line drive from Seattle shortstop Alex Rodriguez and was questionable for his next start. David camped on the phone with Bob Watson, the Yankee general manager, lobbying for his return, and at last the awaited word came: meet us in Oakland.

Replaying the video of Cone's famous start there on September 2, 1996—his first game in four months—you notice how quickly baseball's pliant landscape is altered by a short run of seasons. Darryl Strawberry, young and upbeat, is back at the plate for the Yanks again, with his bat held like a toy behind his attentive gaze, and here is David pitching to Oakland third baseman Scott Brosius, not yet a teammate, and popping him up. Because of what you know in advance, you watch the replayed game in proprietary expectation, waiting for its shift in mood and excitement. Through the early outs you hang warily on every pitch, checking Cone's expression and waiting for what— a wince, a sudden clawing at his shoulder? The setting is everyday—the Oakland-Alameda County Coliseum, with its acres-wide foul ground and ugly new stands in center field—on a dazzling bright afternoon. David, getting the ball back, wipes his forehead with his fingertips, pushing up his cap for a moment, and goes to work on Terry Steinbach, striking him out with a slider. The outs accumulate, and you stop feeling like an E.M.S. attendant. Before the first pitch, Dr. Hershon had said to David, "Just remember, this is only a first few innings. Don't try to throw a no-hitter or anything."

David, for his part, remembers how well he was pitching— ahead on the counts and staying on top of the ball—and, more vividly, being aware of the strange presence of his father, a couple of rows back in a seat just behind the Yankee dugout. Ed had come out from Kansas City for David's post-operative début, which is understandable, but in all the hundreds of games they'd been involved in together—when David was pitching for the Yankees or the Royals or the Blue Jays or the Mets, or, before that, in Omaha or down in Florida—Ed Cone had always been seated some distance off in the stands, which meant that they'd never seen each other face to face, as they did now, each time he walked in from the field after another third out. Every part of this game had begun to carry an accumulation of meaning.

David first noticed the oddity when he came in from his pre-game warmups in the bullpen: there was his father. He gave him a wave of the glove and got a nod and hand waggle back, and the two then exchanged almost furtive glances each time he came in from the mound. "I didn't want to be a distraction," Ed recalls, "but then I began to think this could be an inspiration or something."

Cone's celebrated seven innings of no-hit ball against the Athletics in his convalescent return to action ranks below his 1999 perfect game in the media guide, and perhaps also counts for less than his embattled win over the Braves in the third game of the World Series later that fall, but it bears the Conean imprimatur. David's old teammate George Brett was often sidelined over the course of his twenty-one-year career but always seemed to announce his return from another sojourn on the D.L. with a trumpeting volley of line drives and game-winning doubles or home runs, which Cone replicated here, in his own fashion. Seven hitless innings isn't a no-hitter, to be sure, but the exceptional and mystifying nature of David's ailment and the threatening implications of his surgery had already set him apart from other aching and arm-worn mound practitioners, and now, with this austere back-to-business announcement, he had reestablished himself and caught the eye of fans everywhere. Not yet a year away from his trade from the Blue Jays, he had begun the season as something of an outsider in the Bronx. Most non-fans were aware of him as the most visible and outspoken of the Players Association representatives during the hated strike, which was still fresh in people's minds. Only a masterly public-relations coup—how about seven no-hit innings—could make him noticed in a different way, all in a single afternoon.

David's expression in the video replay, a pale-faced clench of resolution and defiance, suits the melodrama. Tim McCarver, talking about the day later on, said, "David cares and he doesn't mind other people seeing him caring. The combination of the aneurysm and the shoulder surgery, and the way he came back from all that in one game, brought him together with the fans in ways you couldn't have imagined. New York fans are into that stuff. They're a great match, David and the fans."

It nearly didn't happen. With the Yankees ahead by 4–0, and one out in the Oakland seventh, third baseman Charlie Hayes made a whirling play against Mark McGwire, grabbing his hard bouncer just as it appeared to scoot past him on the glove side, and firing across for the out. The next batter, Geronimo Berroa, lofted a drive to deep center field, where Bernie Williams, looking back over his left shoulder and sprinting after the descending ball, took a last bounding stride and plucked it back from the far side of the fence, for the out. Long and svelte, Bernie rarely breaks rhythm as he tracks each fly and liner, but this time he was a mother snatching her baby's stroller from under the locomotive.

Back in the dugout, Torre told Cone that with his pitch count up to eighty-five, he was done for the day. This is the toughest decision imaginable for a manager, of course, but, given the circs—where David had been this season, and where the Yankees were headed at its end, a month away—it's hard to disagree with the call. Joe Girardi, Cone's longtime batterymate and his catcher in Oakland that day, said to me, "David in that Oakland game showed what a great team player he was. He knew that October was more important than his no-hitter. His mind was set right."

Joe, are you *crazy*? Go back and look at the tape of the game. Keep it on to the end—the last shot, almost. There's David on the bench, with his jacket on, and his mouth clamped shut in disappointment. He is frowning, glaring at the ground, almost beside himself over this latest kick in the teeth from fate. Forget the pitch count or the rest of the season: he wants to be back out there, going for greatness.

Cone won twice more as the 1996 season ran down—he was three and one after his return—but was touched up for six runs by the Texas Rangers in the opening game of the A.L. division-als, in October, losing by 6–2 . He did much better next time out, in the second game of the championship series, against the Orioles, departing the edgy scene after six innings, tied at 2–2, in the Yanks' ultimate 5–3 loss, with the decision laid on Jeff Nelson. Seen now, these efforts seem like stretching exercises before the main event or perhaps the ultimate rehab in Cone's endless year: his start against the defending-champion Atlanta Braves in the third game of the World Series. Joe Torre had picked the slot in advance, knowing that the Braves would be coming home to their launching pad at Atlanta-Fulton County Stadium for the middle three Series games (and the last games to be played there ever, before its dismantling). "We wanted Coney for the one game," he said later, "and whether the Series is oh-two or one-one or two-oh at this point, it's pivotal. That park can blow your mind a little, but he'd pitched there many times for the Mets. Plus he was David."

What the manager could not anticipate was that the Yankees would be reeling in the Series at this point, down by two games to none after a 12–1 embarrassment in the opener, up at the Stadium, and then an icy 4–0 gem by Greg Maddux. The careening Braves had won five straight games in the post-season, scoring forty-eight runs in the process.

Cone, with eleven days' rest, established himself early in the game, working low and flashing strikeouts to close out the second, fourth, and fifth innings. Leading the Braves' Tom Glavine by 2–0 in the sixth, he gave up a walk and a bloop, and, with one out, walked Chipper Jones, to load the bases. This produced Joe Torre from the dugout, and a mound conference that has become embronzed in Yankee memory, like a war memorial. Seizing his pitcher by the hips, Torre pulls David close, inches away from his stare, and says, "This is important. You've got to tell me the truth." The famous tight shot, with the dark-eyed Joe peering into the recesses of Cone's soul, is up there in the gallery with Garbo and John Gilbert, or Al and Tipper, but came to a happier ending.

"I'm all right," Cone says, a little startled. "I'm fine. I can get these guys, believe me."

Candor and resolution flow out of him. Who wouldn't go with a guy like this? Torre nods at last, touches his shoulder, and retires. "I trusted David Cone," he says later. "He's the toughest player to read I've ever had because he always expects to do well."

"I lied," Cone says. "I had to make him believe my lie."

Going to work amid the enormous down-home roarings and chantings—the Coneheads here have tomahawks embedded in their rubber scalps—he retires Fred McGriff on a pop to Jeter, then works lengthily against the slugger Ryan Klesko, throwing splitters, but loses him at last on a base on balls, forcing in a run. Umpire Tim Welke's call on the pitch—a not-so-borderline low strike, by the look of it—makes David's jaw drop. After three walks in the inning, he wants a bit of luck now, and gets it when Javier Lopez jumps on a poor pitch, up in the strike zone, and pops it up into foul ground, where Girardi cradles it home for the final out. The Yanks win, 5–2, and David is the winning pitcher. The next day, trailing by 6–0 in Game Four, they stage a fabled comeback built around Jim Leyritz's three-run homer and win, 8–6, in extra innings. The Yankee hegemony has begun— they will be the imperial team of the decade, not the Braves— and Cone's year is complete.

4

Normal Pain

March 1st, Tampa:

Our man is stretched out on a medical examining table
with his shirt off and his left hand ceremoniously folded over his
right on his midriff, while a thin, elegant woman in a plum-
colored tunic pokes needles into his twelve-million-dollar right
shoulder. Each needle comes in its own package, encased in a
little plastic aiming tube. Finding one of the dots she has already
inked on the shoulder, the woman stands the unit upright, pois-
ing it delicately with one white-gloved hand, and tap-taps the sil-
very needle home with flicks of a forefinger. David, the patient,
is breathing gently; his eyes are closed—perhaps he's asleep.
Soon there are ten needles in place, ranging along the curved
muscle from the point of the shoulder and down the outer front
sector of his right arm. The woman's movements are precise,
and she alternates her gaze between the work at hand and
David's face. She has dark Oriental eyes and an expression of af-
fectionate attention. "Do you have some energy back?" she asks.
"Last time you were not so fine."

"My energy is good," David says. "I threw yesterday and I feel
strong."

The woman, Dr. Xin-Yue Jiang, paints a brownish salve onto two small metal paddles connected to a gray metal box on a table beside her, and affixes them, one above the other, in little parking spaces she has left amid the needles. She flips a switch on the box, which emits musical pings. Soon the salve under each paddle begins to ooze down the patient's arm, as the current between these poles makes itself felt, and I can see flickers of muscle moving beneath the skin.

Silence, embellished by pings. A sweet herbal aroma begins to sift around us. On the wall facing the recumbent, porcupined pitcher there is a pinkish anatomical chart of a standing man with one arm outstretched and the other turned so that the palm faces out—an everyday sort of teaching chart except that this one appears to bear a subway map running down its abdomen, with branch lines angling off into the arms and down the legs. There are numerous stations, local and express, with each stop bearing its name in Chinese. Inside the open palm the line turns upon itself and goes into a diminishing circle, a whirligig at the end of the line.

Now Dr. Jiang picks up a cigarlike black tube containing herbs and gently touches its gray, ashy tip to the microscopic knob atop each of the needles, one by one. "Ah, you feel that now?" she asks.

"Feels good," David says sleepily. "I'm picking up some throbs. You can feel the tendon starting to relax—I can't tell you how soothing that is. What's the temperature in there?"

"One hundred eighty degrees," she says. "Yes, now you look!" She is beckoning me forward like a chef inviting a peep at a soufflé. Down the entire upper arm, from shoulder to elbow, I can see twistings and spasms of motion under the skin. Yeeks, David Cone is morphing. We're back in "Alien" and any second now a fanged, dripping Space Arm is going to burst out of its hapless vector and take over the room. The neighborhood will be laid waste, then the city. . . . "Take cover!" I want to yell. "Tell George Steinbrenner, somebody! Get me the White House!"

David has closed his eyes again. Dr. Jiang turns off the gray box, shutting down the pings. Nothing here is mysterious. The box is an ordinary deep-current mechanism, the Electro-Acuscope, which I have seen baseball trainers affix to pitchers' and infielders' arms for years now, in redolent clubhouse training rooms around the leagues. We are not in outer-galaxy space but only somewhere between West and East—here in early March at the Xin-Yue Jiang Acupuncture Clinic, a modest store-front office on Kennedy Boulevard, in Tampa. Cone first visited here a year ago, when he found he was still suffering tenderness in his pitching arm four months after his last outing, the third game of the 1998 World Series, in which he was removed for a pinch-hitter in the seventh inning, with the Yankees trailing the San Diego Padres by 3–1. The Yankees then mounted a success-ful rally, winning the game by 5–4, with the decision going to the reliever Ramiro Mendoza. The next day they completed their four-game sweep of the Padres, to capture their hundred-and-twenty-fifth victory of the year, and their twenty-fourth World Championship.

Cone's contribution to that triumphant season—perhaps the most successful sustained team performance of the century—was that scintillant 20–7 record, with a 3.55 earned-run average over two hundred and seven innings, and two hundred and nine strikeouts. The twenty games won tied him for the league lead (with Roger Clemens, then on the Blue Jays, and the Rangers' Rick Helling) and was a source of pleasure for his friends and fans, who had wanted a measurable reward like this for him af-ter some gruelling recent seasons marred by physical problems. This time, David had pitched brilliantly down the stretch, strik-ing out more than ten batters in three straight starts in Septem-ber. He allowed no runs in the third game of the Yankees' sweep over the Texas Rangers in the divisional series, and one run (in eight innings) to the much tougher Cleveland Indians in the league championship's second game, which the Yankees lost in extra innings, and picked up the win in the title-clinching sixth game, despite an abrupt departure after surrendering five runs in the fifth.

He was running down, in truth, with his successes now depending more on his intelligence and will power, and less on pure stuff. By the time the World Series came along, he had so little left that he required an anti-inflammatory shot before making that third-game start against the Padres. John Franco, who was doing television commentary for Fox at the time, remembers running into Cone in the Yankee clubhouse, a day or so earlier. "He had a sheet-wrap around his arm and he was wearing one of those big hydroxolators," Franco said. "I asked him how he was doing, and he gave me one of those looks—you know, he's saying he felt like shit." When Buster Olney, the *Times* beat writer, asked Mariano Rivera about Cone's performance that day, Rivera became tearful about David's persistence and courage. And Olney told me not long ago that Cone's start against the Padres made him understand for the first time how tough he really was. "He had nothing that day," he said. "No part of his game was in place but he didn't allow a hit until the sixth inning, when the Padres finally broke through. In some ways it was his greatest game."

David, for his part, felt that the shot was an ugly reminder of the prior year, the 1997 campaign, when he had required a number of cortisone shots along the way, and broke down entirely before the second inning of an August game against the Rangers. "I felt a grabbing, biting pain in my shoulder," Cone told me. "It was the first time I'd ever hit the wall. Up to that moment I'd always thought I could pitch through pain."

Cone made a slashing, cut-it-off gesture to his catcher, Joe Girardi, and when Torre came out to the mound he said, "I can't make it," and walked off the field. "It was the most frightened I'd ever been," David said. "I'd heard old pitchers talk about a 'frozen arm,' but up to this moment I'd never known what they meant. I literally couldn't throw the ball to the plate."

Rest and cortisone kept him going—he went on the disabled list from August 18th to September 20th—but in the opening game of that year's divisional series he was bombed for seven hits and six earned runs by the Indians, in three and a third innings, and departed. Less than two weeks after the Yankees were eliminated (the Indians eventually went on to lose the World Series to the surprising Florida Marlins), Cone had undergone an arthroscopic procedure on his shoulder at Columbia-Presbyterian Hospital—a minor cleanup of frayed bursal and labral and rotator-cuff tissue.

This was Cone's second operation in two seasons, coming as it did on the heels of the discovery of the aneurysm in his pitching arm, early in the 1996 campaign, and the surgery that kept him out of action until September of that year. The shoulder arthroscopy, by contrast, was a minor affair, and could be seen as almost a commonplace for pitchers at a similar stage of their careers. By most measurements, it was an absolute success, given Cone's twenty-win season the following summer, but he himself takes a somewhat different view. Looking back at his medical record and performances in this three-season 1998–1996 stretch—the patient's-eye retroscape that we have been following here—he was chilled by the necessity of still another shot to keep him functioning in the late going. "After the experience of seven cortisone shots in two years, I figured there had to be a better way," he told me. "It was time to start getting possession of my own arm." Acupuncture was just ahead.

David's rehab after that 1997 arthroscopy, by the way, found him throwing in warm weather but on a slowly tilting surface, where the occasional bad pitch disappeared into the Caribbean. It was November and he was headed for St. Maarten and St. Thomas aboard the cruise ship Norway, on orders from George Steinbrenner, who had promised to deliver some Yankee stars as celebrity passengers after the end of the '97 season. Operation or no operation, David was expected aboard, and the team dispatched a catcher, Gary Tuck, to handle his careful tosses on the top deck, and trainer Gene Monahan to monitor his arm. David's wife, Lynn, came along, and the touring faculty included Derek Jeter and Wade Boggs, then a free agent and soon to be a Devil Rays player. "Super cruise—I guess," Cone says now.

David had read somewhere that Mark McGwire credited a

regimen of acupuncture to his chronically sore lower back with contributing to his record-smashing seventy-homer mark in 1998, and in an article about Pete Sampras at about this time he learned that the tennis star went to the procedure for relief from a painful long-term elbow inflammation. Some athletes on recent U.S. Olympic teams had been permitted the treatment as well. A massage therapist he knew gave him the name of Dr. Jiang and her partner-husband, Dr. Shui-Guo Zheng, a neurosurgeon, who had emigrated from Guangzhou, in southern China, and in late February last year David went knocking on their door.

Cone told me once that on some mornings when he woke up he could hear crackling sounds inside his pitching shoulder. "It's like Rice Krispies in there," he said. He made nothing of this—it was a passing comment—but it reminded me once again that pitching is not a normal occupation. Pain is an almost daily reality for most major-league pitchers during the season, and an occupational ailment too common to be worth mentioning on the day after they work. Thoughts of progressive or sudden injury and the possibility of some surgery down the line hover increasingly in the minds of veteran moundsmen, marking, like stock options, the evidence of a successful career. Walk into any clubhouse and you'll notice the squiggly little surgical signatures on a number of bared elbows or shoulders—more today than ever, thanks to the greater sophistication and success of surgical interventions. I have already made note of the operation on Cone's old Royals teammate Bret Saberhagen (performed by Dr. David Altchek), who had blown out his shoulder in devastating fashion, severing a group of ligaments collectively known as the capsule. Altchek told Saberhagen not to expect a return to the mound after the extensive surgery, but the patient had other ideas, and after lengthy rehabilitation came back to pitch again. In a *New Yorker* piece I wrote a few years ago, I mentioned some celebrated current pitchers who had successfully come through surgery—Roger Clemens, Hideo

Nomo, Al Leiter, Doc Gooden, and so on—and the list has lengthened remarkably since then, more recently including Kerry Wood and Curt Schilling. Almost my favorite consultee during this tour was the Mets' Al Leiter, who told me that good old "normal soreness" on the day after you pitched felt as if you'd been punched hard in the arm about fifty times. When I suggested to him that his might be one of the few million-dollar professions that could end without warning, in the space of a single pitch, he said, "The nearest parallel I could think of is going down in a corporate helicopter crash."

Another patient I consulted, the reliever Jeff Brantley, discovered that he had been pitching for the previous five seasons with a torn labrum (a shoulder cartilage), and only then decided it was time for repairs.

"When you go out to pitch, you *pitch*," Brantley said. "You can throw through soreness—I pitched great. There's a certain amount of uncomfortability that you're going to have to overcome. The amount of damage you do depends on how long you're going to get the money and how much money you're going to get. When the ninth inning comes along, you just go out there and suck it up. When the time came when I couldn't throw anymore, I knew it was time to go for surgery."

Cone is less stoic or casual than Brantley, but he understands the situation. "There's good pain and bad pain, and one of the big issues for an athlete is distinguishing between pain and injury," he said. "Mel"—Mel Stottlemyre, his pitching coach—"is always saying 'How do you feel today? Is it the good kind of pain?' Good pain is centralized in the muscles and bad pain is an invasion of the joints."

And although David is oddly proud of his tremendous pitch counts and shows a strong aversion to coming out of games before they're finished, he admits to the built-in contradiction at the heart of the pitcher's work. The dilemma shows itself in the parable-plain moment when a manager in a critical late-season or post-season game wants an out or two more or an inning or two more from his famous starter or tough closer, even though he knows the man has nothing left and might be on the edge of a career-shortening injury. He needs to keep him pitching, right now. He wants the win for all the obvious reasons (including career reasons of his own), and the pitcher wants it, too, because he's a pitcher. Each knows what may happen but both take pride in their mutual toughness when the fires of the game are at their hottest.

Cone feels this way, of course, and he cited Orel Hershiser in 1988, when the gaunt, fierce Dodger right-hander electrified the National League Championship Series by allowing three earned runs in as many starts—and returning on a day after he'd thrown a hundred and ten pitches to pick up a save in relief. He went on to win a Most Valuable Player award for his work in the World Series, to go with his Cy Young for the regular season. After another year and a half, Hershiser underwent reconstructive shoulder surgery, as he'd more or less expected.

"It happens," David said. "I can't say enough good things about the man who can perform like that when the price is so high." And he went back again to the 1995 Yankees-Mariners divisional playoff and the moment when the frazzled Mariner ace, Randy Johnson, made an unexpected relief appearance to nail down the series finale. He had already beaten the California Angels in a one-game playoff at the end of the regular season, and he put down the Yankees in the third divisional game, to begin the Mariners' comeback from a two-game deficit. Two days later, he was back.

"This was the game I'd come out of, after that base on balls," Cone said. "I'm in the dugout, thinking how I'd let the team down, but when Randy Johnson comes in I stopped being an opponent. What Randy did—that disregard for long-term effects—is what real players do. I was proud of him. He had back trouble the next year and had to go on the D.L., and there may be a connection, but you don't think of that at the time. What we knew, watching him, was that he'd already beat us on a four-hitter and here he is back again after only one day of rest, ready to pitch some more, because he was their best. I was in awe, watching.

Here's a man about to become a free agent who could name his own price anywhere, and he pitches on like that, regardless of the risk to his career. This came on the heels of a bitter strike, when the players had been hammered in public opinion. I think America began to change its mind about players right there. Sitting in the dugout, I applauded him as a fan."

It came to me that he had been a free agent, too, or on the brink of it, in that same game, when he'd thrown a hundred and forty-seven pitches. Didn't this put him in the identical situation?

"I don't care," he said. "I'd have thrown *two* hundred and forty-seven to win that game."

If this sounds like some warrior's code, with the players in the role of scarred old samurais, it is sufficiently oblique to sustain the image. This particular conversation had come up the previous afternoon, when he and I were sitting beside the pool at the house that David and Lynn own in a gated community called Cheval, on the north side of Tampa. He had been talking in his customarily quiet, almost bland tones, but when again I brought up the hovering question about the athletes' right to their own bodies—whether they or the owners control the fate of their expensive arms and batter's muscles, and are free to make the proper decisions about their limits—he appeared to reverse himself.

"I'm a little more defiant now," he said. "The Yankees hand out this 'New York Yankees Shoulder Program' or 'Pitchers Arm Program' every year. It's a booklet about an inch thick, with different exercises and warnings, and when I get it I throw it into the trash. It's my arm they're talking about."

Did the other Yankee pitchers watch him do this? I asked.

"I guess so," he said. "There's always another copy waiting at my locker when we get back north, before the opener, and I throw that one away, too. No disrespect to Gene Monahan, the trainer, but if you don't know how to train your own arm by this time you're in trouble. I've seen pitchers who come up a little bit sore, and they're in the trainer's room every day. 'Gene, what do

I do today? What should I do now?'—it makes me sick to my stomach."

I asked him about the weight and fitness specialists that some clubs now hire as consultants, in addition to their regular staff.

"I don't need some guy who goes to Gold's Gym and gets a degree, and then wants to talk to me about how to stay in shape," he said. "If one comes into the weight room I will verbally abuse him. I know there's aerobics and all that, and I have a healthy respect for different ideas, but I don't need someone who doesn't even know me telling me what I should do."

I had a flashback to a pioneer training specialist named Gus Hoefling, who'd worked for the Phillies back in the seventies and eighties. A large, dynamic type, with hulking arms and shoulders, he would lean over his prostrate subjects, one by one, before game time, twisting their legs this way and that.

"Yeah, Gus Hoefling—I met him once or twice when I was with the Mets. He was into martial arts. He knew thirty-five different ways to kill a man. All his pitchers were in great shape and they knew martial arts and how to kill people, but they didn't know how to get batters out. Kill, kill! As a matter of fact, I don't remember too many Philadelphia pitchers then who got anybody out regularly. Well, Kevin Gross was there at one point, and I guess he actually was a pretty decent pitcher for a couple of years. I like him."

Dr. Jiang has removed the heating pads and needles. Hovering close again, kneading for each spot with her fingertip, she inserts five fresh needles, twirling them gently into place. David has told her that he threw for twenty minutes off a mound the day before at Legends Field, in his first extended session of the year. Upon awakening this morning, he felt no more than normal soreness. He took a couple of Tylenol and felt pleased that things had gone so well. But "normal soreness" means interior bruisings, he explains to me now, and the doctor, probing and inquiring, has located some likely sites during this early visit, which is David's first of the year. Now she removes one of the new needles and centers a small glass cup over the spot, then briskly sucks the air out of it with some tugs on a small hand pump. A hemisphere of flesh appears within the cup—a little kumquat of rising expectation. As we watch, it reddens and darkens to purple; a drop or two of blood pops up, riding at the top of the dome. "Good," David says, peering down at his shoulder. "This means we've brought up some of the bruise underneath. The whole idea is to create a controlled trauma to alleviate something deeper and more serious." He looks over at Dr. Jiang. "Do I have that right?"

She nods cheerfully and applies more cups—five in all. Not all the wildcatting is successful. When the treatment is over, David bears three suggestive-looking hickies on the site—"I'll hear about this in the clubhouse again," he says—while the other sites scarcely show pink. These will be revisited at a later session. Last year, when his arm was in poor condition, it took four weeks of treatments before some of the suctions brought success. He had twenty-two treatments in all, including some extensive work on his neck—he has a semi-chronic spasm near the fifth cervical vertebra—and in the lower-right dorsal area. Four times during the season he flew Dr. Jiang and her husband (and their sixteen-year-old son, David, who is interested in applying to Columbia University) to New York, for sustaining sessions. David put them up at an apartment he and Lynn keep in Manhattan—they live in Greenwich, Connecticut—and the visitors came to Yankee Stadium to sit with Lynn Cone and some friends and watch David pitch against the Tigers.

We are almost done. Dr. Jiang's husband, Dr. Zheng, comes into the room and subjects David to a massage. A tiny man whose trouser belt seems about to cut him in half, he pulls David's right arm across his chest, up under his chin, and probes here and there along the muscles. With the patient back on the table, he bends the arm another way, opening a deep fold between the packs of muscle, and his white-gloved fingers, kneading and pushing, sink knuckle-deep into the rift. Moments later, with David on his feet again, he seizes him from behind and appears to stretch his torso to a new length while he holds him, amazingly, in midair.

Back in the car, after our extensive, bowing farewells, David tells me that Dr. Zheng's massage just now was the deepest he's ever experienced. "He was touching the bone, it felt like. Felt great."

A faint scent of Dr. Jiang's balm is in the car.

"I feel better at this point than I have in a long time," David says. "I've gotten ready in my own way. I didn't pick up a ball until late January—I want to have something left late in the year this time. I have this stubborn feeling that the best is yet to come."

5

Camera Eye

Spring training began, and a few mornings later I was watching a tall right-hander named Jake Westbrook as he threw off one of the mounds beyond the right-field stands at Legends Field. The sun was out, and a handful of fans lined up along the railing of an overhead pedestrian bridge had a pelican's-eye view of Westbrook and another pitcher, directly below, each working in the little pool of his own shadow. Stimulating sounds of lumber echoed from the semi-enclosed batting cages next door. Westbrook, a rookie sinkerballer who had come over from the Expos during the winter as part of the deal that sent Hideki Irabu across the border, was popping the ball in pleasing fashion, and after a while Mel Stottlemyre stood in at the plate, in the guise of a right-handed batter, where he made a little slashing gesture in front of his belt, inviting Westbrook to show him something inside. The next pitch, a slider by the look of it, broke down toward Mel's knees, holding firm on the innermost corner, and Mel leaned back and squinted his eyes shut with happiness.

A passel of writers—Buster Olney, George King, of the *Post*, Ken Davidoff, of the *Record*, and *Post* columnist Joel Sherman— were hanging in the shade of the stands, not so much checking out Westbrook as keeping an eye on each other. George Steinbrenner was in camp somewhere, and they were engaged in the boring, meticulously observed protocol that Olney calls "mutual nuclear deterrence," which guaranteed that none of them could hope for so much as an exclusive "Good morning" from the Boss, let alone a story.

Cone, who had been getting in a work session just before, came through the chain-link gate from the bullpen area with a towel around his neck and stood with us, watching Westbrook. "Solid mechanics, and you can hear the spin on that breaker," he said. "He's got a little semi-Laredo—a sidearm slider. He's been well coached somewhere."

The writers wrote this down.

Cone, throwing from two mounds over, had showed us less. At thirty-seven, he could bring himself along at his own pace, while Westbrook, who is twenty-two and pitched last summer at the Class AA level, in Harrisburg, Pennsylvania, probably believed—despite cautionings from the coaches—that he had to produce something marvellous here with each fling. David, a couple of weeks along from our day together at Tony Ferreira's, was throwing at perhaps three-quarters speed, but now he finished his pitches with a full flow of the arm and hand, dropping his fingers down close to the dirt at the same moment that his right leg came flaring up astern. His front foot, pointing forward, came down in the same patch of dirt each time. Pulling back his left shoulder at the top of his delivery, he presented his No. 36 on the back of his uniform an instant or two before you saw it again, from the right side this time. He was himself, if not in full.

What I didn't see—I was watching through a little slot between the green plastic windscreens protecting the mound enclosure—was the slider, the bending signature pitch that would be along, if all went well, any day now. Tom Pagnozzi, a twelve-year catcher with the Cardinals who had been hoping to hook on with the Yankees for one more season (he retired, instead), had greeted Cone on the first day with a friendly, "Hey, man, hope you still got that pitch that breaks through my legs back there!" Joe Girardi, David's departed day-to-day receiver, used to claim that the pitch stopped in midair like a driver at a red light and then hung a left.

Watching David work here, idly thinking about sliders, I was struck by a fresh idea about his motion, or physics, and the roots of his work. This sort of clarifying mini-vision—a re-focussing click of the fan's camera eye—is an accepted phenomenon in the inning-by-inning repetitions of the pastime. Jerome Holtzman, the semiretired senior columnist with the Chicago *Tribune*, once told me that he had been covering the Cubs for sixteen years when he was struck, all in the middle of an ordinary midseason road trip, by an entirely new notion of how the game was really played, right down to the base runner's little forward lean as he led off first. Here, noting Cone's one-beat count in mid-windup, I unexpectedly saw the downward drop of his body, still poised atop the mound, as the first stage of the powerful thrust that drove him forward from his bent right leg and into the finishing effort and release. It was the infinitesimal pause that I had noticed or re-noticed, and, once I had it in sight, the delivery could be seen as one of those gleaming, hinged pistons on the flank of a railroad steam engine that take a little hitch and then suddenly slam forward: *Shoom!* Quite a machine, though a different model, say, from Tom Seaver's continuous full-body drop-down, which began at the very peak of his over-hand delivery and ended with the right knee of his uniform scraping the dirt of the mound.

When I tried this out on David later, he looked at me with approval, like an M.I.T. prof with a promising sophomore. "I'd say that's always been the source of my power," he said. "Managers and teammates have mentioned it to me, saying that I stayed over the rubber longer than other pitchers. It's that little moment of gather within your regular tempo. I think I picked that up early, maybe going back to when my dad was coaching me in Little League and showing me how to use my legs. Pitching coaches tried to talk me out of it as I was coming along in the game. We had some real battles. They said it would hurt my arm in the end, but I didn't agree."

David had run into Sandy Koufax over the winter, who reminded him in the manner of a Zen roshi that the pitcher's only connection to the ground in mid-delivery is his back leg. All mechanics and variations began from there.

Lingering forever over the rubber—which is to say for the fraction of a second—had everything to do with a pitch successfully finished, David went on. If he vacated too soon, his arm had to rush to catch up, and he would finish the delivery with an ineffectual snap across his body. If he waited for the gather, by contrast, he could complete the pitch at full extension and tug his fingers across the seams of the slider at the last moment. All this seemed like second nature on days when he had his rhythm, he said, and became wholly elusive when he didn't. Hideki Irabu had once told him that he held on to the ball when pitching longer than anyone he'd ever seen.

I would remember this conversation in the weeks and months to come.

Jorge Posada, at last fully fledged as the Yankee receiver, had caught Cone during this latest session, as he would repeatedly this spring. After three seasons of splitting duties with Joe Girardi, he was considered ready to assume the post full time. A switch-hitter with some signs of real power at the plate, he had appeared in almost twice as many games as Girardi in 1999; with almost any other club but the deeply stocked Yankees, he would have been the full-time receiver by now. He was twenty-eight, and it was time for him to flower, without the hovering presence of the older and more experienced man. Girardi, an eleven-year veteran, had become a free agent over the winter and signed with his home-town Chicago Cubs. But Joe had been Cone's catcher all along, and David was unhappy with the Yankees' decision to let him go. He said the right things about his new partner, to be sure, praising Posada's poise and mature attitude, but I couldn't help noticing how often the other man's name came up in conversation. The pitcher-catcher relationship is a kind of marriage, of course, and David told me once that when he was suffering from arm miseries in the middle of the 1998 season he had been so embarrassed by his ineffectuality during a warmup session in the bullpen that he angrily waved Joe out of there, after two pitches. "He can laugh about it now," Cone said, "but he was shocked. He didn't understand how I valued him. He was the one man I couldn't bear to see me pitch just then."

Girardi, who'd been a major presence in the Yankees' clubhouse, exudes the composure and gravity that attend senior specialists in the grinding trade. Cone had found that Joe was at his best at moments when things weren't going well in the game—after a particularly egregious call by the home-plate ump, say, or when the pitcher had lost his touch. "I'd be out there, with my face all red and the veins popping out in my neck, and he'd walk out and let me scream at him," David said. "I'd say 'Are you working for me there? Are you saying anything to that guy back there?' or something more X-rated than that. He'd just wait—never said anything—and he'd walk back in when I was done, shaking his head and laughing. He was the best in the world at that—no ego whatsoever."

He and Girardi had come to a compact that they would never waste time by second-guessing a pitch selection. It was more important for him to deliver a quality pitch in the right location, no matter what the result. This became the foundation of second-nature feeling between them about sequences of pitches to be rung in against a given batter. More than any other catcher Cone had worked with, Girardi had the ability to read the scouts' advance appraisal of each hitter in an incoming lineup and then to employ this intelligence in a fluid, nonliteral way, which transformed signal-calling and even made the flicked fresh option after an occasional shakeoff feel like an encouraging flow. Adapting to the proclivities and strengths of his partner on the mound came first with him.

"You have to cling to that confidence in each other," David said. "Any kind of second-guessing about pitch selection can drive you crazy, and in time it undermines the relationship." Girardi, he went on, did sometimes come over to him in the dugout and try to take the blame for a misadventure in the previous half-inning, but David would have none of it: "Remember our understanding. It's the quality of the pitch, not the selection. I just didn't throw it right."

Posada and Cone were being optimistic about their coming season together, of course. The young catcher had told me that David was informal and encouraging in their preliminary discussions, and Cone cited Posada's successful partnership with Andy Pettitte, the prime Yankee left-hand starter. But privately David said that he and Posada had different ideas about signals. Posada would put down his sign and then come quickly up into catching position, which meant that he'd have to start the whole process over again if Cone shook him off. David wanted him to wait for the shakeoff, if it was coming, and then put down the next possibility at once. He wanted that flow, not an exchange of letters. (It was this difference in styles that made Cone more comfortable pitching to Chris Turner, the backup catcher, once the regular season began.)

"The one thing I've been telling Jorge is not to take things personally," he said. "A young catcher trying to establish himself can be a little headstrong. He can take offense at me shaking off pitches. Or if I show emotion on the mound, he can interpret it as showing him up or disrespecting him, and that's not the case. Some pitchers need to vent—it's part of their personality."

"Pitchers like you," I said.

"Pitchers like me. But it's never about him—that's all he has to learn."

There was a shared laugh, perhaps about overlapping memories of some of his better eruptions. Just the year before, pitching on Old Timers' Day at the Stadium, he had got into trouble against the Twins, in front of the big afternoon crowd, at one point surrendering four runs after two outs, and came out of the game after five innings. Stalking into the clubhouse, he had found some kids playing there—young sons of teammates or visiting Yankee alumni—and had let fly at this violation of club-house sanctity, yelling and heaving chairs. "A real immature baseball snappage," he called it now. He stomped back to the dugout to collect himself, and when he came back the club-house was a tomb. This was nothing, he told me, compared to some explosions he had witnessed—the time, say, when George Brett demolished a toilet in Minnesota with his bat, leaving shat-tered porcelain and a prettily pulsing fountain. "I'm not real proud of what I did," David said, "but maybe somebody learned what a clubhouse is all about. Actually, I used to do this more, but now I don't have the energy."

Joe Girardi was missing David, too—it worked both ways. "He's brilliant, super intelligent," he said when I talked with him short weeks later—on Easter Sunday, in fact, before a Cubs game at Shea Stadium. "He's the most enjoyable pitcher I ever caught. Every day was something different—even from inning to inning he would change. You never got bored. You know, when he came back after the rain delay in the perfect game—it was a pretty long wait—his stuff was actually better than it had been before."

Most other pitchers—and most other athletes, for that mat-ter—failed to tap their full talents, to Girardi's way of thinking, but never David. "The thing he always brings to the mound, whether he has his best stuff or average stuff on a given day, is the willingness to win. That and his creativity allows him to get outs better than anyone I've seen. I miss him tremendously."

Girardi didn't seem to want to let me go without a full appre-ciation of his old friend. "I hope you know," he said as we parted, "David's become a really important pitcher to the city of New York."

It came to me during our talks about catchers that most of Cone's pitching convictions were not about times when things were going well out there but the opposite. Great games were mindless—you locked in and let it happen. The other kind—"struggle games," as he called them—turned up without warn-ing, even between one pitch and the next in a game that had been strong and easy. "Sometimes it's not being quite comfortable on the mound that can do that," he said. "Or if you get distracted holding base runners on. Any little thing can start you fighting it, making too many adjustments from pitch to pitch. But that's when you become a pitcher—when things suddenly aren't going your way. Those games can be the most gratifying of all if you work them through."

He distrusted pitchers who hadn't learned how to adjust— "low aptitude" types, in his phrase. "That's why I've gone to all these different angles," he went on. "I used to have games in my career where I kept banging my head against the wall, making the same kind of pitch over and over, the same rhythm, the same windup, trying to make it work. I just won't allow myself to do that anymore. I'm gonna throw it underhand if I have to."

Hideki Irabu had almost been both kinds of pitcher, David said. "He'd picked up a slow curve and an occasional changeup, and on days when you played catch with him he showed he could tweak his wrist to get different kinds of movement. But when he got into a game the slightest thing would throw him off—a bad call, some tiny thing with the mound. He'd be lights-out unhittable and in the next instant nothing—gone for the day."

The night before the first full team workout at Legends Field, David learned that another old teammate, Darryl Strawberry, had failed a routine drug test in January, imposed as part of his probation the year before for possession of cocaine and the soliciting of a prostitute. Those charges had led to a hundred-and-twenty-day suspension from baseball by Commissioner Bud Selig—a lenient sentence, in view of a prior failed test in 1995, but one that took account of Strawberry's ongoing struggle against colon cancer, which had required surgery just before the 1998 World Series and extensive chemotherapy. I had seen him in Tampa the following spring, when he was so weak that he had to leave the field after a couple of batting-practice swings and seek the shelter of a dugout. Freed at last of his suspension and

with his strength mostly restored, he made it back to the Yankees in September, playing twenty-four games as a designated
hitter. In limited appearances during the team's swift progres-
sion through the post-season, he batted .333 at each stage, and
drove in all three runs in the deciding game against the Rangers,
down in Arlington, with a first-inning homer.

Now all that was over—or so it felt to David. Driving to Legends Field on the morning after the bad news, he knew what he
would find there, and wished for once that he would not be
placed in the middle of things and expected to say something
wise and defining. There were almost a hundred media people
waiting in the clubhouse, and the TV crews and commentators,
lined up outside, presented "a wolflike atmosphere."

David told me about it by telephone that night—I'd gone
home for a few days—and repeated what he'd said for the cameras and writers. He was not going to abandon Straw now, because of his addiction. He was his friend and he would support
him, but he was extremely worried. This could close the page at
last on Strawberry's career—a possibility that had hung over
him for years now but was still painful for his teammates to
think about.

The surprise was that Straw had turned up that morning and
dressed with the other Yankees. Torre called the standard first-
day team meeting, and Straw used the occasion to apologize to
his teammates. He said he needed their support and then he
broke down—"one step ahead of us," David said.

A strange, sad day. Darryl, out on the field for calisthenics,
was approached by George Steinbrenner, who put an arm
around him as they spoke. Meeting some writers afterward,
Steinbrenner said, "It's a disease, that's what we have to realize.
I'm going to stand by him and see that he rights his life. If it's
in baseball, fine, if it's outside of baseball, fine. But that's up
to Bud."

The commissioner wasn't there, but word soon came from
his office, and Strawberry was told he'd have to leave the field.
Five days later, he was given a year's suspension. At thirty-

seven, outside the shelter of a team and teammates, he had passed from sight. "I hope it's not the end of his career," Joe Torre said, "because I don't know what that would mean."

David reminded me that he and Straw went back together to 1987 and the March day when he joined the Mets, where the twenty-five-year-old Darryl—the boy monster, with his disarming sweetness and sweeping, easeful swing—was already a star among stars on the reigning World Champions, with four seasons and a hundred and eight home runs behind him. "Do you remember how you felt when he came into the room?" David said. "It changed everything, the way he looked."

I asked whether he believed Strawberry's apology had been sincere. I'd heard him talk this way before, I said, and I remembered a time a few years back, when he was with the Dodgers, and he'd said that he'd be all right now because he'd found God.

"I've seen a lot of players who were alcoholics or addicts trying to find a substitute," Cone said. "I always felt Darryl wanted to believe in God, when he went that way. It was never a line for him. He was trying to find something."

And now?

"And now." He sighed. "He'll need his friends. He and I have as much of a history together as anyone. I'll be talking to him— maybe on a different level than others. He knows I don't bullshit him."

There was a silence, and then David said that he'd been very surprised at George. Surprised and touched. "He got right to the heart of it," he said.

A further conversation that belongs in here—an argument, rather—is the one I'd heard from a number of friends of mine a year earlier, when Darryl was faced with the solicitation and possession rap, and was suspended. They were angry at Strawberry and tired of his act. He had subjected us too long to his problems and addictions. He was a wealthy, celebrated figure, they said, with access to the best therapies and counselling, and none of it mattered to him. Sure, Straw had grown up in difficult, even daunting circumstances—he'd come out of an infamous

L.A. ghetto, and had an abusive father—and had had to adjust to the lure of sudden fame and extraordinary financial rewards, but other people in sports had faced similar challenges and had handled them. This was old. Forget Straw.

My own disagreement with this strongly held common view—to me some people appear able to find the handle and others cannot—doesn't matter, but Cone's was more practical, and went back to his beginnings in organized ball. Scouted by his home-town Kansas City Royals, he was selected out of high school in the third round of the 1981 amateur draft, and signed for seventeen thousand five hundred dollars, plus a limited college-scholarship program. He was eighteen, and had already accepted a considerable football and baseball scholarship to the University of Missouri. At the moment of signing, he was practicing for a high-school all-star football game, matching the best statewide players from Missouri and Kansas in an annual game to be played at Arrowhead Stadium, the home field of the N.F.L. Kansas City Chiefs. Cone was a quarterback and star punter for Rockhurst High. The Royals scout, Carl Blando, discouraged him from going ahead with the big game; he was team property now, and too valuable to risk in another sport. The scholarship program—well, he could catch up with that later on. Right now, he was expected at the Royals' Rookie League team, in Sarasota. David signed the contract, gave two thousand dollars to his father, and blew the rest on a down payment for a cherry-red Camaro Z-28. He was on his way.

Not quite the Darryl Strawberry story, but not too far from it, at that. Cone, who had ambitions to wind up as a sportswriter, had already enrolled in journalism courses at Missouri, but winter ball followed hard on the instructional league that fall, and he didn't get home, really, until Thanksgiving the following year. There was no time for college, and no one from the major leagues came around to bring up the subject, then or later.

"Why not have a major-league or a minor-league career *and* go to college?" David had said when we first talked about his early days. "I don't believe that Major League Baseball has any interest at all in the college-scholarship program. They want to develop player skills but not players. Nobody cares if baseball winds up with large numbers of young people who are out of the game by the time they're twenty-seven or twenty-eight or thirty and have no skills and no future."

He said almost the same thing in Tampa now, about his old teammate—he was the only one to make the connection. Strawberry had been signed out of Crenshaw High School, in Los Angeles, for two hundred and fifty thousand dollars, after being selected No. 1 in the national amateur draft in 1980, and was swept at once into the Mets' system. Fame and New York were only three years away. What did we expect Darryl Strawberry to become under such circumstances, David said to the hordes of writers. "Here, be levelheaded about it. Here, handle it"—was that a reasonable expectation?

Cone hasn't decided exactly what he'll do when he hangs up his spikes, but working with the Players Association to improve the major-league college-scholarship program—to give it some practical meaning, that is—keeps coming up when he talks about it.

No Girardi and no Straw this year, then—and no Chili, either. Fans no longer expect a big-league team to go intact from year to year in these fluid times, and though the Yankees have kept a core of front-line players together for years now—Paul O'Neill, Bernie Williams, Mariano Rivera, Tino Martinez, Derek Jeter—another gap in the millennial Yankee roster was the tall, suave, switch-hitting Chili Davis, a d.h. who stimulated the '99 champions with his bat in the first half of the season, and with his cool at all times. Chili for Charles: a smooth-pated, butter-voiced veteran—he'd once been a fixture with the Giants—who'd gone into retirement at thirty-nine, after nineteen years in the show. "No one will know how to enjoy it more," David said.

I can remember dropping by Chili's locker in May of 1999, when he was batting close to .360, and asking him what was going on. He gave the question a serious moment of cogitation, and offered "More *rest*?" He slid off to .269 in the end, with nineteen homers, and I'd watched his at-bats in the playoffs and the World Series with memorial intensity, trying to hold on to him before he disappeared down the dugout steps for the last time.

Chili and David had been a comfort to each other in the late weeks of the season. "We told everybody on the team that we'd carried them for the first half, and it was time for somebody else to step up," David told me. "In August and September, Chili would be the first in the clubhouse every day. He'd get an hour-and-a-half massage from a therapist and then go sit in the hot tub. I'd come by and say how old he looked. That was about the time I'd given up my side sessions between starts—me who'd always been the one who really pushed those, and notoriously threw long and hard. I'd just keep that going until I was happy and satisfied back then. Now I was calling the acupuncturist to get up here for a visit, and I was getting in a lot of swimming. Two old men."

Back in February, on a day when David had stopped off for a moment at the Yankees year-round training complex, a block or two away from Legends Field, I saw a couple of minor-league coaches take him aside for an earnest private conversation, ending with handshakes. Shortly after the season, a security person at Yankee Stadium did the same thing. "I wrote you a letter but I wanted to say it in person," I overheard him say. "You made a difference for us all."

When I asked about this, Cone explained with some reluctance that he and Chili Davis had come up with an idea late in the previous summer before the ritual closed-door clubhouse meeting at which the champions vote on the number of championship-series and World Series shares to be divided up when the players' end was counted up by the commissioner's office. This time, a full share of the three-tier competitions came out to $307,809 apiece for thirty-six champion Yankees. What wasn't announced was that Cone and Chili Davis had persuaded their teammates to vote an extra full share, cutting their own slices a mite thinner, so that some lesser-known members of the Yankee family got a slice of the pie as well. As a result, a dozen minor-league coaches and trainers, scouts, and administrative personnel were startled to receive checks for about twenty-five thousand dollars in the mail. Baseball teams sometimes give the appearance that they're trying to make up for those astronomic player salaries by pinching everyone at the lower levels, but this time, thanks to Chili and David, a few more Yankees could feel like champions when the flags came down.

Cone's charitable donations and extensive work in good causes—notably on behalf of children's care and long-term medical research—are well known, but that handshake says something else about him. His athletic accomplishments require an effort that looks to be beyond the rest of us, but when they're over his first thought is to shorten that distance. Not everyone has this instinct. One ballplayer who pulled off a great personal coup not too long ago called his agent afterward and arranged to have his fee at card shows bumped higher. After Cone threw his perfect game against the Expos, he ordered eighty-four handsome Swiss Ebel watches to be sent out, suitably inscribed, to his teammates, coaches, family, friends, and advisers. The bill came to around two hundred thousand dollars. "I got lucky," he said to me, "and I wanted to remember some of the people who'd helped."

6

David and Ed

The first coach David Cone ever met told him never to throw a ball or a stone or a stick without throwing it at something. Never throw aimlessly. If you're throwing at a tree, pick part of the tree and try to hit it. If you're tossing a ball with somebody, even for fun, pick a target—throw at his belt buckle. If you're chucking a rock into a pond, take part of the pond and chuck it there. Pay attention.

This was early, back home in Kansas City. When David was seven, he tried out for the Spartans, a kids' team in the Three-and-Two, a chain of local Little League clubs. The manager of the Spartans was John Hager, a lawyer who was a friend of the family, so David was pretty sure he had an in. Wrong. He was too young and got cut, but made the team the next year at second base. The following summer, there was a new manager—it was his father, Ed Cone—who put him at third base, where he hung on and got better. Ed had been working with him right along, starting with that hit-part-of-the-pond principle. David kept campaigning to become a pitcher—he wanted to be in the middle of things—and after another season went by Ed took him out behind their house at 5210 St. John Avenue and said, "Never throw as hard as you can. Back off. Always keep something in reserve."

This is good advice for any occupation, but David, one senses, may have figured it out already. He was an insatiable kid athlete, mad about sports. "He couldn't *wait* to play," Ed Cone told me. David's desire and competitiveness had a year-round outlet at home, where he and his brothers and his father played touch football and basketball only when the weather turned too cold for the real game. The Cone house—a crowded old three-story affair with a stone-pillared front porch, next door to an apartment building—was in the Northeast district, a blue-collar Kansas City neighborhood once heavily Italian but by that time, the late nineteen-sixties, with as many or more Irish-American residents, and now with a few Hispanic and African-American families as well. Not a bad place for kids. There was a diamond in Budd Park, right across the street, and if that was in use you could always set up on a dirt diamond behind the tennis courts, not far away, where the grass had been worn away by use, with a big oak tree for a backstop. David preferred this to the formal field, with its fences and parents, and for him and his neighborhood friends—Steve Doherty and Danny Miller and the Hertzog brothers, and the others—it became the place to play. Late in the day, the action moved over into the Cone back yard, where Ed had installed floodlights on the back of the house, converting the space into Coneway Park, in local locution, except when it was called Conedlestick. There wasn't room for baseball—you'd be breaking windows—but ferocious Wiffle-ball games there were scored with Little League rules, except that grounders counted as outs. Loud arguments broke out after each line drive plocked into the air: "A double, a double—and that's another run!"—"Nah, are you *crazy*—that's a single, just ask Dad. *Dad?*"

David, the kid brother, hated to lose—couldn't stand it—and threw himself into the middle of groups and games, trying to keep up with Danny and their older brother, Chris. The oldest Cone child, Christal, told me that when she was in eighth grade she would meet David at kindergarten each day and walk him home. "Half the time when I got there I had to get him out of an argument or a fight," she said. "You could tell where he was in the room because something was always going on around him. It became a family joke. He was ornery, even then. He wasn't aggressive or vicious but he didn't let anybody take advantage. As the youngest sibling, he'd learned not to let anyone push him around."

Within a few years, friends of Danny and Chris got used to this grim-faced, shoulder-high figure cutting in front of them on the basketball court to grab a loose ball, or slinging a weird-looking sidearm Wiffle-ball pitch that made you laugh as it flickered past your knees. If David ever backed off from scrimmages with boys who were four or five years older, it was only for fear of losing it again, getting into another scrap, and then an early bedtime. He loved to pitch, and anyone who has ever thrown that airy white plastic Wiffle ball will know why. Grab it and let fly, with your fingers a little off to one side, and the thing sails and dips like crazy. Whenever David spotted an eccentric or overpowering major-league pitcher on the tube—a Bert Blyleven or a Vida Blue—he ran out back and became the guy in a minute. An epochal affinity for the flamboyant Luis Tiant, who had lately moved to the Red Sox, was just down the line and it influenced him for life.

He was an athlete. When a friend of Chris's handed him an old Jack Kramer wooden-frame tennis racquet, he signed on for lessons in Budd Park and for the first time in his life perhaps slighted baseball a little. Within a year, he had won the Twelve-and-Under Kansas City Parks singles title. But it was hard to fit in another sport, and Ed worried about tennis elbow—a genuine hazard for a kid who wanted to be a pitcher. David abandoned the game and has scarcely picked up a racquet since.

Sports were at the center of things with the Cones—not just for the success and pleasure that they found in their pursuit but as a family lingua franca and world view. Games that the boys played in and games that their father coached were part of the larger web of local school and neighborhood and college sports, and of the stuff that flooded the television screen at home each night and all through the weekends, and had direct connection to the fate of the local K.C. teams—the Chiefs and the Kings and the Royals (who had replaced the Athletics a bit before). David remembers the first game his father took him to at Municipal Stadium, and the excitement he felt when Ed pointed out Lou Piniella, the Royals outfielder, who was autographing cards for some kids just down at the end of their row. But Lou stopped and went off to the dugout before David could get there—a secret relief to him, because he had been so nervous about getting so close to a real player this way.

Ed Cone was a night-shift maintenance mechanic in a freezer at the Swift meat-processing plant, over the Missouri River in the other Kansas City, where he worked a sixty-two-and-a-half-hour week, with a lot of overtime. Before this, he had done the same sort of work at Armco Steel. Maintenance mechanics had evolved from the old craft system—sheet-metal workers, carpenters, electricians, and the like—and the job combined all these skills. There were forty-two Swift M.M.s out of seven hundred-odd production workers, and they installed the basic machines—meat grinders and slicers, conveyers, boxing and packaging units, and the like—and then kept them in repair and up to speed. At Swift, the first stages of meatpacking were done in a cooler, where the temperature was kept at a level below fifty degrees, and the work was finished in the freezer.

Ed went off to work well before dawn—David could hear the garage door slam shut, just under his bedroom window—but the hard hours did free him up for coaching, after the kids got home from school. Days when there was a lot going on Ed didn't get any sleep at all; the second day was strange, bringing light-headedness and touches of nausea around three in the morning, but after that he was O.K. again.

David was the baby, seven years younger than Christal and five years behind Chris, with the other brother, Danny, in between. David showed precocious athletic promise, but there is evidence that his dad had plans for him right from the start.

Twenty-four hours after he was born, Ed and Joan had still not settled on the baby's name, and Ed went home from St. Mary's Hospital at last, convinced that his entry, "Theodore Samuel Cone," had carried the day. "Theodore" for Ted Williams, of course, but the "Samuel," in this case, for Sam Huff, the New York football Giants' linebacker. "Now batting, Teddy Cone"—it had a ring to it, except that when Ed got back to the maternity ward the next morning there was the birth certificate with "David Brian Cone," ready for sealing. "I was kind of upset," Ed admits.

When David began to totter about, Ed gave him a kid-size yellow plastic baseball bat, which he never seemed to let go of, and the coach was happy to see that he could flail it from both sides. "He could still become a switch-hitter if he ever wanted to go back and play in the National League," Ed said not long ago. Chris Cone remembers David as being bratty and a pain, but he laughs when he talks about his assurance. When he was scarcely more than a batboy he got into a game one day as a pinch-hitter. It was a close game, with a runner on base, and a dad-coach named Jim Vochatzer gave him the bunt signal, flashing the signs carefully for the little fellow. David ignored him and swung away: strike one. Vochatzer came down the line glaring, and did it again: watch me, kid—it's a bunt. Another mighty swing and a miss. The sign was flashed once again—you couldn't expect a newcomer like this to work out a walk or a base hit, so make him bunt, even on two strikes—and when David swung again and fanned Vochatzer yelled at him angrily. Ed Cone was watching behind the screen and he yelled at Vochatzer for yelling at his kid. Little League ball, all right.

"David was born for sports," Ed told me. "He had desire and the willingness to work hard. There was a time on an Armco Little League team when we were playing him at third base on days he wasn't pitching, and I told him that the more practice ground balls he could take the better. From then on, he'd make me hit him thirty or forty grounders whenever I had the time to give, and after I'd quit he'd go around until he found somebody else to hit some more."

Pitching was always the goal, and early on Ed persuaded David to hang back a little in the middle of his windup—keeping things together, so to speak—while his arm caught up and came forward in rhythm with his stride. "That made me into a pitcher," David recalls now. "With that, I began to look pretty much the way I look now. It all started with him."

Ed, who had grown up on the West Side of Kansas City, had played sandlot sports in his day. He was a pitcher, too, a side-armer, but found that there were always kids playing who were better than he was. He persevered and played a lot of baseball and basketball, without entertaining thoughts of making a career as an athlete. He missed college, in any case, except for a few early semesters at Southwest Missouri State. His father, Edwin L. Cone, was a well-known figure in the wide-open rough-and-tumble mid-century Kansas City, back when Harry Truman's friend and political patron Boss Pendergast ran things, and cowmen and cattle buyers filled up the Tenderloin bars. He leased and managed a string of downtown hotels. Ed was being groomed to move into the business, but there was an epochal falling-out—Ed won't talk about it—and he went off to work in the Armco Steel plant instead. This was killingly hard work, at low wages, but he could be his own man there. He was married by now, to a smart, capable girl named Joan Curran he'd met after dating a friend of hers at Northeast High. Joan was nineteen and a Protestant, while the Cones were Catholic: another act of defiance. The paycheck at Armco soon meant more than ever, since Ed was supporting a new family.

Ed and Joan were hot-shot bowlers—the house filled up with trophies—but what Ed was best at away from the mill was coaching. He had success with his Little League teams, and in 1975 took an all-star Three-and-Two squad to the Junior Babe Ruth League Tournament, in Wichita, and won it. David, who was twelve and the youngest player on the squad, pitched the second game and threw a no-hitter. Meantime, Ed was developing an amazingly successful junior-high basketball program at Holy Cross parochial school, down the block, where the kids

went. When David started to play there, once again the youngest
kid on the floor, he began to model himself on Tiny Archibald
and Scott Wedman, his heroes on the N.B.A. Kansas City Kings
team, which he followed all winter over the tube at home. In
1974, Ed's squad, the Holy Cross Crusaders, won the seventh-
and-eighth-grade Kansas City Parochial School League championship; two years later, they won it again. At one point, his boys
ran off a string of forty wins and one loss.

"He was way into it," David recalls. "He was highly organized
and technically strong. He wasn't afraid to grab kids and get in
their faces—I'd call him from the Bobby Knight school. He com-
manded respect but there was a fear factor, too. He was a great
coach, you have to say it. We had some legendary battles. I had
a reputation of throwing tantrums in those early basketball
games, and in baseball, too—crying and stomping, ripping my
uniform—particularly if we'd lost, or times in practice when
things didn't go right and my dad had yelled at me. I'd yell back,
defiantly, and he'd order me off the court or out of the game—
send me home. I don't know what that was, me lashing out that
way."

Chris Cone had been a basketball star before David came
along. He had a picture-perfect jump shot. By the time he was a
senior, at St. Pius X, a private Catholic high school, north of the
river, recruiters from some of the Midwest basketball powers—
Kansas and William Jewell—were turning up at his games.
Then, on the eve of a state tournament, he suffered a grand-mal
epileptic seizure during a game and was hospitalized. He recovered quickly—there have been no recurrent episodes of the illness—but the treatment appeared to slow his reflexes. The
recruiters drifted away. Chris took a scholarship to the lower-
level University of Missouri at Kansas City, and dropped out after a time.

David was the better player, no two ways. A strong-shooting
guard and an intimidating rebounder, he regularly played a level
or two above his age—with sixth graders when he was in fifth,
and so on—and soon came to dominate his league and the post-

season tournaments. In his seventh-grade year, he averaged thirty-eight points per game. Steve Doherty, a close friend to this day, remembers that David didn't get into many fights in his Holy Cross basketball games. "Guys on the other team would take one look at him and back off," he says. "They didn't want to mess with him." In one game, David was wearing an aluminum guard on his left hand, protecting an injured finger, and when he fouled out of the game he came at the opposing player who had provoked the call and whacked him with the armor. "It was simple about David," Ed Cone told me. "He couldn't be stopped."

Domineering sportsdads and prodigally talented kid athletes are so much on our minds these days that such tales stir a little cloud of doubt about Ed Cone and his motives, even from this distance. He isn't such a distant figure, at that. He and David talk at length by telephone after some of David's games—the senior Cones, who are retired, live in Olathe, Kansas, south of Kansas City, in a comfortable golf-course development, and pass their winters in a condominium across the bridge from Sanibel-Captiva, in Florida—and David values his judgment about pitching technicalities. This pattern is a common one in baseball. Joe McIlvaine, the Mets' mid-eighties vice-president who was thrilled by scouting reports of this loose-armed kid relief pitcher named Cone on the Kansas City roster and then pulled off the celebrated trade that filched him away, told me not long ago that he didn't know about other American families but wherever there was a promising young athlete you almost always found a strong father in the picture as well. "Keith Hernandez's father was the example," he told me last summer. "Whatever was great about Keith—and there was a lot—you have to credit in some part to his father. And whatever wasn't so great, in your opinion, you could also—" He waved the thought away.

David told me that Davey Johnson, the Mets' manager in the eighties, was mystified one summer when he kept finding pine tar on the receiver of the telephone in his clubhouse office. Then it dawned on him that Hernandez, his great first baseman and team captain, was sneaking in there and calling home for mid-game counselling.

Sports fathers count for so much that McIlvaine, who now scouts for the Twins, always finds it useful to bring them up in his first conversations with a young high-school or college player he is tailing: "'Tell me about your dad,' I say, and whatever they say then will fill me in in important ways about that player and his future."

David talks about Ed, too, but has no doubts about his father's motives. "There was never a suggestion that my success in sports, if it came along, would be some kind of an avenue to financial success for him," he said one day in Tampa. "He wasn't proving anything through me. With him, sports was an avenue for his kids to get a better education. We were sports-crazy in my family, but the real obsession was always school. You might say it didn't work out that way with me."

David knows that his father has a satellite dish at home, so he can keep tuned to his starts, wherever his team may be, and another, smaller one, mounted on a bit of plank, that he takes with him if the Cones are travelling, so that he can zero in on David even from a motel. Ed also comes East to catch some games each year, and to the big post-season series, as they come along, but this affiliation and attention doesn't weigh on their relationship. It's almost the other way around. "My dad has been perfect in all this," David said once. "He's never interfered. He's been the model. I only wish I'd remembered to bring him to more games or to call him more times after I'd pitched. I know he lives and dies with every pitch, but sometimes three or four games have gone by and we haven't talked. My mother has called me at times, to remind me. I wish I'd kept him closer. It's only that I've had to be independent."

I heard this, in other variations, throughout our summer together, and always found something disturbing and familiar in it, a thread of mixed colors that may run through many American family tales. David often ends such a conversation with a reference to his independence, and his tone brightens when he does so. He is a reflective but not a particularly intuitive man. Without being cold or self-bedazzled or downright nasty (anyone in baseball can fill out an All-Star roster in each of these categories), he can show flashes of the smooth disregard of others that comes with celebrity—but there is a persistent something within him, a knot of honesty or anxiety, that sends him back over things in his mind, where he tries to find a resolution. Lynn Cone once told me that baseball has allowed David the luxury of not feeling things, but I notice that when he talks about his family, feelings—or at least sadness—are what come out.

Ed Cone said, "I'd love to have had the talent that David does, but I never felt I was living my dreams through him. It wasn't that way at all. I tried to encourage him and maximize his skills. I always felt he'd make it, but of course I didn't anticipate this level of success. Never ever."

The Northeast neighborhood of Kansas City has changed since 1979, when the Cones sold the house and moved to the more up-scale South Side of town. The unpretentious closely adjoining family houses are divided into rental units now, not recently painted, and though there are still some plants hanging from porch beams here and there, the place has a tired look. The grass at Budd Park, across the street, is patchy on the edges and there are empty plastic Pepsi bottles in view. A drugstore and a café just up the street from the Cones' on St. John Avenue have vanished, and the house itself may be vacant now as well. There's a broken wire gate in the middle of the front yard but no fence to go with it, and you can see planks stored in what used to be Christal's room, on the top floor. Driving around the neighborhood, Ed picks out the house where David's friend Danny Miller once lived, and the Hertzogs' house, which is set back a little in its row, but he doesn't know anyone here anymore. "This was an old-fashioned working-class sort of place," he says at one point. "You knew your neighbors and there was a lot of conversation in the evenings, porch to porch." A big, eight-story gray building, down the hill, that was formerly a Montgomery Ward distribution center looks mostly empty—the company moved out in the eighties, taking more than a thousand jobs—and there are four baseball diamonds in the space behind it, where once there were five. The dirt on the base paths has been recently rolled, though, which is a good sign.

"Back then, we'd practice here starting around four o'clock, and games began at six-fifteen," Ed says. "With each diamond, there'd be a couple of teams waiting to play as soon as the first game ended, and then the late softball leagues moved in after that. The stands would be filled up, and there was horseshoe pitching in those spaces over there. Families everywhere. If you asked somebody at work 'Where were you yesterday?' they'd say, 'Down behind Ward's.'"

There's an idyllic, Norman Rockwell sound to this, but the truth of those times is less sunny. Work was the reality. Joan was a secretary and later became a travel agent, but when she got home nights she was worn down and in no mood to put anything fancy on the table. Sometimes they all went out to McDonald's instead. David wore jeans and shirts handed down from his brothers, and Christal recalls that there were times in the early days when it was hard to find milk for the kids. When Joan was working at the T.W.A. business office downtown, she and Ed would save up their vacation times and go out to the airport, where they could pick up freebie seats for a family trip somewhere—maybe the big one to Disneyland. The trouble was that T.W.A. flights with six empty seats were hard to come by, so the Cones kept getting bumped at the last minute. David remembers coming home again that way, with their packed bags. "I was only four or five," he says, "so it was hard for me to understand. But we finally made it to Disneyland—I still remember the trip. My dad got sick on the plane."

He also remembers, as kids do, a day when he was very young and knocked over a glass of milk on the table when the Cones were eating at a good restaurant, for a change—and the way everyone came down on him for it. "My parents were disciplinarians," he says. "They'd get angry with you and show it.

They grabbed you. There were rules—it was the old-fashioned way of raising kids. If you complained or got out of line they said, 'This is the way things are done in this house. If you don't like it you can get out.' That was a refrain."

School was old-fashioned, too, and the nuns at Holy Cross didn't hesitate to slap the kids, even the ones sitting in their chairs, to keep order or get attention. As often as not you got slapped in the face. One lay teacher was famous for coming up behind a kid who was talking in class or peeking around during a test, grabbing the boy by the hair and working him over. "It was called 'woolling,'" David said. "He was an expert at it. You could do that then."

Ed Cone had his rules, too. If David or one of the others talked back or cursed during practice, he'd be banished: "That's it—get home." Steve Doherty remembers the Cones as being tough but close-knit. "If there were any troubles with the family they'd never let it show," he says. "They kept it at home. They were proud that way."

When David or his brothers got into a fight or cursed or broke something at home they knew what was waiting. "That's it—get the stick," Ed said, and the boy would go upstairs and find the stick he kept behind the bedroom door—a heavy, flat thing, like a bed slat. Then Ed would come up the stairs, too. "You'd hand him the stick and bend over and take your swats," David said. "It got your attention—it left welts. I remember that long walk up the stairs, how dreadful it was. Going to get the weapon he was going to beat your butt with. That was the way he had been raised, you know, but imagine anyone doing that nowadays . . ."

The stick wasn't a daily or even a weekly event, and the ritual began to wane after Chris, in his middle teens, took a stand one night and offered to fight his father if it went on any longer. They fought, but then the two backed off, realizing what they were doing, what they'd gotten to. "It didn't happen again," David said, "but I'll never forget my brother making that stand."

Ed Cone is notably quiet and polite today—he speaks in low,

careful tones—and it's hard to imagine his earlier self in these tales. He appears to have been a different person then—Eddie Mack, as he was called in the neighborhood. He liked to take a drink with his friends, and while he didn't go around picking on people, he had a temper and was quick with his fists. Not a man to mess with. Lynn Cone told me that she has seen the Cone anger in David at times but that while the two of them have had their red-faced screaming fits, like any other couple, she knows it would never come to more than that with him. David once told her that everything he had done in this world was in order not to be like his father.

This is a dark picture, and David has been at pains to fill it in for me with warmer colors. Christmases were big—it was the only time the Cones went to Mass, and there was a big family meal somewhere—and birthdays strictly kept, always with a cake. A favorite grandmother—Ed's mother, Cleo, known as Ha-Ho, from some infant's mispronunciation of her name—came through with calls and gifts on such days, and with sweetly inscribed cards that contained a nice twenty-dollar bill. Ha-Ho was on David's side, and when she and her sister Clova died, both in 1999, it left a big hole in the family—the last connection to a different world, in his estimation. The Cones are of Irish extraction, but they've been in this country for a long time. A great-great grandfather, Orvando Cone, died of a musket wound at the Second Battle of Bull Run. There is a persistent story in the family that another forebear was a Cherokee.

Ed and Joan were dog people and always had at least a couple in the house—a German shepherd, Bandit, and a beautiful bluetick hound named Little Blue, and many others—but there was a sad turnover because of the traffic on St. John Avenue. David was out there the day when Sam, a favorite terrier, got nailed and took off yelping, leaving a trail of blood. He ran after him, crying and calling, and finally chased him down a mile or more away, then went knocking on doors to find someone to call his father. "We saved him," he says. "I saved him."

The Cones were into things—sports and school, politics and

family—and they brought an immense energy to everything they took on. They were hard-rock Democrats and union loyalists. "Bleeding-heart liberals," Christal says. "Still are." Harry Truman, whose house was in nearby Independence, was a household god. When Ed was a young man, his first job was as a messenger for the Commerce Bank, in Kansas City—exactly the same job that Truman had held in his youth. A few years ago, Ed was reading the David McCullough biography of Truman and was startled to find a claim that Dwight D. Eisenhower's brother Arthur had held down the same post as well. "The hair stood up on the back of my neck," Ed says.

David remembers his father going out of his way to persuade African-American kids in the neighborhood to come out for his Little League squads. When one of these kids was affronted by a racial slur he'd heard or sensed during a practice workout and walked off, Ed found out where he lived and went and talked to his parents that night, and won him back. The union affiliation ran almost as deep. Late in his career, and a senior master mechanic by now, he got into an argument about overtime with the management at Swift and walked off the job. Confident of his seniority and his status in the United Food and Commercial Workers Union local, he had actually booked a flight to New York to go and see David pitch at Shea when the management called him and backed down.

Joan, one senses, had the harder path always. Married young, she had four children in short order. She had grown up in a family without men—her father disappeared when she was young—and here she was in an acutely male sports-crazy family, with never enough time or money to go around. Cancer took her three sisters early, and then her mother—she herself had a cancerous growth removed from a lung a few years ago—but there was reserve or sternness to the Currans' makeup even before that. "Four harsh women," David once described them. On another day he said, "I really feel for my mom. I think how tough that must have been for her trying to break out of a world like that and then finding herself married and with children right away. There were always us kids to take care of while she was working and worn down."

The insistence on a good education for the children came as much from Joan as from Ed, and the family found enough money to send all the kids to private Catholic high schools—Christal to Glennon, an all-girls high school, Chris and Danny to St. Pius X, and David to Rockhurst. Rockhurst always fielded powerhouse football and basketball teams, but David and Chris both say that David was sent there for the academics, even though he was far and away the best-known freshman athlete in the region by the time he entered, in the fall of 1977. Ed had wanted Chris to go to Rockhurst, too, but he didn't know any of the kids there and refused. Joan had got her way about the importance of school—both parents did, really—but the cost of it was something she often brought up in family conversations. The family was always close to the line, and twelve hundred dollars for a year at St. Pius and more than fifteen hundred at Rockhurst, on top of that, was almost too much to be borne. When David was drafted by the Royals, in 1981, and gave up the scholarship at the University of Missouri to begin his professional career, she thought at first that it was a mistake, a defeat for the whole family.

Before this, when Ed was starting his junior-high basketball program at Holy Cross, only seven kids turned up to play—not enough for a scrimmage. He went on with it, though, gathering recruits bit by bit as the team began to win, and by the time David reached eighth grade some youngsters had to be turned away because there weren't enough uniforms to go around. They'd also started a girls' program. Chris told me that not many parents in his old neighborhood seemed to do much for their kids when he was growing up but that his parents made up for it. Joan came to all the Holy Cross games, and she and some other mothers started a small concession. Ed brought franks from Swift, and she found a wholesaler who gave her a nice price for candies. They put in a popcorn machine. Joan ran it all and swept up afterward. With the extra money, they bought more uniforms and shoes and basketballs, and, in time, put up extra poles and backboards out in the schoolyard.

In spite of all this optimism, there was a sense that the Northeast neighborhood was running down. Jobs had thinned out, and families the Cones knew began to move away. Enrollment at some parochial schools was dwindling and in the early sixties the diocese announced that Holy Cross would be closed and its students consolidated elsewhere. Joan, Protestant or no, was outraged. Aware of the crumbling public-education system in Kansas City—the city schools are currently struggling to regain accreditation—she felt that parochial schools would be more in demand in years to come, not less, and she and some other Holy Cross mothers demanded meetings at the school and won a reversal. (Later, in the seventies, Joan and other parents staged public protests over downsizing at Christal's Glennon High School, with placards and picketing that got them on local TV, but that battle was lost.) Holy Cross, with a modern school plant tucked behind the church itself, is still in business, and now there is a state-of-the-art computer lab, thanks to a donation by David Cone.

David had entered Rockhurst, while his friends were going to St. Pius X, or to public high; there was less time for Wiffle-ball games out in back of the house. David's room, upstairs and to the right on the second floor, looked like any teen-ager's—there was a steamy poster of Farrah Fawcett Majors on one wall, and he'd made a basketball hoop out of a coat hanger jammed up over the closet door, with a tank top hanging from its rim—but his descriptions of the Cone place at this time become shadowed. More than once, talking with me about it, he called it a haunted house. One night in 1977, Danny came home after he'd been in a wrangle up the street, and then his opponent, a large man with a high, crazy voice, turned up in the front yard screaming. The Cones peered out—he had something shiny in his hand. Now he was up on their porch and banging on the front door. "I'm coming in!" he shouted. "I'm coming in and I'm gonna kill you!"

He hammered again on the glass-paned front door, shaking it in its frame. At any moment he'd be in. Ed ran upstairs and grabbed his rifle, a little .22 target model. Still shouting, the intruder burst through the door—the thing in his hand was a knife, not a gun—and the Cones were screaming now, too, in terror. David, weeping, was huddled behind his dad on the staircase when Ed fired and the man went down.

Things got quiet in a hurry. The crazed man, shot in the side, was not seriously injured, and the police, when they got there, sorted it all out and exonerated Ed. Never was there a clearer case of self-defense. Within days, Ed and his assailant came to an agreement: no charges would be pressed, either way, and the man and his family would leave the neighborhood for good. It was over. Today, an air of embarrassment surrounds the affair. David would just as soon not talk about it, but he admits that he was shaken. He had to beg off some classes at Rockhurst for the next few days, and he received counselling there. In time, the Cones sold their house, for twenty-five thousand dollars, and moved away, too. This didn't happen until 1979, two years after the break-in, but in David's accounts it seems to come almost immediately. Home had stopped. When Ed sold the place to an African-American family there were complaints up and down the street, but Ed didn't care. "He made a point about that," David says proudly.

On a cool, windy day in April I sat with Ed Cone in a reserved-seat section up the first-base line at Yankee Stadium, while we watched Orlando Hernandez briskly do away with the visiting Texas Rangers. Ed is the quietest man I have ever encountered in a ballpark. He sits with his hands in his lap, taking everything in but without exclamations or gestures. He doesn't keep score. He has a closed-down look to him, and when he talks you have to lean close to hear him. In time, he began to tell me about his working days at Armco Steel, back when David was a baby. Armco, with its rolling, clanking presses and enormous vats of molten steel, fitted all your preconceptions. Workers there, sweating and toiling in their hard hats, seemed dwarfed by their surroundings. Ed was a millwright at first. With seniority, he became a maintenance technician for the two-hundred-ton overhead cranes, inside the huge electric furnaces. Temperature up there hovered around a hundred and twenty degrees. "So I ended up moving from the furnace into the freezer," Ed murmured, making a little joke out of his departure from Armco in the mid-seventies and going to work at Swift. More than once in our conversations, though, he called Armco "a good job" or "a good place to work," but then said he was happy to get out of there when the time came. Armco had been shut down during the bitter hundred-and-sixteen-day steel strike of 1959 (Marvin Miller, who later represented the Players Association over two decades of negotiations and battles with the owners, did the same services for the United Steel Workers of America in those days), and it became clear afterward that hard times were coming for this kind of rock-solid American industry. People started to drift out of the Cones' neighborhood after the strike. The Ford plant closed, then Montgomery Ward. When Armco shut down, stage by stage, in the early eighties, it cost three thousand jobs, and the shock was immeasurable. Only a few years before this, the mill used to hold popular Open House days for its employees, and the visiting families could see the place in full swing, with the cranes whirring along overhead and molten steel being ladled out, to thrilling showers of sparks. Ed remembers Danny as a small boy watching him pack up his lunch pail in the morning and saying, "Some day I'm going to work there, too."

Swift was less dramatic, but the work exacted its penalties. Ed had suffered a spinal injury in 1967, when a drunk rear-ended his car at a traffic light; four-year-old David, in the adjoining seat, suffered a broken nose. As the years went by, Ed began to find his duties in the freezer almost more than he could handle. He was suffering from rheumatoid arthritis—he still takes daily medication for it—and sometimes a co-worker had to help him to his feet after he crawled out from under a machine he'd been working on. He stayed on, though, even after the kids had grown up and gone. In 1990, when David won a salary-arbitration award for $1.3 million from the New York Mets, he came at once to his father to tell him that his working days were over. "Nothing I've done in my life has meant more than that moment," he said to me.

In the Yankees game, El Duque had gone into high gear, cricking up his front leg like a deck chair as he bent the Ranger batters to his will and the Yanks moved off to a 5–1 lead. Ed was talking about Armco, unwilling for me to get the wrong impression of the place. "The people I worked with there were salt of the earth," he said. "We had an engineer at the mill who had won the Congressional Medal of Honor. He was on his way up, you could see that, but you never caught him standing around telling someone what to do."

Without explanation, he began telling me the plot of an old Spencer Tracy movie he remembered. The scene was wartime Europe, perhaps in Norway—I think the movie is "The Seventh Cross"—where Tracy is a member of a band of patriots fighting an underground war against the occupying Nazis. "In the movie, somebody gets captured by the Gestapo and they wonder what's going to happen," Ed said. "They're afraid he's going be tortured and that he'll confess—give up information that will give them all away. Somebody says to Spencer Tracy, 'Do you think he will talk?' and Tracy says no, he'll never do that, he'd die first. The other man says, 'Better men than this have said that and then talked,' and Spencer Tracy says, 'There are no better men than this.' That's exactly how I feel about the people I worked with. There are no better men."

I was touched that Ed Cone would produce this vivid scene for me—I'm older than he is, but I also find scraps of old movies leaping to the fore in illustration of something private or complex that I am trying make clear in my thoughts—and I ventured to say to him that his whole family story struck me as being part of history, something central to the times he and I had lived through. American heavy industry had disappeared from our landscape, taking good jobs and good neighborhoods and some apparently impregnable routines of life with it. Nothing could be done about it —it just went ahead and happened.

He agreed, of course, and provided me with some of the examples I have set forth here. It seemed that the Cones were now participants in a different American story, the current one—the supplanting of our industrial empire with the equally broad and all-consuming entertainment business, which almost overpowers us with television, movies, video, music, sports, and celebrity, diverting our attention and language and changing the way we dress and think and pass our time. David Cone, a local boy transformed by his skill and luck and enterprise into a national sports celebrity and a multi-millionaire, is no less a figure for his time than his father was, piloting his crane above the open hearths of Armco. I mumbled something about this but then gave it up, perhaps sensing that neither of us would want to go very far in this direction. David has earned thirty-eight million dollars in the past five years, from his salaries and signing bonuses alone; his father, at the end of his tenure with Swift, was earning twelve dollars an hour, before overtime. David has transformed his own life and considerably altered those of his parents and his brothers and sister. David worries about them. "There's been a role reversal," he said once. "I'm the father now, at least when it comes to money. I didn't expect this."

I mentioned this thought of David's to Christal in a phone conversation, and she agreed only up to a point. A director for Sprint PCS, she is independent and direct in manner. "David was the youngest child and an athlete, and nothing was expected of him in other ways," she said. "He had no responsibilities to others. He's been very giving in financial ways but he was never there for me emotionally. But my father has been there for me all along, big-time. David's had to postpone an emotional life because of what he does, but I'm starting to see glimmerings in him and it's nice."

People I've met who complain about the money that ballplayers make and how easy they've had it while being rewarded in such astounding numbers for playing a game may find a bitter pleasure here, but for me this American family memoir has enough grief and irony in it to silence conclusions. Father Chris Pinné, a Jesuit priest who once taught David theology at Rockhurst—he was a lay teacher back then—told me that he'd run in to David in St. Louis one day in the nineteen-eighties, where his old student, a Mets starter now, was getting ready to pitch against the Cardinals. "I was glad to see him—I'd always liked him," he said. "I asked David if he was happy and he said yes, he was. He was making more money now than he'd ever imagined possible. More in a year—or maybe he said more in a month—than his father had earned in his entire working life. 'What nobody tells you is how to handle all that,' David told me. 'How do you do that without embarrassment? I wish I knew the answer.'"

7

Get a Grip

Tuesday, May 8th, Yankee Stadium:

There's a small fan turnout on this mild spring evening, maybe because the game is against the hapless Tampa Bay Devil Rays but more likely because the Knicks are on television, facing the Miami Heat in an N.B.A. conference semifinal. A couple of times lately I've heard David murmur, "Thank God for the Knicks," meaning that Patrick Ewing and Latrell Sprewell have been diverting attention from his gruesome year. The Yankees aren't playing so hot, either, but not many people have noticed because the team is still suspended up there in first place, as if by levitation, three games ahead of the Red Sox. Back on Friday, Jorge Posada fumigated a poor effort by the pitchers with a walk-off three-run homer in the ninth, good for a 12–10 win over the Orioles. But Mariano Rivera ruined Sunday with an uncharacteristic failure, blowing a two-run lead in the Yanks' 7–6 loss. Derek Jeter is two for seventeen on this home stand, and Shane Spencer, one of the aspirants in left field, has gone hitless in three games. "We're fortunate to be where we are," manager Joe has been saying. "We need to get better." He's measured and statesmanlike, but sometimes I miss Earl Weaver, whom I remember saying once, "We've lost six and our ass is about to hit the water." At least Chuck Knoblauch is back tonight, leading off; he's been out for a week with a recurrence of his wrist problems.

Cone himself has been a cause for concern and speculation. He was rocked for eight runs by the Angels in his first start, surrendering a homer to his first batter of the year, Darin Erstad. After a couple of no-decision efforts, he was brutally treated by the Blue Jays at the SkyDome, where he left after three innings, eight runs and three homers to the bad. Not what he expected, but, as everyone keeps saying, it's still early times. Here, wrapping up his pre-game tosses from the mound, he gets his signature musical welcome—the dark "Woke Up This Morning" theme, from "The Sopranos," which he has picked himself. It amazes me that he and the broadcaster Michael Kay are the only big "Sopranos" fans around the Yanks.

Cone is still using the rocking-horse pre-pitch motion that he inaugurated two starts ago, on April 28th, when he shut out the Blue Jays through seven innings on three hits, for his first win. I spotted the change while he was warming up in the bullpen for that game. There's a rectangular screened opening in the outfield wall, down at the pitcher's end of the Yankee pen, and looking out there I could see him in sections, as it were—his head above the wall, parts of his arms and waist in the window, like one of those split-page children's books—doing something new and comical during the early part of his delivery. He was a kid horsing around in a schoolyard game of catch. When he brought it into the game, the altered motion caused the early batters to back out and stare. Standing with his left shoulder facing the batter, he looked at the ground and made two formal-looking half-bows before continuing as usual. It reminded me of John McEnroe's pausing pre-service ritual. In that same game, David also began pitching from the extreme first-base side of the rubber—another rabbit's foot for him. When he was struggling in 1996, he did it the other way around, shifting to the third-base corner of the slab, and found instant success. But the new motion and departure point didn't help much in his next start, at Cleveland: five runs and eight hits over six innings' work, but no decision in a game that the Yanks pulled out after he left.

Tonight, I'm looking for a better fastball from him—something inside to right-handed batters. That critical pitch has been drifting out over the plate, with ugly results. David believes that the misshapen little finger on his pitching hand, broken in 1987 in the bunting mishap, has been making it difficult for him to set the ball up properly within his grasp. Over the years, the injury has imparted a small twist to his hand, tilting it a few degrees to the right. With the underside of his wrist no longer square to the plate as he throws, the sinker loses its integrity. To correct this, he and Mel Stottlemyre have slightly altered his grip, hoping to achieve a "one-liner"—so named because the batter sees a single dart of red stitches on the side of the ball as it arrives. (The slider, by contrast, announces itself with a red dot.) For Mel, this is just getting back to basics. The one-line delivery, which is meant to hold to its path under the batter's elbows with the persistence of a deerfly, was once known as "the Drysdale pitch," after its Dodger practitioner.

Watching the Tampa Bay batters from the pressbox, I can sometimes pick up this pitch by its line of flight—I can't see the red slash—but I always check myself on the TV monitors. I don't know how many writers or fans still stop to think how much the screens and replays have added to our expertise; television has made scouts of us all. The *Times* has a prime left-hand slot in the front row of the Yankee pressbox, but whenever there's a serious pitch or at-bat coming up Buster Olney leaves his seat there and moves to the steps directly under the nearest overhead set. That way, he can catch the pitch and the play live from the field, then lift his eyes and find out what he's seen. Whenever I sit in the stands with my wife and friends now, I look around for the monitor for the first couple of innings. Without it, checking the location of the catcher's mitt as the ball arrives is the best way to see what a pitch is doing, but I don't always remember this. I want my replay to tell me if that was a hard slider—

lately "the cutter"—or what. The curveball, more of a curio
these days, is easier because it breaks downward, roughly on a
twelve-o'clock-to-six-o'clock path. A lot of people in baseball,
including writers, drop these ballistic terms with absolute
savoir faire, as if you could guarantee at a glance what a given
pitch has been, but I've noticed that old hands seem to throw in
a qualifier—"looked like that little cutter there, to me." Anyone
sitting next to you in the right-field top deck who says "Back-up
slider, just off the corner" is after your money.

David gets through the first inning without harm but also
without establishing anything that looks like a rhythm. He walks
Fred McGriff in the second and gives up a run-scoring double to
Vinny Castilla, struck off a flattish breaking ball—a slider without much slide. In the third, there's a double by Miguel Cairo,
and after Cone gets behind in the count to the dangerous Greg
Vaughn he throws an up-pitch—maybe a hanging curve, but a
meatball by any name—that is whacked to left for a two-run
homer.

Another disaster impends, but David regroups. The pitch
counts go down and a sense of pattern comes into his work.
Cairo, leading off the fifth, looks at a slider for a called strike,
fouls off a fastball, lays off another slider that just misses, for
ball two, and is out on an easy bouncer to third. Gerald Williams
hits a double, but after another out Vaughn fouls off an up-fast-
ball (whew) and then flies out to left, to end the inning. Eleven
pitches, and then David requires only nine more to whiz through
the sixth.

Esteban Yan, the Devil Ray right-hander, has been rushing
through the Yankee batters in impressive fashion, but Shane
Spencer smacks a two-run homer in the fifth, and two innings
later Jorge Posada, red-hot at the plate this week, hits the ball
over the center-field fence, tying the game at 3–3. Coney is back
in business. Working briskly, fighting off fatigue and inattention,
he rings up Dave Martinez on a fastball, to begin the eighth, and
retires Vaughn on a grounder. I'm pulling for him to finish the inning, but there's a single by Jose Canseco, and here comes Joe

Torre up out of the dugout. The catcher and the infielders encircle David on the mound, thanking him as he turns over the ball and departs.

It's another no-decision for Cone—the Yankees win it, 4–3, in the tenth, when a bases-loaded walk to Paul O'Neill forces in the winning run. Not a memorable game, except for its two hours and forty-seven minutes, which counts as a flashby these days, and I offer it only to suggest the sort of everyday, bourgeois hard work that goes into a pitcher's pretty good outing—the kind of office day that eluded Cone so often this season but kept him in good standing with his manager and still in the rotation. His ninety-five pitches included only four strikeouts, but he looked almost at home on that little hill this time and free to enjoy the tasks. In the clubhouse, he was semi-elated. He'd hung some sliders, he admitted, but then he got better. "It's all tempo and rhythm," he said.

The afternoon after the Tampa Bay standoff, Cone and I sat in the Yankee dugout, each of us with a slithery new white baseball at hand, while he tried to explain how he holds the thing for each pitch and what's meant to happen next. It was raining a little (the game that night would be called), and he was wearing an open Yankee warmup jacket and, underneath but outside his shirt, a black Nikken shoulder harness around his pitching arm. This slinglike gizmo contains magnets, said to benefit the arm, and Cone wore one every day in this part of the season, in the semi-conviction that it was whispering to his prime asset. He looked young and rested—he had no pain from the previous night's exertions—and, with the ball in his hand, ready for another six. Cone has normal-sized hands and fingers, nothing like the meaty paw of a Clemens or Pedro Martinez's lizardlike digits, which weirdly bend thirty or forty degrees upward from the middle knuckle at the end of the delivery, but the ball appeared to have become part of his anatomy. While we talked, it slipped from one position to the next on its own, it seemed, as if in response to his thoughts.

That one-line sinker, I said—how did he grab that?

"It's basically a two-seam grip, as against the four-seamer," he said.

This was easy, and it would be easy here on the page if we had morphing capabilities, or if the reader could put down this book for a moment and root around the house for an old baseball. The ball, it will be seen, keeps presenting a natural horseshoe curve of stitches when rotated—there are four of them. If we grab a horseshoe so that the first- and middle-finger fingertips just slip over the broad topmost curve of the stitches, a red row of stitching will appear to run down the outer side of both fingers, as if to frame them. With these two fingers now slightly parted, the odd conviction comes that you're on top of the ball. To be sure you've got this right, look for the commissioner's signature just under the "Official Major League Baseball" stamp, and let the top joint of your fingertips cover it—ah, there, Bud—at each end, above the seam. This is the two-seamer—you've got it. Slip the ball toward you or away from you and two red seams will brush under your fingers while you complete a full rotation.

Now, still with two fingers just over the seams, turn the ball a quarter-rotation to the left—clockwise, that is—so that the broad part of the horseshoe is just to the right of the knuckle of the middle finger. This is the four-seamer: roll the ball gently toward you or away for a full rotation and this time you'll feel four seams go by. You're armed now: you're a pitcher.

"You know all this stuff," Cone said. "Four-seamers are meant to cut the wind—it's the rider—while the two-seamer tends to sink. The one-liner is just a variation on the two-seamer—your fingers slip a little toward the wider white area of the ball, and you press down more with your forefinger. I like where my thumb is now, underneath." He waggled the ball up and down a little, envisioning the drift-free pitch holding its line now, even moving inside a little to Frank Thomas, inside to Alex Rodriguez. "Ten years ago I never worried about sinkerball grips," he said lightly.

We moved along to the curve—rotate the four-seam grip a quarter-turn or less, until you're splitting a seam, with one finger on either side. "For the slider, you slip both fingers on top of the seam," he went on, "but with mine the forefinger is dominant. El Duque throws his a little bit the same way. Everybody has his own style. Catfish Hunter told me that when he had trouble with his slider he'd hold it with a fastball grip."

Discouragement crept over me. With effort, I could arrange my fingers in the right configuration for each delivery but I had to study them while I did. I was a dancer watching his feet. Worst of all, I wasn't throwing the ball—I ruined my arm more than sixty years ago, throwing curveballs—so none of this meant much, and David didn't suggest that we get out there and play catch. Too bad—at least I could have shown him my old knuckler.

We wound up the seminar with the splitter, which I knew about because I'd spent time with Ron Darling and Roger Craig, back when the pitch was a thrilling novelty for pitchers everywhere. They'd happily showed me how you forced your forefinger and middle finger apart over the shiny parts of the ball, so it was ready to slip free, almost fall upward, as your arm came through. "You can always move your thumb sideways a little, to give the pitch some movement," David said now. "Along with a well-placed scuff."

I gave him a glance.

"I've never scuffed, cross my heart," he said. "But if one comes along in a game, so be it. I'd find my own way of cheating, if it ever came to that." He waggled his arm, smiling. "Maybe with the magnets."

What was strange about this part of the season was that even while Cone was taking me through this baby curriculum he'd been encountering a frustrating, wholly unexpected difficulty in executing the stuff in action. The slider, in particular, was eluding him, and I noticed that we'd stopped talking about the pitch as much as we once had. It had become a sick relative. This in turn made it hard to talk about strategy—what he had in mind when he faced a given hitter in a given situation. Early on, I'd thought of sitting down with him before one of his starts and going over the other team's batting order—the wily, good-contact up-front hitters, the scary left- or right-handed power in the middle, the over-swingers and scufflers down below—while he told me each man's strengths and weaknesses. Then we'd check out the Yankee scouting reports and he'd confide his plans to me. It was a dumb idea, though, and I was glad I never brought it up. What we both knew, of course, was that each hitter and turn at bat presents the pitcher not with a fixed offensive array, like those boxy divisions on a war map, but with something fluid and conditional, a cloud chamber of variables: the count, the score, the inning, the number of outs, the position of base runners, the umpire's strike zone, the capability of the outfielders, the quickness of the catcher (how much you can trust this particular receiver to handle a splitter in the dirt, with a runner on third), how this next batter was swinging in his last at-bat and the one before that. Getting into all this, David told me, was the main event and mattered more to him than remembering what the scouts were saying.

"You can get caught up in information and overpreparing," he said. "I go more on feel. Vinny Castilla is a terrific fastball hitter. Last night, I hung a slider and he hit a double. Third time up, I threw a fastball up and he backed away and looked at me. I nodded to him: yes. Then I threw him another and he popped it up."

Videos aren't high on Cone's list. "More and more, the hitters rush to the video room to see how somebody's just gotten them out," he went on. "They don't trust what they've seen. If I'm not pitching on the first day of a series all I do is sit in the dugout and read the bats. As soon as a batter swings I'm looking for body language. Have you ever seen Don Zimmer during a game? He sits there next to Joe and never moves—except for his eyes. His eyes go everywhere and they tell him all he needs to know."

Beyond this for David—before it, actually—comes his arm

and the availability of his repertory on a given day. Most days, he is past the middle of his pre-game warmup, out in the bullpen, before any thoughts about the early batters begin to stir. If nothing comes he'll have to wait until he's taken the mound before the first inning, making his final tosses. The hell with it: he'll think of something.

Mike Stanley, who caught David for the Yankees in 1995—he started this season with the Red Sox, then moved along to the Oakland Athletics—told me, "He gets out there and he has such a sense of what's working for him, what he can throw on any given count. I'm thinking game plan and he's shaking me off. It doesn't matter what the guy at the plate's strengths are—he doesn't care about strengths or weaknesses, it's just a question of what he can rely on. How's my slider today? How's the sinker feeling? How much life in my fastball? He's extremely intelligent."

Coney's old sidekick Bret Saberhagen agreed. "He's got so many looks," he said. "Every time a hitter sees him, it's like he's developing some new rotation on the ball or he's found a new arm slot. He'll go down sideways or throw harder or slower. He must have about twenty pitches he can throw at any time, speed, or arm angle. Each time we come to play the Yankees I'm excited to see what David's going to show us this time."

Between them, Stanley and Saberhagen have thirty years in the majors, and know the hard turns and heartbreak that the game can offer—Sabes was looking forward to getting back in the rotation with the Red Sox after two major surgeries for his horrific pitching injuries—but I don't think anything in their experience could have prepared them for the depth and duration of their friend's tortures as this summer wore along, or make them believe that the resources of his they eagerly cited, here in late May, would turn on him, viperlike, and compound his troubles before his year was done.

Cone's problems with his slider embarrassed him. So unexpected and puzzling was its defection that I began to envision him taping up hand-drawn flyers on the corner lampposts and back alleys of the pastime:

LOST PITCH

"Slider"

Faithful 14-year-old breaking ball last seen at Legends Field, Tampa, late March. Owner heartbroken. Finder call D. Cone, Bronx, N.Y. *Reward*

The missing animal, it should be understood, was not the frisky mid-count pitch that Cone threw to right-handed batters, which breaks sharply over or just beyond the outer limits of the plate, darting away from a right-handed batter's swing, but its partner, the delivery aimed at the same man's hip or haunch that bends late, just into the black, and is mostly taken for a called first strike. This was Cone's trademark, and is a standby of contemporary pitching. You used to see batters watching while it checked in under their fists, and almost nodding in recognition: yup, that's the one. Cone's admired "back-door slider," by the way, is nothing more or less than this second pitch, thrown to a left-handed batter. Tim McCarver, who likes to get things right, once musingly said to me, "You know, the outside of the strike zone can't be the back door, can it? Couldn't we call that the patio slider?" Inside or out, swung at or taken, the Cone slider has won enough certifications to merit presentation to the New York Landmarks Commission. Ralph Kiner, the hoary Mets broadcaster and Hall of Fame Pirates slugger, says that the pitch reminds him of Sal Maglie's old scimitar, back at the Polo Grounds.

"I can't get a good feel for it," Cone told me now. "I can't throw more than two or three decent ones in a row. I don't know where it's gone, that old bread-and-butter of mine."

This was puzzling, because throughout his troubles Cone's side sessions—his regularly scheduled, extended throwing dates in the bullpen, two days after his latest start—had been upbeat and revealingly useful. He and Mel Stottlemyre kept working on ideas and arm slots, concentrating on whatever had gone wrong in his most recent appearance, and always found solutions or variations he could carry with him from there. He still had no pain or physical problems. These were some of the best side sessions of his life. The slider, though, refused to come along. It was exempt or something—not a pitch you could expect to tame or recover in the bullpen. You almost needed game conditions to summon up the intensity to get it right.

"Your hand has to be way out there for the slider, really extended, and the seams have to rip off your fingertips at the end," Cone said. "That's what I've not been doing, but I think it'll come back with the summer weather, when you can really get a grab on the ball." He made a little gesture out away from his chest, and I was reminded of a time, years ago, when he had told me that the slider had to be finished like a painter's brushstroke. Then he'd made a little de Kooning swash through the air, smiling as the invisible pitch went away.

Stottlemyre confirmed all this, but made me feel better about it at the same time. He was undergoing chemotherapy for his myeloma, but resisted undue sympathy or medical chitchat. He had given up none of his duties with the club at this point. He made the road trips, hanging with his guys in their hard times and triumphs. Tall and private, he aimed his squinting, kindly gaze down at everyone and moved on.

Mel remembered, of course, what it had been like thirteen years earlier, when he was the pitching coach for the Mets and David had suddenly come into view like a Queens sunrise. "His stuff really jumped at you then," he said. "He was excitable, always into the game, and at times, as he'll tell you, a little out of control. He threw harder then."

What about the fastball now? I asked.

"He needs to throw it a little more often—enough to keep the batters off the breaking ball," Stottlemyre said. "It's not that he's a completely different pitcher this year. It's just that the slider, the lack of the dominant slider, has made him make a few adjustments. I think his arm has felt good enough to throw it with some authority but he hasn't trusted it enough. He's dropped down on it, and it's become a little bigger, a little flatter. He's made a lot of mistakes with it to the right-handers."

He put this almost positively. Crinkling, he said that he looked forward to the day—any game now—when the old reliable would come back for David, because the batters would be in such trouble then.

But what if it didn't come back, I said. Was that a possibility?

"Pitchers don't go on forever," Mel said equably. "Sometimes it's hard to keep the feel for a pitch. If you've got more than one good pitch, like a slider along with a curveball, you might lose track of one of them and not get it back. I lost my curveball when I was twenty-three. It just went away, and then I had to come up with something else."

I didn't pass this along to David, although he probably knew it. What he had to face was that the missing slider wasn't just one pitch out of his full array: it was critical. Joe Girardi used to point out to him that he had far more stuff to throw at left-handed batters—the splitter and fastball, the back-door slider, that sinker falling and fading on the outside corner, and so on—while the right-handers had to be subdued mostly with the slider-fastball combination. Without it, he was half a pitcher.

Reminders of his frustrations and changing status in the record books were never hard for Cone to find, of course. Each time he pitched, the Yankee media notes for the day bristled with then-and-now stats that told the story like a running news-ticker under an earthquake. When he pitched against the White Sox again in the middle of June, below the boldface "**TODAY'S STARTER: RHP DAVID CONE (1-6, 6.49)**" and "**CONE BY THE NUMBERS**," you found ". . . **opponents are batting** .294 (79-for-269,11 HR); LH .261 (35-for-134, 5 HR); RH .326 (44-for-135, 6 HR) . . . **in 1999 opponents** batted .229 (164-for-715, 21 HR),

second-lowest in the American League." Farther down, your eye
would fall on a line like "**Night: In '00** is 1–4, 6.56 (8 GS, 46.2 IP,
34 ER) . . ." and over at the other end "**in career** is 119-67." And
so on. He was aware of this withering record, of course—every
player has this gnat swarm of numbers around him, all year
long—but except for a wry passing line now and then I never
heard him hold forth about his past brilliance or importance, or
his place within the Yankees story. He was too busy with the
struggle for stuff like that.

The other puzzle he couldn't get away from was the state of
his arm, which was amazingly, almost defiantly free of pain.
"With me it's always been about pain management," he said. "All
these years, my biggest wish has been, boy, if I could only have
one healthy, sound year. Just get my arm under control—manage it for a whole year. The way I feel now goes back to my
warmup before my very first start, in Anaheim. I hadn't done
anything over the winter, just let my arm rest, and now I felt as
if my whole plan was right on target. I was thrilled, warming
up—this is where I want to be! Wow, no pain! I can do things
here—this could be the greatest year of my career.

"I remember hearing about an old pitcher who said 'My only
wish is to hold the ball in my hand and master it.' That's really
the way I felt, warming up in Anaheim that first day. I didn't
know that my fifth pitch would be knocked out of the park for a
home run by Darin Erstad. That started everything."

Oppressed by such realities, Cone had begun to take on a
slightly hunched look, it seemed to me, and when I checked this
with the MSG broadcaster Suzyn Waldman and the *Post's*
George King they said they'd seen it, too. Along about this time,
David got up in the middle of the night to go to the bathroom
and found himself going through his pitching windup and delivery there, naked in front of the mirror.

Cone's early difficulties—the season was not yet a third done—
appeared to elate some of my friends who weren't baseball fans.
They found it almost funny that a famous athlete with such a long

record of success couldn't win anymore or defend himself better. "It's all over with him, isn't it?" they said cheerfully. "He's old. He looks terrible out there." He was no longer beyond them, and they seemed relieved and released by the change. I didn't feel this way. While I missed the air of brisk hostility that once set Cone apart, I felt closer to him and began to sense, in glimmers, that I was getting a better sense of pitching than I'd had. The difficulty and complexity of the work showed itself in absorbing and excruciating detail, now that he was struggling, while the boring mystery of success still shone in my mind, even as I saw it slip away.

This was not what I'd anticipated when I'd first made plans to write this book, but I hadn't understood then how quickly we fans can turn our backs when our old heroes go south. This wasn't what we wanted from them, this bumbling and struggling. Get away—don't you know why we're here? Show us how to win again—get out there and be great! And if the Stadium fans did not, in fact, get down on Cone at any time in his tormented year—there was scarcely a boo—that told us what his true value was. He'd have happily missed that message, but still . . .

The more I saw Cone in confusion and pain, the better I liked him. Was it because I could see something fallible and unguarded in him, now that he couldn't control the games and batters and turn them to his bidding, or was it because he'd become more like me, to myself? Was I patronizing him now? Did I share in that same sneaky schadenfreude that I'd heard from my friends, now that he wasn't on top of things? Will the Yankees stay in the Bronx? I gave up.

Almost from the beginning, Cone was aware that the book wasn't going to turn out the way I thought it would. Instead of an inside look at a wizardly old master at his late last best, this was going to be Merlin falling headlong down the palace stairs, the pointy hat airborne and his wand clattering. "Any time you want to change your mind," he kept saying, but I didn't agree.

"We don't know how it's going to turn out," I said. "This is more interesting."

"I can see that," he said. "I guess."

* * *

Through April and the better part of May, Cone was contending grimly not just with the batters but with his earned-run average, which embarrassed him. "It's going to take all year to get decent," he said. After his second loss, back in April, that 8–2 shellacking by the Blue Jays, which left him at 10.70, he whittled away at the E.R.A. over his next six starts—a win and two losses and three no-decisions, lowering it with each start, and at last, after a 4–1 loss to the Red Sox on May 26th, finding a more respectable 5.68 at the end of his pitcher's line.

In the Boston game, a Friday-night date at the beginning of the Memorial Day weekend, he appeared to slip out of trouble when he speared Brian Daubach's hard come-backer to the mound, with one out and runners at first and third. With an inning-ending double play at hand, his attention was caught by the glimpsed front runner, Jeff Frye, darting plateward, and he unaccountably instituted a rundown and tag out. One out instead of two—blame it on nerves, blame it on David's mad resolution never to give up any more runs, ever. Carl Everett's bloop single, hit off an excellent pitch and scoring two runs, felt like a deserved punishment. "Good players anticipate situations and make the right play," Cone said in the post-game standup. "I blew it." This was balanced and Conean, but in the dugout after the half-inning ended he'd been plainer: "I should have my fucking salary taken away."

The next morning, in the clubhouse, manager Joe slipped a consoling Havana cigar—a Cohiba—into Cone's hand and murmured, "You looked exactly like Bob Gibson out there. I can still hear him: 'Forget the double play—that runner's *never* going to get home!'"

Cone's hopes that a decent season was still within reach now took a jolting downturn, with two miserable starts in a row. Throwing a drifting fastball to Oakland's Matt Stairs in the first inning, at the Stadium, he gave up a three-run homer, and departed midway in the fourth, seven runs to the bad. And then, up in Montreal, struggling with his control, he repeatedly fell behind in the count and saw another homer go out, again in the first, whacked by the electric Vladimir Guerrero. David had better moments after that, including a couple of stylish K's with the back-door slider, but quickly in the sixth he gave up a single, hit a batter, and was taken deep by Orlando Cabrera for three more runs. The disaster was not much noticed in Canada, where the Expos offer no English-language radio or TV broadcasts of their games, but it counted. The Yankees, beaten 6–4, had fallen into a tie for first with the Red Sox.

I had a hard time sleeping that night. Cone appeared to be at the end of his string. Only the absence of another viable starter was keeping him in the rotation. But when he called from Montreal he sounded calm. "I feel the pressure's off," he said. "I've reached rock bottom. I've been pretty angry but I told Joe last night, I'm through with self-pity. We'll see what happens next." There was a pause and he said, "Or is this massive rationalization?"

David had stood up for the press again after that Montreal game, as usual (the writers were shocked to find him there), and that night the bullpen pitchers and a couple of position-player invitees—Chuck Knoblauch and Tino Martinez—said "You're with us," and took him out on the town. They walked the late streets, dragging him along. "The best suicide watch I've been on in quite a while," David said. "It was like the old Mets days."

They ended up in a spot called Sir Winston Churchill's, on Crescent Street. When I asked him if it was a bar or a restaurant, he said, "I wasn't in the mood for food. I saw the sun come up. Nobody else lasted that long."

In the Bronx again—it was a quick road trip—Joe Torre said, "Every day is a big day with David now. The theatre of tomorrow can get to you." He also went back to some Conean history—the third game in the 1996 World Series, the day in 1997 when he walked off the field, unable to throw another pitch—and then, almost offhand, said, "David has enough in the bank for me to retire on. If there's doubt now, it's not because he can't face the struggle."

Torre's mixed figure stuck with me and brought back a line of his at the very beginning of the season, when I'd asked him why so many players and writers and fans seemed to care about this particular player. "He's real," Joe said.

David, I'd noticed, had begun to skimp on his interviews a bit—who could blame him? A big Mets series was coming up, in which he'd pitch the ESPN Sunday-night game, and on Saturday afternoon a little group of us writers, not the main beat people, unexpectedly found him in front of his locker, where he'd just finished a radio interview. Seeing us approach, the third or fourth wave of the day, he started to leave but then sat down on his chair instead, with his cap in his hands.

"I'll deal with whatever comes my way now," he said. "I've tried a lot of things to get myself untracked. Then something happens when I'm out there and lose it, and the damage is done, usually in the form of a three-run homer. I come in and tell you guys afterward 'It was only a couple of bad pitches,' but it's more than that. I need to grasp onto things. I've had a little bit of self-pity going—the 'Woe is me, this shouldn't happen' mode, but—"

He made a "What's the use?" gesture. He'd been talking in pauses, turning his cap around and around in his hands.

"I know my last two starts have been just terrible," he went on. "And you know what—forget about that. I'm trying to get my mind set to what the team needs. Forget your numbers. Forget what you've been projected to do this year. Try to help this team right here, right now. That's all that matters."

He looked up. "Good enough?"

Yes, good enough, and after he'd left we looked at each other and said, "Did you *hear* that?"

It was a heavy, threatening evening when Cone took on the Mets, and he pitched like an avenging earlier version of himself. In a rush, he retired the first two batters on grounders and struck out Alfonzo, swinging, with the slider away. Mike Piazza, leading off the second, stared at the inside fastball that rang him up, and, with two outs, Jay Payton went down looking, on a live fastball: three pitches, three strikes.

A little rain had begun, and the Yankees managed an undawdling run in the second, against Mike Hampton. Cone, back again, was brusque: a walk, another strikeout, a lined double play to Bellinger, at second. All his doubts and pauses had gone. The slider had come back and he was himself again.

In the third, there was an orange lightning bolt and a clap of thunder from somewhere beyond left field—"Ooohhh!"—while Paul O'Neill was batting, and the rain came. It poured down, that whiteout effect, and the game was called—it had never happened—and Cone, besieged by the writers about this latest turn of luck, shut the door. "No good came out of that," he said. "I lost the opportunity—it went away."

8

Young America

When Chris Cone was in his mid-teens, he was shooting baskets out in back of the house one afternoon with a school friend, Frank Garcia, who prided himself as an athlete. Garcia said something about his fastball, and Chris said, "That's nothing, you should see my kid brother—he can really throw." Back and forth it went, and when Garcia demanded proof Chris yelled upstairs for David. "He was only about ten years old and Frank was big and full-grown, six-four or so," Chris told me, "so he just laughed when he saw him. Trouble was, we couldn't find a ball anywhere—it wasn't summer—and there wasn't room out in back to measure the distance. We ended up in the little alley between our house and the apartment building next door—it was so close that an old guy up there had been hollering about us making so much noise with our hoops."

Still no ball, but then Chris remembered the can of Campbell's tomato soup that their mother had left on the kitchen counter for the boys to heat up with their lunch. He and David couldn't stand tomato soup, so the next step was easy. The door of the apartment house became the strike zone, and Frank Garcia, winding up, threw the red-and-white missile on an arc from about seventy-five feet away and bounced it off the door, bango, for a strike.

"David ran and got the can back from the porch," Chris said, "and when he let fly from the same distance it was a rocket—a real flat fastball that almost took the door out. No question who had the better pitch."

When their mother got home that night, she asked the boys if they'd had their soup and the boys said yes, yum-yum, it was delicious. Funny, Joan said, producing the dented evidence, that's not what the man next door says.

"And so we got busted at home," Chris said.

There was never agreement about which sport David Cone was best at—tennis or basketball, football or baseball or Campbell's. "He had a natural excellence," his high-school basketball coach, Douglas Bruce, said. "Knowing about him now, you're not surprised, but he was better than that. He was very good, very gifted."

This was at Rockhurst High School, the élite Jesuit academy on the south side of town—it's called Out South—just across State Line Road from Kansas, where David entered in the fall of 1977. Academics at Rockhurst are rigorous, but the school takes pride in its athletics—soccer fields and diamonds and a football field, Dasta Stadium, range lengthily beyond the school building on the hilltop campus—and so it was noticed when David made the Hawklets' basketball varsity, as a guard, in his sophomore year. On the football team, he played safety and punted for the varsity. By his senior year, in a natural sort of way, he became the quarterback as well. That fall, his team upset Raytown, the No. 1 high-school team in the state, in the district finals, then lost at last to Raytown South, a Kansas City suburban school, in the semifinals of the state tournament.

Before this, David, with the encouragement of his football coach, Al Davis, had enrolled in a local summer football camp for kicking seminars, and turned into the best punter in his circuit. "You'd see players on the other team looking over at him during the pre-game warmups," Davis recalled recently, "and if there was a little wind going they'd see these forty- or fifty- or sixty-yard spirals, over and over." At about the same time, Ed

Cone got word of another coach whose specialty was field-goal kicking, and got him to take on David for a couple of late-afternoon sessions. When the man got back to Ed, a bit later, he was talking in whispers. "You're not going to believe this," he said, "but he's hooking forty-yard field goals already. Like the N.F.L."

We expect our professionals to have compiled these early scrapbooks, of course, but it's tantalizing to pick up the thread of excitement from those who were there on the sidelines and can bring back a shining evening, twenty years gone, and our man in the middle of things. Chris Pinné, who taught theology at Rockhurst, remembers the blinders-on look that came over David at game times. "He was violently intense," he said. "He had a disgust for losing that didn't have anything boyish about it. It was the feeling that I can do better, we can do better, if we just keep at this. But he was more than that—there was something attractive about him in the middle of the anger that everyone saw. There's a sensitive inner self in David that we all need to protect." Other friends of David from this time remember his temper, too—and a vein that bulged on his forehead when he was about to lose it. Main Vein became a nickname.

Doug Bruce—he's now the athletic director at Rockhurst—brought up the district basketball semifinals in 1981, when David, a senior shooting guard, took on the six-foot-ten center, Jon Koncak, of Center High, who had almost single-handedly eliminated Rockhurst the year before, closing down the Hawklets' 22–3 season. The two boys had been facing off on the court since early parochial-school days, when David was at Holy Cross and Koncak the star at St. Thomas More. Koncak went on to a respectable career in the N.B.A. with the Atlanta Hawks, but he came off second-best in their rematch, after Rockhurst won the game, just as David had promised. Seconds before the first-half buzzer, Cone pulled up short and knocked in a thirty-five-foot jump shot. "He didn't just heave it up there, the way kids do," Bruce said. "It was a jumper to dream about—I can still see it."

David knew hardly anyone among the eight hundred and twenty boys at Rockhurst when he arrived, and he senses that his suburbanite classmates spotted him as a Northeast kid, somebody from the wrong side of town, and looked down on him a little at first. But he was a super-jock—his celebrity had preceded him—and his feats and his charm quickly won a place for him in the school. He became the Coner. He was a little spoiled, perhaps, but his teachers also remember him as an easy B-average student. Doug Bruce, a math teacher as well as a coach, had him in sophomore geometry. "David always claims I carried him through that class," he told me, "but I don't agree. I thought he was pretty good. Listen, just getting through a Jesuit-school curriculum is real pressure. He was a leader—the kind you want to put up front."

Father Pinné, who is currently teaching in Belize, had him in a senior theology course, where David relished the bantering exchanges between the boys and their teacher that accompanied their best days. "I think of him as all boy," Pinné said. "In class, he was like a young athlete who hadn't yet reached his peak. He wanted to succeed in academics, because his parents wanted that so much."

When David and I talked about Rockhurst, I began to notice how often he mentioned his morning trip to school each day with his sister, Christal. She was attending the University of Missouri at Kansas City, and she'd drop him off on the way. Most mornings, they'd take along one or two other Rockhurst boys from the neighborhood, too; it was a car pool. "She had a new Dodge Colt, and Rockhurst was way out of her way, but she never complained," Cone said. "I think the trip was part of the deal with our parents—they'd get her the car if she'd bring me to school. I was fourteen or fifteen and she was twenty-one or so, but we got along. She was great." The arrangement lasted only for his freshman year; after Christal graduated and went to work he had to find a different morning ride. By his senior year, he had his own wheels—an ancient yellow VW.

Rockhurst was male and then some, and one could be forgiven in assuming that those morning trips with Christal, in all seasons and weathers, may have been a significant part of

David's curriculum. He didn't know many girls, but, as a sports star, he never had trouble finding girlfriends—Jill Cleveland and Mindy Hicks, to name two. When I asked him one day if he'd ever been close to any young women, back then, whom he saw as friends, not girlfriends, he said no. A couple of days later, he brought up the matter again and said he'd remembered one, Julie Magerl. Or some such name—he wasn't sure how it was spelled. But my question was loaded. David was charming and boyish, and if he'd gone to a coeducational school there would have been more. He and Jill talked on the phone every day. One snow day, when classes had been cancelled at Rockhurst, he made it all the way through the drifts to Jill's house in his yellow Bug, to go sleighing. Then they stayed indoors and played quarters instead.

In the mid-seventies, the Kansas City Royals and the Yankees faced each other three years running in a succession of violently contested American League championship games, and on one of those October days Chris Pinné came down the hall at Rockhurst and overheard David, on a pay phone, in conversation with the Dean's office. "This was funny," Pinné said, "because the phone was right outside the Dean's office—the secretary there was about five feet away. As I came along I heard David say, 'I'm Mr. Cone calling to say that David needs a dismissal today to go to the dentist.' His friends saw me coming and skedaddled, but David finished the call and when he hung up, beet red, he said, 'What are you going to do about it?'

"I thought it was tremendous—he could see me laughing—and I said that if he could get away with it I wouldn't say a word. So he got to stay home and watch the Royals game, and the next day he brought in a note, probably signed by the same parent who'd made the call."

David's favorite class was French with Father Michael Marchlewski—Father Marco—with its Culture Day each Thursday, when the boys sampled cheese and sipped wines out of tiny paper cups from the infirmary. Father Marco talked about de Gaulle and Victor Hugo and the medieval Gothic explosion and how to tell Bordeaux from Burgundy—the Bordeaux bottle had hips. Now and then he took David and a classmate of his, Mickey Miller, down to the Gates Bar-B-Q, on State Line Road, for what they called executive lunches. Years later, David met up with Father Marco in St. Louis, where he was teaching—he's still there, at De Smet Jesuit High School—and introduced him to Doc Gooden. "I've seen you on television," Father Marco said, "and I see your lip still trembles when you're angry."

"Just the way it did when you'd get on me about a homework paper, in front of the whole class," David came back.

"A proud man," Father Marco said to me now. "I think he's still sore about losing that football game to Raytown South."

David wrote about sports for the school paper, *Prep News*, and in his junior year he launched a school petition—he collected more than seven hundred signatures—to force the school to restore its baseball program. Rockhurst had given up baseball in 1966, in an economy move. Al Davis, the athletic director, developed a strong track program in its place, and tried to recruit David for it, but he wouldn't go along: Rockhurst had to have a ball team. The school had two good young pitchers besides him—Jerry Rauschelbach and Tommy Daniels, a left-hander—and he knew they could clean up in their league. He found a little-used park diamond nearby that would do for a field, and even lined up a local sports manufacturer to donate uniforms. Three or four Rockhurst teachers told him they'd volunteer to coach spring ball.

He got nowhere, of course. Al Davis, who is retired now, has no memory of the uprising. Rockhurst baseball was restored in 1989—Cone was pitching for the Mets by then—and the Hawklets are doing well in the sport. In 1993, Cone made a sizable donation to Rockhurst—it was one of the largest in the school's history—with the perhaps ironic direction that a major portion be spent on improving athletic facilities.

The odd part of the no-baseball circumstance or roadblock is that it appears not to have handicapped him in the least. Kansas City in the sixties and seventies was an Eden for junior ball, with

the Three-and-Two supporting six flourishing Little League divisions. The Three-and-Two complex, at Ninety-fifth Street and
Blue River Road, offered five diamonds and a nice little stadium,
and a boy in his upper teens who had progressed stage by stage
from Midget C ball all the way through the Senior Division could
matriculate in the Ban Johnson League, and play all summer
with college-age amateurs who were entertaining serious baseball dreams. It didn't hurt if you had a coach living right at home
with you during this journey.

David remembers how protective his dad always was about his
arm, casting an eye over at him from the sidelines or, when he
was younger, from the front porch, to make sure he wasn't making like a Koufax out there. He has the impression that his father
never did let him cut loose, but Ed doesn't agree. "When I was
coaching him in the Three-and-Two, I didn't want him going all
out in the early part of the season," he told me. "He'd been playing basketball in the winter and his arm wasn't ready. And he
was young—just getting into his teens. But as the season went
along I'd keep him throwing fastballs harder and harder. I
wanted him to finish strong and then not throw at all over the
winter. That's the way you build strength."

When David was thirteen, he let go with a curveball in a
game and hurt his arm, and Ed moved him to third base for the
rest of the season. The next summer, he struck out nineteen batters in a game—nineteen out of twenty-one, that is, in these
seven-inning affairs—and a Dodger regional scout (a "bird dog,"
in the parlance) noticed him. David was no more than average
size for his age, about a hundred and thirty pounds, but the
scout told Ed that he'd rated him at the upper levels nationally.
After another year—David was fifteen and at Rockhurst now—
he was throwing in the mid-eighties, and Ed agreed that it was
time to add a curveball. It was a slurve, really—not yet a slider—
which David threw with his fingers hooking a seam but the in-
dex finger pressing hard, to make the ball break. Ed liked the
pitch, but every other coach David encountered, all the way up

to the major leagues, said no, son, *that's* no way to throw a breaking ball: throw it so it breaks off your middle finger. Do it our way.

Somehow David's way worked, and later that summer he took his repertoire into the Ban Johnson League, where he began to pitch against grownups. "I was fifteen but I looked about twelve," he recalls. "These were college-age guys and here was this skinny kid pitching for Boyle's Famous Corned Beef. They didn't look happy about it."

The Ban Johnson League had commercial sponsors, and the Boyle's Famous uniform featured shamrocks and white shoes (just like the Royals) and a leprechaun on the sleeve. The manager, Pat Nolan, had been at the work for thirty years or more, and sustained a sense of high purpose on the field. At five o'clock, he'd repair to the Brooksider, an Irish beer parlor, for beers and smokes and go on talking baseball. Nolan died this past year, but the Boyle's Famous pitching coach, Joe Presko, remembers David as a strong kid, pretty polished, but with control problems. Presko had pitched in the majors for six years, and one of his sons, Tim, played with David on the Boyle's team, while another, Joe, Jr., helped coach.

Presko, whom I'd found by telephone, told me that baseball wasn't anything like it used to be in Kansas City. "You never see a pickup game anymore or anybody playing scrub," he said. "Everything is more organized now." Neither of us wanted our conversation to end, and before it did Presko, relenting a little now, said, "David Cone was the best for his age I ever saw."

Another summer came around, and David, doubling up, went back to pitching for his father in the Senior Three-and-Two, but stayed on with Boyle's Corned Beef as designated hitter. He went to a Cardinals tryout camp at the Three-and-Two Complex, and to another, staged by the Royals, at Royals Stadium. "Two or three hundred kids showed up," David recalls. "You got ten throws, and if they liked what they saw they'd let you have a few more." He got the few more, and became what is known as a "Follow." At the Cards' tryout, one of his fellow-aspirants said, "Just think, if we come back next year we'll be able to *drive* here."

Early in David's senior year, Ed Cone asked him if he'd given much thought to his choice of college yet, and to what kind of life he envisioned after that. David, incredulous, said, "Dad, how could you forget—I'm going to be a major-league pitcher."

"It scared me," Ed told me. "All that time, he had it figured out. He never wavered."

Scouts had been at the tryouts and the Ban Johnson games, older guys in windbreakers and dark glasses—Ed Charles, from the Mets, the Royals' Carl Blando, and the regional Cardinals' man, Mike Roberts—and in May they turned up at a game at Crysler Stadium (it's pronounced "Crissler"), in Independence, to watch David pitch four innings for Boyle's against a strong Milgram's supermarket team. Not much was said afterward— "You did good" was the most David heard—but Ed, more optimistic, thought that the Royals were lying in the weeds, to throw off the other clubs. Sure enough, Kansas City spoke up in the third round of the national Free Agent Draft, on June 8th, and took him in the third round. The Cardinals were set to make a bid for him at the same level but had to pick farther down the line. The Royals had a great draft—Mark Gubicza and Tony Ferreira in Round Two, and then David Cone. Ed and Carl Blando were old friends, but of course there wasn't any chance that David would turn down the seventeen thousand five hundred bucks and go to college instead. Within a week, he was on his way to Sarasota in the red Camaro.

The first summer of pro ball, at Sarasota, dragged on into the fall instructional leagues, and it was Thanksgiving before Cone got home from Florida, back with his parents in their house at Birchwood Estates, a development in the Southeast part of Kansas City. The first night home, he went out to celebrate with friends and got drunk, almost as if it were expected of him. "I thought I was king of the world," he says now. "I was a pro

ballplayer, eighteen years old, and completely out of control."
He brought a girl home from the party and when Joan awakened
and heard them, up in David's room, she threw him out of the
house. The offense took a long time to heal, but what David felt
at first was relief, even joy. "I was free," he told me. "I was on my
own at last and it meant everything to me."

Next spring found him in Charleston, South Carolina, in low
Class A ball—a step up the ladder. He and his Charleston Royals
roommate, John Bryant, a righty from Irvine, California,
scrounged around and found themselves a little duplex not far
from a military base. It was a dump, with dirty windows and a
million cockroaches. They had no furniture until they came
upon an old love seat that one of their neighbors had put out on
the street. They dragged it in and sprayed it with Lysol, and after
that he and John took turns sleeping there, with the lucky one
curled up in a ball for that night, his folded jeans making a pil-
low, while the other made do on the floor. More often than not,
dinner came down to peanut-butter-and-jelly sandwiches,
washed down with Old Milwaukee beer. "We were living the
life," David said. "The club paid no attention whatsoever to anything we did away from the field. In some ways, it was the best
time of our lives."

Things picked up for the players when the Royals went on
the road, busing their way to Asheville or Gastonia and the rest
of the clubs on the Sally League circuit. (The acronymic Sally, a
tingling old baseball address, derives from the South Atlantic
League.) This meant seven or eight dollars a day in meal money,
plus a motel room at night, with beds and sheets and a television. The money was handed out in a lump at the beginning of
each two-week trip, and that day the whole team went wild at
Waffle House. These were boys, after all. On one trip, a teammate of David's took along a bamboo bong, carefully wrapped in
a shirt on top of his travel bag, but was discovered when the
manager inadvertently unzipped the bag at a bus stop. Fired on
the spot, he disappeared from baseball forever.

The Royals' home games were played at crummy College

Park, a steel-post relic that had also served as varsity field for cadet teams at The Citadel. Thanks to its indefatigable pork-barrel congressman, Representative Mendel Rivers, the region abounded in military camps, and David remembers Wednesday Beer Nights becoming a huge draw with the sailors from the Charleston Naval Base and the Charleston Naval Weapons Station, airmen from the Charleston Air Force Base, and contingents from The Citadel.

"Were they big fans?" I asked.

"They were drunk," he said. "Beer was twenty-five cents—big glasses—and the fans got their money's worth. The deal for us was that if we'd won the game we got to hang around after and finish up the kegs, and maybe meet the usherettes."

The Camaro Z-28 had disappeared by now. David hadn't kept up with the payments, and on his first day in Charleston he drove it to a local dealer and traded down on a blue Buick Regal. "Signing bonus completely gone," he says, lingering on the moment. "That time was huge for me. It was a busting out. I thought I was king of the world, living by myself and supporting myself and playing ball. We were all the same, a bunch of kids trying to figure things out. Every night on the road, we'd go straight to the hotel bars and look for girls. Wild and partying on the surface but we were desperate to meet someone, we were so lonely. We were carousers but we weren't very good at it."

He was working hard, building a 9–2 record by midseason, with an elegant 2.06 earned-run average. Richard Jablonski, who covered the Royals for the Charleston *Post-and-Courier*, still remembers those '82 Royals—Mike Kingery, catcher Roger Hansen, and a third baseman named Pastornicky. Danny Jackson was the ace of the staff, but Jablonski recalls a 1–0 shutout that Cone pitched against somebody—a one-hitter and maybe the best game he ever saw. "We had an idea where he was headed," Jablonski said, "and you could tell he'd do whatever was needed to get there. A lot of guys with his talent came through here but pissed it all away with drinking."

Jablonski's father ran into Cone, years later, at a card show in

Rome, New York, and David was glad to sign a baseball for him. The younger Jablonski looked for the ball not long ago—it had been tucked away in a closet—but a rodent had eaten the cover, signature and all.

David enjoyed his manager, Roy Tanner, known as T-Bone (who was later a scout for the Phillies), but he battled hard with suggestions that he convert to a drop-and-drive fireballer. He got the same advice later on from the Royals' touring minor-league pitching coach, Bill Fischer.

"A typical brat," Fischer says of that David Cone. Currently the pitching coach for the Devil Rays, he fills the heavy-faced, thick-chested, kindly-gruff Old Coach mold as if straight from the kiln. "Flighty," he went on. "Wild but an above-average fast-ball. I was tryin' to get his hands farther away from his body. I saw him only the one summer. He became a much, much better pitcher than I ever thought he'd be." He and Cone came to a standoff, I sensed, but it should be added that Fischer is reverently admired by Roger Clemens, who came under his tutelage when he was coaching the Boston pitchers.

The lonely life in the Sally League warmed when David had a visit from Jill Cleveland, his old high-school sweetheart. They had met at a basketball game back when he was at Rockhurst and she a senior at Raytown South, and she'd come to Florida with Ed and Joan the year before, when they visited David in Sarasota during his rookie summer. "Five-ten and a redhead," David said, telling me about her. "She made quite an impression. Big Red."

Jill Cleveland Sweazy is an entrepreneur, who lives in Orangeburg, South Carolina. One of her four businesses involves finding corporate sponsorships for NASCAR racing teams. She is married to Dr. Scott Sweazy, a urologist. They have a five-year-old son and an infant daughter.

"David—" she began when we talked, and then stopped. "Well, David chased me and then I ended up chasing him." She said this with infinite affection.

"When I went to Charleston to see him, I had a little time off from the University of Missouri," she went on. "My mother had bought the air ticket, and I got down there and the first thing David said was that he and John didn't have much—how right he was!—but he'd just found a nice second-hand mattress. We'd drive to the park every day, along with John—I don't remember those games—and spend all the rest of the time together. David was always funny. He had a knack for that, making us laugh. Leaving Charleston after those few days was one hard time—hard for me, not for him. It took me a long time getting over that."

They saw some more of each other the following year, when David unexpectedly found himself living back home again in Kansas City, but he was seeing other women as well. "He was open about it," Jill said. "He was always a good guy. He didn't want to be settled yet, and I respected him for that. It was funny because another one of his girlfriends, Mindy Hicks, came from my home town of Sugar Creek."

Jill Sweazy and David have lost touch with each other, but for a number of years he would call her up whenever the Mets came through Houston, where she was living, and they would see each other. "Not to *see* each other," she said, "but just to say hi. I was so happy everything had gone so well for him. He was my first love."

In the middle of that summer, David was bounced to a higher Class A level, at Fort Myers, and finished his year there. His combined 1982 record came out to 16–3, with a 2.08 earned-run average: tops among the Royals' young prospects. He could hardly wait for another spring. In March, on the threshold of Class AA ball or better, he was pitching an exhibition game against the Pirates, at Pirate City, when he let go with a wild pitch that went all the way to the screen. His catcher, Mitch Ashmore, scurried after it—there's a short backstop at that diamond—and fired the ball back to the plate, where David, covering, got his legs tangled as he attempted to tag an onrushing Pirate runner. There was a collision, and he felt a searing

pain in his left leg—"a bolt of electricity," as he put it. Rolling in
the dirt, in complete disarray, he heard the runner, a young Hispanic catcher, saying "*Lo siento, lo siento*"—"I'm sorry, I'm
sorry"—over and over. But nothing could undo what had been
done. He'd severed the anterior cruciate ligament, the stabiliz-
ing band of tissue at the center of the joint, and the reconstructive surgery that followed was extensive: you can still see the
white lines on either side of Cone's knee. He had fallen off the
fast track and would not pitch again for a full year.

The only scrap of good luck was the Royals' decision to allow him to pursue his prolonged rehabilitation at home—at
home in Kansas City, with the big-league club, that is, where the
team's trainer, Mickey Cobb, could work with him every day.
He'd just turned twenty, and here he passed a full season in the
company of elders, a notably grizzled, veteran pack that included George Brett, Frank White, Hal McRae, Amos Otis,
U.L. Washington, Dennis Leonard, Paul Splittorff, and Vida Blue.
David had no baseball duties—he was in a hip-length cast for
the first months—but the Royals put him to work manning the
third-base-side video camera that provided scouting footage on
left-handed hitters. It was nice work, pegging out there each day
on his crutches and feeling almost in the middle of things, and
David was disappointed when one of the equipment people left
the camera out in the rain by mistake, terminating the gig.

Rehab was appalling. Cone, who has encountered his full
share of it down the years, always makes a dismissive gesture
when I've asked him to talk about his physical travails, but he
admits that this stretch was gruesome. He was putting in work-
days away from the stadium now, as well. Still earning no more
than the minimal, minor-leaguer's forty-five-hundred-dollar
salary, he had taken a job at the Webb Belting plant, where he
worked full shifts slicing and gluing thick strips of rubber. "Hard
work at minimum wage," he says now. "I can still hear the sound
of the steam presses there. And of course it entered my mind
that this was going to be my future after all—doing the same
kind of work that my father had done all his life." By the end of

each shift he'd find knife cuts on both hands, and when it came to him at last what risks he was taking with his future he quit.

Jack Etkin, a *Star* beat writer (he has since moved along to Denver, where he covers the Colorado Rockies for the *Rocky Mountain News*), remembers a youthful pitcher grinding away on a flexible bike in the K.C. training room that summer—oh, yeah, that kid who played for Rockhurst, the one who's always tagging along after George Brett. Dennis Leonard, an eminent right-handed starter for those Royals, still sees Cone up on that stationary bike, too. "He rode it from here to California and back," he said. "Surgery is part of the deal for pitchers, but nobody who hasn't done it can understand what rehab is like. He was on that thing for so long that they had to rig a horse blanket on the saddle, with gobs and gobs of Vaseline on it because of his blisters. Little did I know that in a few weeks I'd be up there beside him, on the next bike."

Facing Cal Ripken in Kansas City late in May of that year, Leonard tore the patellar tendon on his left knee, in mid-pitch, ripping it off the kneecap—the sound was like Velcro tearing loose, he said—and had to undergo multiple surgeries and three years of rehab before he could get back to his work. People with the club have told me that only a notably determined and tough-minded star would have gone through a siege like that, particularly since Leonard's contract would have allowed him to draw full pay for the next three years if he'd decided simply to call it a career. But he would have none of it. "I didn't need to prove anything except to myself," he put it to me.

This is not a sidebar to the Cone story. Listening to David, I became convinced that weeks and months passed in the company of such men had a powerful formative effect on the later, grownup David Cone—the one that fans came to recognize and count on in big games. This was his college, and he paid attention. He becomes animated when he talks about the large, toupeed Lee May smoking a cigarette and sipping a cup of coffee on a clubhouse Sunday morning back then as he watches a batch of fresh-faced young Royals filing past him on their way to

Baseball Chapel. "What you gonna do in there, pray for base hits?" May growls. "I know why you're in there—Jack Morris is pitchin' today. You think God's going to help you with that?" He laughs fiercely and takes another drag.

David doesn't think much of Baseball Chapel, either. "This isn't my favorite day around here," he murmured on a mid-summer Sunday morning in the Bronx. Some of his close colleagues—Paul O'Neill and Joe Girardi—have been churchgoers, to be sure, but he himself favors a more unitarian view. "With a small 'U,' I mean," he said. "I'm for some kind of church that doesn't exclude anybody, any group or belief—if that's possible." He didn't pursue the thought, but on another day said that the hovering chaplains and do-gooders who turn up in the clubhouse on Sundays were notorious green flies—autograph pests and souvenir seekers, in the lexicon.

Cone also had a run-in with the fervent Yankee outfielder Chad Curtis during the 1999 World Series in Atlanta, after Curtis informed the media that the Yankees would no longer talk to the NBC reporter Jim Gray because of the way he had battered Pete Rose with questions about his long-standing suspension for gambling. David and a couple of other veterans took Curtis aside and told him to bag it. He didn't speak for the Yankees—he hadn't got there yet: O.K.? By the next spring, Curtis had been traded to the Rangers.

The 1983 Royals had an air about them. At their core were the stars or fixtures who'd battled the Yankees through those grinding American League championships of the seventies and made it at last to the World Series in 1980, where they'd lost to the Phillies—lost to Steve Carlton, really—in six close games. They were on the way to another World Series and a World Championship in 1985, but darker headlines would intervene. David, involved in the team's night life almost as a mascot, tried to stay cool when he noticed that cocaine was a regular part of the scene. Everyone else took it for granted, but there were some who liked it more than others. (Not all the Royals appear to have been in on the drug scene; George Brett, for instance, told me that heavy cocaine use by his teammates came as a surprise to him when news of it broke, later that year.)

One of the party people, an established star, often arrived late at the clubhouse, after another hard night. He brought a little brown paper bag with him, carrying it into the training room, where he lay down on a table with a towel across his middle, and fell heavily asleep. When the towel fell off, as it generally did, he would snore on, with a full erection in view. "That must have been from the cocaine, but it sure got your attention," Cone said.

"Drugs were different then," he went on. "At the parties we'd be drinking and talking, having fun, and somebody would pass cocaine around on a kitchen plate. It was 'Here, kid, you want to try some of this?' and then it would move on. Nobody made anything of it, the way they do now—it was like a picnic."

One of the users was Vida Blue, the left-hander who had burst like a nova on the baseball scene in 1971, his third year with the Oakland Athletics, when he won a Cy Young Award at the age of twenty-two. "Vida was so classy—such an elegant man," David said. "He treated me better than anyone else on the Royals. We'd sit together at some of the parties and talk all night about life and baseball—things I'd never heard of or thought about before. Sure, the cocaine was part of it but it wasn't the main part."

These easy nights went away in midseason, when it became known that the Federal Bureau of Investigation had begun tracking some major-league teams for cocaine use. Players became wary, even paranoid, about their parties and habits, and things began to change. Dan Quisenberry, the straightest of straight arrows, once expressed to me the admiration he had for Lonnie Smith, who had kicked cocaine on his own, before the investigations and testimonies began. It was time he stopped, Smith told Quis, but he'd always be glad that he'd had the experience. Smith was one of the players who testified when the full drug story broke and fans across the country had to make up their minds about the real lives of professional athletes, on the road and after dark, as against the shining images of them they'd held for so long. Drug use and enormous money—the average major-league salary went to three hundred and thirty thousand dollars in 1984—became blurred into a single issue, a horrendous shock, in the minds of many fans, and began a seismic alteration in the way we viewed these talented, perhaps not so lucky young men.

The hearings and investigations went into 1985, and became the first order of business for the incoming commissioner, Peter Ueberroth. The trials of drug dealers in Pittsburgh and Philadelphia had brought a parade of grim-faced stars and spear-carriers to the witness stand—Tim Raines, Lee Lacy, Dale Berra—who testified before a grand jury about cocaine use in major league baseball. Seven players, including Dave Parker, Joaquin Andujar, and Keith Hernandez, were suspended for a year but then permitted to play on instead, with fines and community-service penalties. Four Royals players— Willie Wilson, Jerry Martin, Willie Aikens, and Vida Blue— went to jail after federal convictions relating to cocaine possession, for terms of three months and fines of several thousand dollars. The sentences were the most serious imposed on any players at that time, even though the implicated Royals had been seen as lesser offenders in a major sting operation that the F.B.I. had launched against regional drug operators. It was believed that suspended sentences for the accused Royals, or fines and a warning, would limit prosecution of the larger case when it eventually came to trial. From this distance, it seems unlikely that the Royals front office could have been entirely unaware that some of the team's celebrated players were using hard drugs. Jim Frey, who had been released as manager in 1981, told me recently that he'd brought up the cocaine issue with the club's management before his departure but got no response.

Cone had wrapped up the worst of his rehabilitation by the end of that winter, and he put in a semi-convalescent 8–12 season with the AA Memphis team. He reached Omaha the year after that, almost ready for the majors. What had happened during that summer in the Royals' clubhouse had an effect on him, to be sure, but I can't believe that his boyhood was damaged or snatched away there. This was the eighties, after all, long after Vietnam, when the edge had gone off our American sweetness for good, even in the heartland. I'm not one who holds that it is baseball's job to preserve innocence or wall it away, and those who feel that way, including all the owners and players and hard-bitten beat writers who wept into their popcorn over "Field of Dreams," when it came along a few years later, were wishing in the dark.

David, in any case, appears to have kept his boyhood, or some essential parts of it—you can see it in his eagerness for combat and lighthearted manner elsewhere—along with a side that is worldly and hard-eyed. Both are there, both are true: he is a grownup. That summer, he had plenty of time away from the Royals—they were on the road half the time—and he passed it with his family and his girlfriends and his old buddies from school. One day Jill pushed him into a pool with all his clothes on, plus the heavy brace on his injured leg. For a moment she was horrified at what she'd done, but when she leaned close to where he was thrashing and flailing about he made a grab and pulled her in, too.

Video games were big just then, and no one could beat David at "Space Invaders." Steve Doherty stayed up with him all night sometimes, drinking beer and playing Atari. "What he liked was sitting around a pool in his jammies, drinking bourbon and eating barbecue," Steve said. "That was a perfect day for him. That and doughnuts."

9

Revivals

Tuesday, May 16th, Yankee Stadium:

Alert readers who recall that Cone was last seen here disconsolate after a rainout against the Mets in June will be able to make a small backward step to pick up some other Yankees during the same late-spring stretch. The White Sox, coming in for a midweek two-game visit, offered the tall righty starter Cal Eldred, who had not seen a winning season since 1992 but made like a Don Drysdale on this particular evening, shutting down the Yanks (with a bit of their help), 4–0, and extending the champions' losing streak to five games. O'Neill, given a bases-loaded opportunity in the fifth, flied out feebly to left and sent his helmet scuttering across the infield like a chicken in the rain. Five losses equalled the longest string of Yankee defeats the previous year, and, like that dry spell, which had come at the same point in the season, it allowed the Red Sox to step past the Yanks in the Eastern Division standings and into first place. This slump felt worse than that one, because of the absence of Derek Jeter, who had missed four games now with a strained lower abdomen and was perhaps headed for the disabled list. Even before the injury, Derek had looked unhappy in his at-bats, swinging at too many pitches off the plate and looking a fraction late on tough inside deliveries that he characteristically muscled over second base or into short right. His struggles seemed to afflict the whole top half of the order; the Yanks' team .267 at the plate was the third-worst in the league.

When I consulted Cone about the losing streak, he was less sanguine than I'd expected. "This could be an ugly one," he said somberly, and he reminded me of the schedule—a weeklong road trip against the Indians and White Sox just ahead, and then the incoming Red Sox for three, over the Memorial Day weekend. "You don't want this stuff to go on much longer," he said.

The emaciated offense was enough to bring some senior columnists up to the Bronx on the following evening, where they bent over the champion's bedside before the game, holding their little mirrors up to the patient's mouth. "When do you know that the Yankees are . . . through?" *Newsday's* Steve Jacobson asked Joe Torre, cocking his chin and staring over his spectacles in his familiar Chief of Neuropathy manner.

The manager, surrounded by a couple of dozen other mediafolk during his news conference in the dugout, took this and similar questions in customary fashion, laying down a comforting blanket of calm. The lineup for this little daily newsmaker puts the seated Torre, generally in his Yankee warmup jacket and nursing a cardboard container of green tea, in the middle of the bench, with a couple of newshawks leaning in from either side like coaches. The rest of us face him in straggly rows, with the latecomers teetering on the unroofed first step of the dugout (sometimes in the broiling sun or daunting drizzle), while they aim their tape recorders past the ears and hairdos of their scribbling colleagues. Because the manager is good at his work, one's Torre notes read almost like finished copy, with the meatier quotes up on top in the pre-game filler grafs, and the rest trailing off interestingly in the dot-strewn foot.

The biggest problem the management had right now, Torre started off this time, was trying to relieve some of the pressure the players were accruing just by trying so hard . . . You never

ask your players to do something different at times like this . . .
Five losses in a row isn't as important as where you are after five
losses in a row [in second place, as noted, a game behind the
Red Sox]. . . . Yes, we miss an accomplished d.h. like Chili Davis,
but we didn't have Chili for most of 1998 [when he was on the
disabled list for the better part of five months, with a bad ankle].
. . . Yes, Ricky Ledee [the pale, unconfident, left fielder and d.h.,
hitless in his last fourteen at-bats, and sinking toward the .200
level at the plate and a rumored tradeaway to Baltimore or Oak-
land] must be feeling concern. What Ricky needs to remind himself is what he did against Kevin Brown and the Padres in 1998
[two-run double in his first World Series at-bat]. . . . Yes, a lot of
teams do measure themselves against us—it's a great compliment. For the Yankees, winning is the only expectation. Right
now we're dry, but if I had to choose between a team that can hit
and not pitch and a team that can pitch and not hit, I'll take the
team that can pitch [i.e., us]. . . . You can't make an evaluation of
this club against the Yankees of the past two years at this time.
You make that evaluation at the end of the year. . . . Jeter's not
easy to replace, and no, we don't have Luis Sojo [the affable
Venezuelan utility man, gone to the Pirates] this year. The last
time Luis replaced Jeter he played great, but I couldn't convince
anybody of that because he was batting .210. . . . Our identity has
been our pitching. And so on.

The competition for the left-field position between Ledee, a
multitalented left-handed batter, and the blond right-side slugger Shane Spencer was waged for almost half the season and
came out miserably for them both, but my notebook filled up
with samples of Torre's peacekeeping on the touchy subject
whenever he talked to the press. "It takes six or seven months to
play this game," he said once. "There's enough pressure just putting on the uniform in this city, without our telling a guy that
we're on his side or not. Commitment is commitment—it takes
time to allow someone to play."

This remark had to do with Ledee, who'd been slumping, but
of course Spencer would draw equal sustenance from it when

he read it the next day. And Joe's next thought reached wider: "Having that support when you go into the clubhouse is what counts. This club is remarkable in that way. As separate as Hideki Irabu was from start to start when he was here, the players would defend him to the death. Kenny Rogers had the same experience."

No contemporary manager is better at this chat form than Torre, and none faces a tougher audience. He is suave but not remote, and unlike some managers not a thousand miles from the Bronx he is able to describe his emotions without displaying them. Given a Brioni suit and some late briefings from the Balkans, he could replace James Rubin, the departing State Department mouth. Joe, with his long face, dark eyes, and ruminative pauses, exudes the wisdom of an elderly hunting dog—a celebrated bluetick, with memories of fabled night runs and ancient treeings to call up at will. This presence gives him time to pause before each answer, though there is never the sense that he has framed something to avoid the truth or to placate a particular questioner. If he is admired equally by the beat writers and his players it's because he gives them the same responses, which appear to be a reasonable facsimile of what he himself is thinking, subject to the necessary diplomatic shadings and omissions. The players trust him because of his eighteen prior seasons as a manager, and even more for his eighteen years as a player, with the Braves and Cardinals and Mets (the two roles overlapped for eighteen days when he was a player-manager, at the beginning of his Mets term). They know about his .363 batting average and Most Valuable Player award in 1971—and, because he always brings it up, his next season, when he dropped seventy-four points in the standings. He also celebrates the anniversary of the day in 1975 when he contrived to bat into four double plays in a single game. When a writer in this particular confab remarked that Joe, as a slugging catcher with the Braves, must have batted behind Hank Aaron from time to time Torre held up an admonitory hand and said, "Well, they had to bat *somebody* back of Hank." I've known Torre ever since he was a

player, and now and then in his talks he'll throw in a compli-
mentary "Roger can tell you," when recalling some dusty bygone
inning, as if he and I had somehow become equals in the annals.
Most managers are sanctified once they've survived the first two
or three seasons on the job, but few are more informal than Joe
or more appreciated.

On the day of this small spring crisis, Torre had chosen the
old-fashioned, Momlike remedy of shaking up his batting order,
benching Ledee, moving Bernie Williams up to No. 2, and giving
the cleanup slot to Shane Spencer, who'd put some good swings
on the ball in his recent at-bats. The new lineup got the clubhouse chattering, which might have been the main idea. "Hey,
Bernie, you're batting second today!" Chuck Knoblauch called
down happily to Williams, at his corner locker, and everyone
turned to watch. "I *am*?" said Williams, scooting over to look at
the batting-practice rosters on the clubhouse door. "Hey, cool."
The last time Bernie batted No. 2 he ran off a twelve-game hitting streak.

"And you're playing short, too," Knoblauch threw in.

Don Zimmer, in the coaches' locker room, recalled a time
when he was managing the Red Sox and tried to bring them out
of a bottomless slump with a pure batting-order shakeup,
pulling scribbled name slips out of his cap. "Seven out of the
eight came out in the same place they'd batted in the day before," he said. "That's how bad I was going."

A bustle of writers had assembled at Shane Spencer's locker,
across the way. "Lou Gehrig, Joe DiMaggio, Mickey Mantle, and
Shane Spencer?" murmured Jack O'Connell as I arrived. But the
beat guys, of course, love a chance to talk to someone besides
the regulars, who must be written up at length ten or fifteen
times in the course of the season and made to sound fresh and
interesting. Not interviewing Paul O'Neill is a day at the Lido.
I've extracted useful information from him over a few widely
spaced intervals, but whenever he sees me edging closer to him
at his locker at the far end of the clubhouse he will flinch and
mutter, "Not *again!*"

What's no longer news about Shane Spencer is that he was a "replacement player" in 1995—one of the minor leaguers and semi-pros dragooned by the owners to fill out their rosters during the latter days of the players' strike, when management proposed to open the season with scabs on the field. The experiment didn't go beyond spring training, and was stopped by a federal judge's injunction, which in effect ended the walkout. The handful of the fill-ins who later made it up to the majors, including Spencer and the Mets' starter Rick Reed, have not been admitted to the Players Association. Cone is player rep for the Yanks, and when I asked him about Spencer he said that they'd worked out a relationship. "I know he got himself stuck in Class A ball for a long time, and thought he had to take any chance he was offered to improve himself," he said. "I told him other young guys had been in the same position but hadn't given in to the pressure they were getting from management. On their side, you have to say that the pressure was unbelievable. They were told they'd be fired if they didn't go along—never be allowed to play ball anywhere. This came down from the top, even from some of the managers. The coaches were in the worst position of all. They're union members, too, but we gave them a free pass back then—it was too complicated to work it out any other way. It was bitter for a long time, but time does move on. Shane plays hard."

Spencer, in any case, was the story of the day. "I've gotten a little more patient," he said to the writers circling his locker. "I'm not the best athlete in the world but I come to play every day." He said he'd taken heart lately in some balls hit to right-center field—he bats right, taking a massive, full-bodied cut at the ball that reminds you a bit of Mantle, at that. "I'm a gap-to-gap hitter," he went on. "I'm not *thinking* pull, but even when I think hit it to right I'll probably still pull it."

What you remember first when you look at Spencer is his nonpareil September in 1998, when, summoned up from Columbus for the fourth time in the season, he batted .421 for the month, with eight homers, including three grand slams. Shane is blond and mild, with plump cheeks that push up a boyish pad of flesh under his pale, wide-spaced eyes. He is twenty-eight but looks twenty, and will still look that way, in all likelihood, ten years from now. With his good looks and sloping shoulders and dramatic, down-dropping cuts at the ball, he becomes Roy Hobbs, every time up.

Spencer has avoided Columbus so far this year, but it's never far from his mind. "When you get sent back," he said, "everyone comes around and asks what it's like up there. And I say, 'Tell you what, I'll do anything in the *world* to get back there.'"

Shane had missed the news about Bubba Carpenter, a teammate and friend of his on the Clippers who had put in nine years in the minors, with the last full five at Columbus—long enough, he once said, to make him consider running for mayor. Over the winter, his contract had been purchased by the Colorado Rockies. Called up to the show at last, he'd had a game-winning, pinch-hit eleventh-inning home run at Shea Stadium the night before, against the Mets.

"Is that right?" Spencer said, his facing lighting up. "I'll give him a call tonight after we're finished here." Carpenter, by the way, had echoed, or pre-echoed, what his buddy had just told us about escaping the minors: "If I had to play another nine years to get to the big leagues, I'd do it."

The slumpy weather was clearing already, here in the clubhouse. At Chuck Knoblauch's space, my final stop, the hunched, intense lead-off man was tilting a bat, twisting and waggling it, tautening his grip. He had been in and out of the lineup since April 23rd, when he sprained his left wrist against the Blue Jays, and those absences, coupled with the sidelining of Derek Jeter, his accustomed backup in the order, had much to do—perhaps everything to do—with the Yankees' feeble scoring of late. Last year, the two combined for two hundred and fifty-four runs, the most potent lead-off pairing in the league.

"All we need is a little bitty hit, for something to happen," Knoblauch said now. "A walk, a bloop, anything—one big inning." Achilles and Ajax may have muttered the same words during one of their little down-spells.

Reminded that he'd had a walk and a stolen base the day before, in the first game against the White Sox, Chuck borrowed a pencil and wrote in a tiny star against the date on a team schedule taped up on the side of his cubicle. "That's for the walk—to remind me. Last night was the most pitches I've seen, which is a sign maybe. Last night was the best I've felt this year."

An hour or so later, leading off against the Chicago starter Jim Parque, Knoblauch banged a triple into the right-field corner, and shortly came in with the first of nine Yankee runs for the evening. Shane Spencer went three for five, and Bernie Williams, batting in the two slot and not playing short, hit a home run from each side of the plate, the second one a grand slam. The Yankees' slump was over—for today, anyway. Nothing to it.

Red Sox at Yankees, May 26th, 27th, 28th,
Athletics at Yankees, May 29th:

The Memorial Day weekend needs a name of its own on the baseball calendar, marking as it does the dividing line between spring excesses (nine hundred and thirty-one home runs this April) and something more serious for the rest of the distance. In olden times, the delicious Monday holiday was seen as a perfect excuse for a full schedule of doubleheaders in both leagues, but I noticed that four teams in the American League had actually been given the day off this time, and two more in the N.L. Never mind; perhaps "traditional" should now be reserved for the rosin bag and the seventh-inning stretch. The Red Sox-Yankees weekend games, up at the Stadium, with the anticipated Pedro Martinez–Roger Clemens matchup as their finale, fulfilled every expectation except childish, fanly hopes for a sweep, but I sensed that the passions of this dandy rivalry have dimmed a fraction, even in Boston. *Mets* vs. Red Sox—now, there's a rivalry!

The contortions of scheduling brought about by expansion and interleague play would bring the Sox and Yanks back together again all too soon, for seven games in June—three here in the Bronx, and four the following week at Fenway Park—and the two clubs would conclude their business with each other with a blurted last three in Boston in September. The Yankees' 2000 schedule is inexplicable, except to a computer. How else to account for two separate trips to the West Coast in August, or the Yankees and Indians wrapping up all their games at Jacobs Field with a pair of series there in May? ("Might as well leave our clothes at the hotel," Paul O'Neill said.) The existing, much reviled balanced schedule, which has all the teams in the league facing each other for the same number of games, regardless of geography or divisional affinity, will give way next year to a long-discussed unbalancing built around twenty or so meetings between each of the teams within a division, and about half as many with everyone else. In theory, the scheme is attractive to the players, who hate road trips; the writers, who hate road trips and weird deadlines imposed by time-zone warping; and the owners, who hate the high cost of airplane fuel. Realignment has been relentlessly plugged by Commissioner Selig, who sees all such disadvantages magically wiped away by the new plan, plus a golden chance to restore traditional rivalries and guarantee more of those good old late-September pennant scrambles. His fondness for such solutions has given rise to a suspicion that some of the weirder quirks in the 2000 schedule were allowed to stand unrevised by Major League Baseball to make the Commissioner's plan shine forth in comparison. Even Joe Torre suggested this in one of his dugout media meetings.

I think Bud's plan is sentimental at heart, and depends on a sunlit backward view of crowds thronging the local ballyards in the twenties and thirties to see the same handful of teams repeatedly and happily playing each other all over again. (In truth, the throngs turned out mostly for the Sunday doubleheaders.) Judging by what I pick up from station WFAN, I am in a minority in holding such doubts, but it's hard to believe that modern-day ticket buyers will love the unbalanced schedule, once they see how it works. Try as I may, I can't see the fans—much less this fan—besieging the gates to catch the eighteenth or nine-teenth Marlins-Phillies game of the summer, or the Twins and Royals over and over, or the traditional Rockies and Padres again, huzzah. Nor do I think they will fail to note that most September games will have no particular bearing in sorting out two wild-card qualifiers for the first post-season go-round. Baseball in the old days—I was there—produced heated rivalries here and there because of proximity; there were only eight teams in each league then, clustered a city or two away from each other on this side of the Mississippi. We saw the same faces and batting orders all the time, God knows—for eleven dates each in our own home park—but never complained since there was no other option. When chance and valiant play now and then produced a genuine late-season pennant thriller (the Yankees and the Red Sox in 1949; the Giants and the Dodgers in 1951; the Red Sox and Twins and Tigers in 1967) you watched breathlessly because of its rarity and because of the oblivion that awaited the losers. There were no wild-card second chances, and no one had to wonder whether baseball was holding its own against the N.F.L.

Baseball wasn't better then; it was just different. It may have felt traditional, or more likely just frozen, since the sport had changed at such a glacial pace. The Giants and Dodgers hated each other because they were both in New York, and the Giants and Cubs because of something that had happened between John McGraw and Frank Chance in 1908. Modern-day rivalries have sprung up more quickly—the Yankees and the Braves, for instance—but mostly slip away. The Yankees and the Kansas City Royals developed a nice fear and loathing of each other when they went head to head in the American League championships four times between 1976 and 1980; then it stopped happening and nobody gave a damn. Traditional rivalry is O.K., Bud—all you have to do is wait until it happens. Interleague play has brought out big crowds, but the "natural rivalries" it is intended to promote have diminished our speculative appetite for the Mets against the Yankees or the Cubs against the White Sox, and so on, that had persisted because those games could be played only in the imagination. Interleague play is like eating pie in the morning.

What feels modern about modern baseball is multiplicity and distance, and the flowering of some exorbitant talents, and we've got used to it. What I know for sure is that I'm going to feel suckered next year when I look in the paper and see that I only have today or tomorrow to rush out and catch Randy Johnson or Barry Bonds or the Dodgers as they flash through town for the first and last time this summer.

The three Red Sox-Yankees games at the Stadium, to get back to where we started, felt *sort of* traditional, but it was the promise of events and stars to come—Derek Jeter and Nomar Garciaparra together again (both had been sidelined with injuries and were due to return); and Pedro against the Yankee batters he had wholly dominated, back in September; and the proximity of the teams at the top of the American League East—that brought out 165,480 roaring customers and made it seem that it was baseball's time of year again. The festival then stretched itself on into the Monday-afternoon game, against the dashing young Oakland Athletics, which was Beanie Baby Day and Unassisted Triple Play Day in the Bronx.

Cone's loss in the Friday-night opener—the game where he made that impetuous early rundown play—would have felt worse except for a distraction in the bottom of the third, when a fan fell out of the upper deck and onto the high foul screen behind home. Up close, where I was, it shook you up—a horizontal figure passing through our pressbox field of vision, top to bottom, twenty feet away, with an accompanying, instantly exhaled journalistic "WHOWW!" The view from the suddenly crowded front row disclosed the fallen aviator prone, off on the right side of the sloping screen, with his cigarettes and wallet arrayed at his side. He was alive but semi-conscious within his own dent, framed by a circle of empty blue seats directly below, where the fans had belatedly scuttled away. The victim looked all right at first but then passed out. He was breathing bumpily, and his outspread arms, angled head, and motionless form took on the suggestion of a crucifixion. Joe Torre, emerging from the dugout, said a word to home-plate ump John Shulock, who called off play at last, and the players, bystanders now, stood staring in a deepening well of silence. No way to bring help seemed at hand, and the thought came to me—and to others, I'm sure—that this man, weirdly and beautifully suspended in the air behind home, was about to die.

He stirred instead, opened his eyes and took an addled look about, and then, amazingly, sat up, his arms pointing upward in a vapid and infuriating "We're No. 1" gesture. He pumped again, eliciting roars, and we turned away in disgust. You're not dying, dude—you're drunk. Changing our minds, angry that we'd cared, we wanted him gone. He crawled at last to the mezzanine row at the top of the screen and disappeared into oblivion. We went back to the game and the gags—"his first screen appearance," etc.—with the last coming from the *Post* columnist Joel Sherman, who said, "I thought it was Cashman"—the frail and anxious-looking Yankee general manager, fired at last and flung into the void by the Boss.

I pointed out the dent in the screen to my wife, Carol, and my son, John Henry, the next day, from our lower-deck seats at the Saturday matinée, not much of a game but a perfect entertainment for the gazillion kids there, bent almost double under their layers of Yankee gear, who saw the good guys fall behind, 3–0, in the early going, and then win it back and take the game, 8–3, in delightful fashion—bing, bung, bong, yow—with four neatly spaced home runs by the Mssrs. Spencer, Ledee, Posada, and O'Neill.

The action couldn't start soon enough for some of these junior fans. We had scarcely taken our seats when a Mizuno-mitted lad in our row piped, "What's the score, Dad, what's the score?"

"It's nothing-nothing," said Dad. "Geez, this is the third batter."

Consumerism was at a high pitch around us, and I got a kick out of the smaller girls and boys, with their hands and mouths stuffed, twisting this way and that as they took in the customs of the country: the man up in back with the earsplitting two-finger whistle; the Asian family in front who weirdly kept pelting each other with Cracker Jacks; and the deep chants rolling across the sunlit grass. The Yankee management, reacting to a nasty near-riot in the stands at Wrigley Field, the week before, had just issued an edict cutting off beer in the bleachers (the A.C.L.U. has yet to respond), but the creatures appeared to take it in good part. The first-inning cries and responses at the Stadium have assumed the precision and formality of the Japanese tea ritual, with the bleacher fans greeting the Yankee players in the field one by one—"Paul-*ee!* Paul-*ee!*" . . . "De-rek Jee-tah! De-rek Jee-tah!" (all four syllables are stressed)—and so on, while the greetees, between pitches, respond with a friendly half turn toward the stands or a wave of the glove. The intimacy that enfolds you during a fifty-thousand-plus turnout in the Bronx or at Shea is a more complex sociology than anything you can find in Baltimore or Samoa, and more debilitating. On this day, our sector was assaulted inning after inning by the yattering of a Red Sox fan-dad, just off to our right, who knew more baseball than Bobby Valentine and John McGraw put together, and told his wife and kids and the rest of us about it, non-stop. "You don't send this runner here, no, you don't run him on this count, you wait for two-and-one, the two-and-one . . . yes, here's the two-and-one, *now* they send him, you'll see—jeezt, why din' he go? This Torre never did know how to handle his runners, just like the Yankees always, can't run, can't play. Won't run, wait for the bomb—is that baseball, I'm asking you, is that ball or just Yankeeball, like I been saying? . . . Here comes Tino, inning over, inning over . . . There, din' I tell you?" We took this for pitch after pitch, batter after batter—took it like soldiers, like Mennonites—only exchanging a martyred rolled-eyes message with our frazzled neighbors now and then, but when Paul O'Neill's three-run dinger in the bottom of the sixth suddenly made it 8–3, Yankees, our tour-guide unexpectedly got up and took his hapless family home, and a beautiful smiling peace descended on our rows.

Bye.

Pedro and the Rocket, on the next night, Sunday, was pure. Clemens looks larger each time I see him, and the pressbox-monitor view of his back and shoulders from the center-field cameras is like coming up behind a sixteen-wheel Mayflower rig below the crest of a hill. Ever since his arrival on the Yankees, in 1999, Roger had given enervating attention to the corners of the plate, as if his work in New York would require a more intellectual array of stuff, but tonight he was free of all that. Pedro's horse-wide eyes give him an expression of supernal attention and intelligence as he looks in at his catcher, and the economy of each delivery, when taken with the startling motions of the ball, appears to complete an idea, a plan confirmed and flashed into view. This was Clemens the five-time Cy Young holder, who had twice struck out twenty batters in a game, paired up against the Pedro whose seventeen-K effort against the Yanks in his last start here was called the best game ever pitched at the Stadium.

This one lacked only September. With nothing to choose between the two starters for eight innings, we could only sit back and wish it weren't rushing by so quickly. Martinez threw a curveball to O'Neill in the fourth that took a dive under his fists, and he struck him out in the sixth with a change of pace—it was his knuckle curve—that went past like a sigh. Clemens, more emotional, shouted something—"That's a strike!" it turned out—at the Sox' right fielder, Trot Nixon, when he struck him out, looking, in the first. After six innings he had faced the minimum eighteen batters, dismissing ten of them on strikeouts. Nixon, up again in the seventh and perhaps still irritated by that advisory shout, cracked a one-out triple to left in the seventh, but Clemens got Daubach on a called third strike, and when Garciaparra went down swinging, the Rocket came straight up in the air off the mound, with his arms over his head.

The break, the awaited oddity, came in the top of the ninth, when Roger couldn't find Jeff Frye's little one-bouncer behind him on the mound. Nixon, back again, smashed the fourth pitch deep into the right-center-field bleachers, silencing the argument. The Yankees loaded the bases in the ninth, but that was all. Yes—well, O.K., then. A comeback would have smudged the memory of these two pitchers on a great night, which was all we wanted in the end.

The Monday holiday celebration, against the brash, attractive Oakland Athletics, suffered by comparison, and starter Andy Pettitte may have reflected that his 4–1 win might have been the only two-hitter in Yankee history that felt like an anticlimax. History, in any case, arrived in the sixth inning, but so quietly that its observers or acolytes—the Yanks and A's in the field and we in the stands—could manage no more than a murmured "Wha'?" . . . "Huh?" when a low batted ball to Oakland second baseman Randy Velarde became three outs before our eyes. Velarde, completing the four or five steps required, flipped the ball to an umpire as he trotted toward his dugout, while realization and a great gabble of conversation and explanation rose from every side. The situation had been routine—no outs, Tino Martinez on second base (he'd been hit by a pitch) and Posada on first after an infield error. When the pitcher, Omar Olivares, allowed the count on the next batter, Shane Spencer, to reach three-and-two, both runners took off with the next pitch, as expected. The ball, an undemanding chance, was gloved by Velarde at shoulder height, and he tagged Posada, in front of him on the base path, and unhurriedly continued to second, in plenty of time to step on the bag and double-off—no, triple-off—the returning Tino. Velarde, who is a former Yankee shortstop, had turned the same trick in spring training against the Dodgers five years ago. Practice makes perfect.

The play required so little skill and hustle that one's first impulse was to think it was ordinary—something that the game must crank out every week or so in its endless rounds of circumstance. But this was only the eleventh unassisted triple play in baseball history, and the first in any New York ballpark. I had not imagined such a thing and could claim memory of only two prior and assisted, unfabulous triple plays in all my years at the game. The next morning, I remembered to look in the box score, and there it was: "**TP**—Oakland 1 (Velarde)." An accompanying item listed the ten previous players who'd pulled off the chance—baseball is the only sport that keeps this word in its lexicon—going back to 1909, and including Bill Wambsganss, who did it in the World Series of 1920. Most of them were short-stops or second basemen, of course, but Johnny Neun, a first baseman with the Tigers, on May 31, 1927, grabbed a line drive struck by an Indians batter, tagged the next man on the base path, and, glimpsing history, ran all the way over to second to beat the other base runner to the bag. There had been an unas-sisted triple play pulled off by the Chicago Cubs in Pittsburgh on the afternoon before Neun's; the next one arrived forty-one years later.

I couldn't get over what we'd seen—and that the players ap-peared to have barely noticed it. "Yeah, strange" . . . "Nope, never saw one" was the most that came out in the clubhouses. Shane Spencer, who had started it all, said, "It happens." The play, I began to realize, had next to nothing to do with the par-ticipants: it was a statistical widgit, an idea more than a play. Len Berman, the sports anchor at New York's Channel 4, was scornful when he ran the clip the next evening, and called the moment less exciting than a hit batsman. I am still in the grip of it, though, and find myself foolishly murmuring, "I can't *believe* it" when it comes back to mind. The unassisted triple play may confirm something that lies deep within the sensuousness and near-seriousness of baseball: the notion, so boring to non-fans, that in fact anything *can* happen out there if you wait long enough, and when it does you will be struck by a bolt of luck that never showed itself, here in New York, to Casey Stengel or Ring Lardner or Red Barber or Babe Ruth.

10

Meet the Mets

Cone was on top of the wave when he reported to the Royals' camp in Fort Myers in February of 1987. It was his sixth spring at palmy old Terry Park, but this time he was coming back almost as a major leaguer. The year before, he'd gone 8–4, with a 2.79 earned-run average, at the Royals' AAA club in Omaha (it was his second year there), while trying to learn a new role as a relief closer. He lived at the Interstate Inn, a sixteen-dollar-a-day efficiency off U.S. 80, which he shared with Rickey (Buster) Keeton, along with a Rent-a-Wreck car. Keeton, who'd made it up to the Brewers for a cup of coffee as a setup man for Rollie Fingers, was twenty-nine years old and headed in the opposite direction. For David, Triple-A was almost cushy, because you got to travel by plane. True, the road trips lasted for sixteen days and you were forever being waked up at dawn to get out to the airport in time to grab another commuter flight, but it sure beat the bus. Much of David's Omaha time was spent with Jamie Quirk, a thirty-two-year-old left-batting Royals third baseman-catcher who'd dropped down to the lower level to improve his catching skills and perhaps lengthen his career. (The plan worked—everybody needs catchers—and he got in six more seasons in the show.) Quirk, once a late-night companion to George Brett, now holds the calming, character-building post of bench coach with the Royals. "David had a fastball and a slider back then," he told me. "He was almost there but he kept trying to strike everybody out. I wanted to persuade him to be in the strike zone more and set the batters up—let them hit the ball now and then but where you wanted them to hit it. He got the idea some days."

Before we leave Quirk, who was victimized more than once in his career by sportswriters who couldn't help describing some play or at-bat of his as "the strange fate of Quirk," I will challenge readers to put one hand over the bottom of today's surprise test.

Q: Which major-league record does Jamie Quirk share with Babe Ruth and twenty-four others?

A: Most lifetime homers—forty-three, in his case—for his letter of the alphabet.

Cone was called up to Kansas City in June of '86, after Mark Gubicza got conked on the head in the outfield there during batting practice and had to sit out some games. A story went around that Mark had faked his dizzy spells so that his buddy David would be pulled up onto the big-team roster at last. David got into four games with the Royals, working in relief, then went back down, but he returned late in August for the rest of the way: twenty-two and two-thirds innings in all. There's a nice video shot of his first big-league strikeout, when he gets rid of the Angels' George Hendrick, swinging, on the Laredo.

Back with the Royals again, David was no longer the wounded Class A pitcher doing his rehab in the big club's training room but a budding major-leaguer, here on his own merits. He kept his eyes on the veterans, trying to learn the life. Meal money was thirty dollars a day, and when he came into the clubhouse one afternoon carrying a bag of Chicken McNuggets with fries he was yelled at. McDonald's was bush. "The Royals were always saying, 'Be a big-leaguer! Act like a big-leaguer!'" he recalls. "They'd look me over and say, 'Hey, big-leaguers don't wear shoes like that. Big-leaguers don't dress like that—go out and buy yourself a sports coat.'"

It was demeaning to be treated like a newcomer, and when he complained about the lack of attention from the coaches and the dumb little errands he was asked to do, Dan Quisenberry, the ochre-mustached closer and philosopher, took him aside and told him to understand that all this was expected of him now. It was his role to play the rookie.

"At that point in my career this was profound," David says. "I was learning how to belong to a team. The way Quis delivered it, it was like a big brother talking."

He had other models on the club as well. George Brett played and batted with electric ferocity—his drooping-bat, Charlie Lau style at the plate, with his body surging forward and opening as the pitch arrived, held every eye—and did not hold himself aloof from the lesser players in the clubhouse. In 1984 (this was before Cone's arrival), when he learned that Mark Gubicza and Bret Saberhagen were sharing a motel suite, he insisted that the two rookies come and live at his house instead. George, with his sunburst grin, was always ready for another drink or another party afterward. Before long he began to invite the new rookie to tag along on some of his night outings. Brett was like nobody else, and when David unexpectedly changed teams, a year later, he talked about his old hero so often that he became known as "George" in the Mets' clubhouse.

David loved the life with the Royals—how could it be otherwise, with his old sidekicks around him, here at the top? One day there was a great-looking girl watching batting practice from a front-row box, and Saberhagen and Gubicza dared him to go over and ask her to flash her breasts for them. Of course he would. He turned on the charm, and though she didn't exactly go along with the plan she gave him a hug and let him rest his head down there, just for a minute. "Gubie and Sabes were dying laughing," he said. "It was after that that Quis took me aside and told me a little about what it meant to be in the majors."

Cone believes that stuff like this was one of the reasons the Royals let him go. "They felt I was a little off the wall, so they were ready to listen when the Hearn trade came up the next year," he said. "Little did they know that the Mets were going to be a perfect fit for me, and that I'd do anything in the world to fit in with that wild group of guys."

Cone's euphoria this spring of '87 was built on his conviction that he was a complete pitcher now, thanks in great part to what had just happened during his second year of winter ball in Puerto Rico, where his two and a half months' performance with the Ponce Leones won him the Player of the Year honor. Down there he'd polished his split-finger under the tutelage of pitching coach Diego Segui, an early master, who showed him how to make the pitch bend or back up with different finger placements. His parents came down for a long visit and loved the vibrant atmosphere at the games. That sweet season, David lived in an apartment called the Marbella, facing the beach in the Isla Verde section of San Juan. His Ponce teammate Eddie Olwine lived next door. You could walk right out the front door and jump in the surf. One day that January, standing in the warm water, he fell into conversation with a slim, striking young woman with dark hair and green-brown eyes. She'd just come out of the surf, and she looked about fourteen, but when they began to talk she said she was there on winter break from Wheaton College. She was Lynn DiGioia, a junior-year arts and economics major and a competitive amateur figure skater, from New Haven. They went out for a beer together that night. Her mother, who was vacationing with her, mentioned the date to Lynn's father on the phone, and he said, "What! You let her go out with a *ballplayer*?" But there were more meetings on the beach and more dates. "He had a very easygoing way," she told me. "He was adorable. The other guys I knew were still trying to figure out who they were going to be, maybe a doctor or something in business, but they were perfectly willing to wait until after school to find out. But David already knew who he was. He had this determination and incredible drive. I'd never met anyone like that."

David enjoyed his Ponce teammates, who included the pitcher Terry Mulholland and a free spirit named Mambo

DeLeon, and he found friends on other teams as well, including the eighteen-year-old Robby Alomar, who played for the Caguas Criollos. Eddie Olwine knew his way around, and sat at David's side at the craps and blackjack tables. The Leones' stadium was way over on the other side of the island, but David cut a deal with his manager, Orlando Gomez, allowing him to show up only on days when he was pitching or needed to get in his side-work. The traffic-clotted drive over to Ponce took forever, but Olwine says that David, behind the wheel of their white rental Mitsubishi, sometimes neared a hundred miles an hour driving on the shoulder. "After a couple rides, I insisted on being the designated driver," he says. When the Mitsubishi was stolen from a casino parking lot one night, David realized that he'd failed to check the insurance box on the rental form; thus began a lengthy relationship with Charlie's Car Rental. "We've all got to be young once," Robby Alomar says of this time.

Caguas captured the Puerto Rican Winter League pennant, and, after adding Cone and five other stars, including Candy Maldonado, to its roster, went on to win the Caribbean World Series, which was played in Hermosillo, Mexico. Bars in Hermosillo had a 4 A.M. curfew, and the Criollos players' festivities were such that manager Tim Foli was fired, right in the middle of the series, for lax discipline. But the Puerto Ricans survived an early loss and came back to take the championship, shutting out the Dominican Republic (and its star catcher, Tony Peña) in the penultimate game, before bombing the team, 13–2, in the finale. David, coming on in relief of Juan Nieves in the earlier game, got the save. Alomar remembers the great stuff Cone had on call back then—sliders and curveballs thrown to the corners—but the fastball still burns brightest. "He threw hard and up high," he told me. "Ninety-eight, ninety-seven—I mean *hard!* He was a fierce, pure talent at that time."

Back in Puerto Rico, David, packing up and getting ready to fly home, couldn't find room for his ornate, four-foot-high Pitcher of the Year trophy, and gave it to a nine- or ten-year-old boy he found hanging around outside Charlie's Car Rental. "I've often wondered where that thing is now," he says.

There were a couple of open weeks between the end of winter ball and the beginning of spring training, a little window, and
instead of going home David flew to Boston—Wheaton is in
Taunton, nearby—and he and Lynn had a happy winter weekend
together. Then she came down to Fort Myers, with her mother,
to see him in a Royals uniform; his parents were there, too. She
and David never discussed the future, but they were beginning
to look like a couple.

Cone had arrived at Fort Myers in shape to pitch a full nine
innings, but hoping, more realistically, to win a place as the
eventual successor to Dan Quisenberry as the Royals' closer. He
had drawn even with his peers at last, after his injury, and was
prepared to join Gubicza and Saberhagen and Danny Jackson as
the final piece on a young staff that Royals fans had been antic-
ipating for half a decade now. Late in spring training, manager
Billy Gardner said, "Give him the glossy"—take his picture for
the media. He'd made the team. The next day, general manager
John Schuerholz called David into his office and told him that
he'd been traded to the Mets.

The transaction—David and a catcher named Chris Jelic to
the Mets in return for catcher Ed Hearn and the obscure right-
handed pitchers Rick Anderson and Mauro Gozzo—still glows
in the annals like a rotting stump. Schuerholz, who later moved
along to build the remarkable Atlanta Braves team of the
nineties, always cites it when he's asked to pick his worst trade
ever. The Royals had won the World Series in 1985, knocking
over the cross-state Cardinals in seven games—Bret Saberhagen allowed one run in eighteen innings and was named Most
Valuable Player—and their fresh assemblage of arms now
promised more glory ahead. The centerpiece of the deal, to
their way of thinking, was Hearn, an up-and-coming receiver
whom they saw as a potential counsellor to their young
flingers. Working in the shadow of Gary Carter in New York,
Hearn had been better known for his game-calling than his
bat—he hit .263 lifetime, with four homers—but Royals scouts
who had trailed him during a Mets West Coast swing the previous summer may have been dazzled by an uncharacteristic hot

streak at the plate. The trade, in any case, went sour at once when Hearn suffered a shoulder injury and appeared in only six games that year.

Steve Fehr, a Kansas City lawyer who is Cone's adviser and agent (he's the younger brother of Donald Fehr, the executive director of the Major League Baseball Players Association), believes that the Royals had concluded that David probably would never get his great stuff together. Fehr has worked in close tandem with Cone down the years, while negotiating lucrative contracts with the Mets and the Royals and the Yankees, but he admits also to being a lifelong Royals rooter, who holds season tickets behind the visiting-team dugout at Kauffman Stadium. That fanly part of him still mourns both of Cone's departures from the club—in 1987 and, after his return for a two-year second stint, in 1995.

Schuerholz was struck by Cone's poise when he got the dismal news, and the way he handled the news with the K.C. writers, but David doesn't remember it that way. "I went to my locker as quickly as I could and packed my bag and left before I began to cry," he said. "I'd been a Kansas City player all the way. It was my home town, and I'd played for them at every minor-league level. Now I was ready and I was gone."

He went back to the hotel, where Mark Gubicza found him. The two went out to lunch at Bennigan's restaurant, and David called home. What he feared, he told his distressed dad, was that this meant another trip back to AAA—he wasn't a major-leaguer after all. But when he reached Lynn, at Wheaton, she said it was great news. He'd be coming to New York, the perfect place for them. She'd been hoping for something like this all along. He was made for New York, she said.

David's first appearance in a Mets uniform came a few days later, on an early afternoon at Al Lang Stadium, in St. Petersburg. It was against the Cardinals, who shared the park with the Mets. "No one there knew me," David says—no one, perhaps, but Joe McIlvaine, the Mets' vice-president for baseball operations, who had just eaten Schuerholz's lunch. The trade had been made on the word of a Mets scout, Carmen Fusco, who'd seen David pitch earlier in the spring. "General managers are always getting credit for guys they never saw," McIlvaine's boss, general manager Frank Cashen, told me, and I recall his explaining to me once that the Schuerholz disaster was the kind of thing that comes with the country for G.M.s. "We've all done it and we'll all do it again," he said. "With trades you gotta do what you gotta do. You're looking at a man who traded Jeff Reardon to the Expos for Ellis Valentine. Mea culpa, mea maxima culpa." And he smote his breast.

Two or three weeks before the deed, Jack Lang, the veteran *Daily News* writer, had been sitting in the sun with McIlvaine one morning while the two idly riffled through the new American League Red Book—the sprightly annual that first lists the spring rosters. They came to the Kansas City pages, and McIlvaine's finger stopped next to Cone's name. "I'd never heard of him," Lang told me, "but Joe asked that if I had any plans to mention him in my stories to please take it easy or maybe not mention him at all. 'We've got great reports on him,' he said. 'He's just a kid but we've got something in mind.' Nobody else knew, but after he got there and threw for the first time everybody knew."

There was a little breeze off the bay that afternoon—the kind of day at Al Lang when pelicans hang in the air near third base— and David, warming up, had such tremendous stuff that his catcher, Barry Lyons, couldn't hold his pitches. "They had this huge break, so they went past me and right back to the screen," Lyons recalls. "I'd never seen stuff like this in my life, and I thought, Hey, you'd better start to read this guy before you lose your job."

Cone keeps his own visions of that game. "I struck out five or six batters in three innings," he said. "Everything I had was on call. I looked around at Mel Stottlemyre—he was the Mets' pitching coach, but I didn't know him yet—and his jaw was literally dropping. Jack Clark was the big Mets nemesis in those days, and I struck him out in the first on four pitches, ending with a Laredo that buckled his knees. He went back to the bench staring at me, and later he's quoted as saying that with all the great pitching talent that the Mets had already it was unfair for them to come up with a new kid like this."

Watching the ball being whipped around the infield after each fresh out, David saw disbelief at every corner. "Keith is like, where did *this* kid come from," he said, "and Wally Backman is laughing, with the glove over his face. I had a great game, a really solid day, and I just remember walking back to the dugout and Davey Johnson, the manager, almost running up the steps to shake my hand. I'd never seen a manager do that. As if to say welcome—welcome aboard."

Not to mention Keith. "Keith Hernandez made me feel more welcome in one day than the Royals had in six years," David said.

New York already knew these Mets by heart, and a bright mantle of affection and confidence and attachment hung about the defending World Champions as they began their new season. It wasn't just the astounding way they'd won, back in October, after the reprieve of that little ground ball hopping between the legs of Bill Buckner, the Red Sox' first baseman, with two out in the tenth inning of Game Six of the World Series, and then, with defeat averted and reversed, the championship snatched away from the foredoomed Boston team two days later. Besides this, or beyond it, was the vivid assemblage of characters on this young, hard-playing and hard-partying and extravagantly talented home team—Doc Gooden, Keith Hernandez, Darryl Strawberry, Gary Carter, Lenny Dykstra, Ron Darling, Wally Backman, Mookie Wilson, Ray Knight, Kevin Mitchell, Bobby Ojeda, Howard Johnson—each of whom was talked about among the New York fans and semi-fans by his first name or nickname only: they were ours. That Red Sox loss was taken hard not just in New England but right across the country, because of a deeply felt envy and semi-hatred of New York and New Yorkers and their unfairly brilliant ball club, who summed up the arrogant big city as no team has done since.

Finding a niche on a club like this looked daunting for an out-of-town semi-rookie, but there were early omens for Cone that this year wouldn't be like the last one. Before Opening Day, the reliever Roger McDowell required a hernia operation, and Dwight Gooden, in a sensational turn of events, entered a drug-rehabilitation program for cocaine addiction at the Smithers Institute. Then Bobby O. went down with damaged elbow ligaments. Cone, who had begun as a reliever—McIlvaine had not quite decided whether he or another newcomer, Randy Myers, was best suited for the pen—got his first start on April 27th, at Shea, and flopped spectacularly, losing 11–1 to the Houston Astros. It was a nightmarish, Murphy's Law sort of game, in which he walked in a run, balked in another, and surrendered a monster two-run homer to Astro first baseman Glenn Davis. With McDowell ailing, Davey Johnson found no reason to save his rookie from a pounding. David and the whole country got to see the gruesome replays on television that night, including a moment when he appeared to be cowering on the mound with his hands up by his head. (He has noticed a weird similarity between this and the posture he fell into after his best game ever, the perfecto.) When Stottlemyre finally came to rescue him, David was saying, "What's going on here? What's happening to me?"

The next day, he found a softball on the chair in front of his locker—from Wally Backman, he thinks—with the message "This is what your fastball looked like yesterday." His fears that he was ticketed for a trip back to the minors deepened, but Davey Johnson called him in and said he was still in the Mets' plans. Days later, he pitched strongly in an in-season exhibition against the Red Sox (Don Baylor, who was with the Bosox then, remembers his feeble swings against the new kid that day), and on May 12th he notched that first win, 6–2, in a Riverfront Stadium start against the Reds. Grimacing, Cone still recalls that he had a shutout going until Paul O'Neill, pinch-hitting, took him deep. Then Kal Daniels whacked another.

Lynn, to go back a bit, had been at Shea for the Houston debacle—she'd driven down from Wheaton for this, her very first major-league game—but the sight of David standing out on the mound for the anthem meant more to her than the ugly stuff that came after. Another member of the Cone cheering section was Andrew Levy, a classmate of hers at the Hopkins School, in New Haven, who'd brought along a gang of his college friends from Lehigh. Levy now helps promote David's charitable affairs, and he is also the No. 1 Conehead—the first fan to turn up at Shea, a few weeks later, wearing in tribute the pointy skinhead look, right out of "Saturday Night Live." David had found a home.

Two weeks after the Cincinnati game, matched up against the Giants' Atlee Hammaker at Candlestick Park, he squared around to bunt and took the pitch full on the little finger of his pitching hand, shattering several small bones. He had extensive surgery and missed two and a half months.

Tim McCarver and Ralph Kiner had been in the booth at Candlestick when Cone broke his finger, and a day or two later they ran into him at a crab house in San Francisco. "I didn't know this young man with his hand in a cast," McCarver recalls, "but I had a lot of feeling for him because of what had happened. Secretly I felt he was the quintessential flash in the pan."

Cone sat for a few minutes at their table—McCarver remembers his great smile—and the impression changed. "He was smart," Tim said, "and there was nothing phony about him—no artifice. What I saw that day was his disappointment—and the fire in that disappointment. I thought he was ready to grow up."

The '87 Mets finished second to the Cardinals by a slim three games, and at one point actually stood on the doorstep of first place, late in a game at Shea in September, when the Cards' third baseman Terry Pendleton drilled a low line-drive home run over the center-field fence that turned the thing around. The homer, which hangs like a sword thrust in the middle of my Mets-mind—David can't get rid of the painful moment, either—reca-pitulates the disappointment and insufficiency that afflicted that Mets that year and in the years just ahead.

The accident certified Cone as another wounded hero in a

year when injuries were taking down the Mets pitchers like so many members of the Lafayette Escadrille. David, in a huge cast, hung in the dugout with the team on home stands, but didn't make the road trips. He was rooming with the dumpy, delightful Sid Fernandez and Sid's mother in Port Washington, but some weekdays he went up to New Haven and stayed with Lynn's parents there. Lynn, having graduated from Wheaton, was working with a design firm in New York; she had less time on her hands than he did. David returned to the lineup on August 14th, and finished with a respectable 5–6 year, in twenty-one games, and a 3.71 earned-run average.

Life was sweet for the new young pitcher in New York. He and Lynn were seeing a lot of each other, and when she moved up to Boston again in the fall, to complete her studies for a retroactive double-honors degree at Wheaton, he followed her when the season ended and moved into her apartment. She remembers coming home one afternoon to find him seated at her computer, editing her honors thesis, on Le Corbusier's Chandigarh project. "He didn't know the subject but he made it much, much better," she said.

Lynn impressed him. She knew her way around SoHo and where the best little restaurants were everywhere. When she took him to the Guggenheim Museum she'd be excited about the latest show there, and passed that along to him. He liked confidence and expertise. Both he and Lynn told me that nothing would have survived of their relationship if he had stayed on in Kansas City with the Royals. It was New York and New York City life that kept them together. "Lynn," he said to her one day, "you never gave me a chance to leave you."

The 1988 Mets won a hundred games, captured their division (over the Pirates) by fifteen games, and thrived behind a pitching rotation—Gooden, Cone, Darling, Ojeda, and Fernandez—that led the league with a 2.91 earned-run average and eleven hundred strikeouts. Catcher Gary Carter, always insufficiently prized for his game-calling, played a strong hand here, extracting the best, game after game, from a memorable mélange of starters. Doc Gooden, the best two-pitch hurler in baseball, still brought the air of a gentle genius to his work, which contrasted with the pale ferocity that batters saw in Cone and the flagrant variety of his stuff. The left-handed Ojeda, it was said in the league, had three different changeups, while Darling, a perfectionist, in Tim McCarver's words, "appears insanely intent on throwing an inches-away oh-two splitter on the first pitch to every batter." The other lefty, Fernandez, had breaking stuff that emerged from behind his capacious middle at the last moment, like a cab around the corner. These Mets excited you and drove you bananas by turns. Darryl Strawberry had hit twenty-seven homers by the end of July but hit only twelve thereafter, and finished second to the Dodgers' Kirk Gibson as the National League's Most Valuable Player. Bobby Ojeda, who finished at 10–13, accounted for five shutouts, almost out of necessity: in eight of his starts the Mets scored a total of ten runs in support. On September 21st, he nearly severed the middle finger of his pitching hand with an electric hedge clipper—it was rebuilt by microsurgery—and was excused from further frustration.

Cone's resplendent 20–3 year—an .870 won-lost ratio, which led the league and still stands as his career best—was backed up by two hundred and thirteen strikeouts and an earned-run average of 2.22, both second-best in the league. Headlines pursued him. He pitched a one-hit shutout against the Padres (Tony Gwynn doubled in the fourth) and a two-hitter against the Phillies. Out in L.A. one day, the Dodger slugger Pedro Guerrero threw his bat at Cone after being struck in the helmet by a pitch, and won a four-game suspension. "But that was a curveball!" David cried indignantly as the fracas began.

Keith Hernandez, who missed most of June and July of '88 with a hamstring injury, recently reminded me what Cone was like in that first great season, when Mets fans were in such a frazzle of pleasure and discovery about each new strikeout of his and his rush of late-season victories. "What I loved about him was that he never got cute when he was in trouble," he said.

"He had this array of great pitches, but they didn't distract him. In a tough spot the look on his face would change and it was three fastballs and go sit down. That high cheddar inside—he was never afraid of that."

He was nearly untouchable at the end, winning six games in September and barely missing two no-decision efforts that went to extra innings. When he came off the field with his twentieth win, on September 30th, with the Shea cheers showering down around him, he was startled to find former President Nixon waiting for him, there in the dugout, with his hand outstretched. (Nixon was a genuine fan, and I recall two or three evenings that summer when I unexpectedly came upon him rounding the corner in one of the tunnels at Shea or Yankee Stadium. It was a Coney Island effect—wooo!—and it got me every time.)

In most seasons, David's 20–3 record would argue for Cy Young consideration, but this time the award went almost by acclamation to the Dodgers' Orel Hershiser, after his 23–8 season, which culminated in fifty-nine consecutive scoreless innings at the season's close: one of the great sustained performances of the century. This unarguable circumstance—another "yes, but" dimming another remarkable Mets feat—seemed to hover about the team through the season, and it infected the ensuing National League Championship Series (there were no divisional post-season games as yet), when the Mets lost to an admittedly inferior Dodgers team, in seven games. "The Mets were the most dangerous team I've ever seen, here or in the minors," the Dodger reliever Jay Howell said afterward. "We were tremendous underdogs—which is a huge advantage."

The Mets go melodramatic in October, it's in their genes, and, taken together, the middle games of that 1988 playoff at Shea Stadium have probably not been matched for atmospherics—"more 'Macbeth' than baseball," as I wrote at the time. And "A full autumn gale postponed Game Three and, on the drizzly, icy morrow, produced vivid and memorable images: Kirk Gibson losing his footing on the rain-sodden turf in left field but somehow staying aloft through three long, sliding steps as he flung out his glove and pulled in Mookie Wilson's drive; and Keith Hernandez stumbling on the base paths and then, imitating by turns a sunstroke victim, a swimmer, a turtle, a supplicant, and a corpse as he scrabbled toward third, at last falling still, inches short of the bag." There was more, of course, including the taunting fans' chants—"OR-EL! . . . O-RELLLL!"—while the Mets, helped by some slovenly Dodger play, clawed back against him and his successors and won by 8–4 in the end. This was also the game of the great Pine Tar Crisis, a bit of umpirical deduction that banished Jay Howell from the field after the gummy stuff was found on his mitt; he was subsequently suspended for three days (lightened later to two) by the league president, Bart Giamatti, though it was agreed by all parties that the tar was there not to load up his pitches but only to improve his grip on the ball on a day when wiser men or children would not have dreamed of going out to play.

Only baseball creates this kind of high-protein fan nourishment, and the 1988 N.L.C.S. will be talked about decades from now, I believe, not just because of these Halloweeny antics or because of Hershiser's three starts—he won only the last one, and the pennant, with Game Seven—and his save in another; or because of Mike Scioscia's ninth-inning homer against Gooden, which helped capture the fourth game for the Dodgers; or for Cone's complete-game 5–1 win in the sixth; but for what happened to him, befell him, in Game Two.

Hungry to fulfill readers' burning interest in the new young pitcher, the *Daily News* had signed him up to write a first-person column during the post-season. "Dave Cone has a skeleton in his closet," an accompanying box began on the first day. "He was the sports editor of his high school newspaper in Kansas City and would love to write sports professionally some day . . . Cone is settling in behind a typewriter to give News readers a first-person account of his experiences. Good luck, Dave. Just make deadline."

Good luck, indeed. The column was ghosted by beat writer Bob Klapisch, who by agreement would talk to David after each

game and then put out something under his name. There would
be no shortage of material, it turned out, starting in the very first
game of the N.L.C.S., out in Los Angeles, where the Mets, rally-
ing against Hershiser, finally scored in the ninth—the first run
he'd surrendered since August—to bring the game to 2–1, and
hung the loss on his successor, Howell, when Kevin McReynolds
bowled over Scioscia at home plate with the game-winning run.
The visitors' dugout was a wild scene, with the young Mets exulting in their rough treatment of the untouchable Hershiser and
then baiting Howell as he tried to wriggle free.

"The clubhouse was a pandemonium after that," Cone recalls. "Klap quickly appears and asks me what was going on in
the bench in the ninth inning, and I say we'd all known that our
guy, Doc Gooden, was the better pitcher today. We were ragging
Hershiser and calling him lucky for all he'd done, and yelling,
'Throw another curveball! Throw another curveball!' at Howell,
like he's a high-school pitcher. When things get calmed down,
Klapisch breaks out the pen and pad and says, 'O.K., now we
gotta do this article,' and I say yes, I'm looking forward to it."

What appeared under David's byline the next day wasn't
what Klapisch jotted down in his notes but the richer stuff that
had come before. There's a head shot of David at the top of that
column, with his cap pushed back, and underneath, in the fifth
line, comes "Hershiser was lucky, Doc was good. . . . We knew
about Orel's 59 zeroes, but none of us thought he was invinci-
ble." In the next paragraph, our ghosted, hapless journalist-hero
says, "I'm not a psychologist but I have an idea what's going
through the Dodgers' minds right now. It isn't good." And then,
"*This* is the Dodgers' idea of a stopper? . . . Seeing Howell and
his curveball reminded us of a high school pitcher."

Reading this stuff now makes you wince. "So tonight my moment comes"—Cone was starting Game Two. "I've freeze-
framed the image a thousand times. Cone stands on the mound.
Cone takes deep breath. Cone winds up. . . ."

Cone gets his ears knocked off. The Dodgers, of course, read
the *News* column the next morning and passed it around the

clubhouse. Copies were pasted to the dugout wall by game time. Ed Cone, there to see David in his first post-season outing, was seated nearby and recalls a level of anger and obscenity he'd never heard on a ball field. All the people in Dodger Stadium seemed to know what had happened and were licking their lips over what was to come next—all but David. Deep in his pre-game preparations, he had not read his own firebrand stuff, and only became aware before he took the field that something was up. Keith Hernandez, noticing his red face and strained expression in the dugout, sent Ojeda over to ask if he was all right. "I should have gone myself," Hernandez says now. "He definitely was not himself." Davey Johnson, the Mets manager, blames himself for the debacle as well. "My greatest regret about that season was David Cone's literary career," he said. "I should have screened him more carefully. He got the Dodgers riled and for that one game he was a hundred miles away."

Cone, to bloodhound bayings from the stands and the dugout across the field, gave up a run in the first inning, and four more in the second, on a pair of singles and a two-run double by Mickey Hatcher. Then he was gone. The Dodgers won, 6–3, and the Mets lost a game and eventually a series that had appeared easily within their grasp. They never recovered—more than one baseball columnist gave it as his opinion this summer that Cone's ghosted column and tainted, unfortunate defeat in the second game had cost the Mets a pennant and a World Championship not just that year but perhaps another one or two after that, because they were so strong. To some degree David has not recovered, either. Until the perfect game, in 1999, this remained the most famous outing of his career.

The grotesque circumstances of the loss also obscured what Cone did in his next start, Game Six of that playoff. Back at Dodger Stadium and still in the thrall of his earlier humiliation, he began shakily, bouncing pitches and surrendering a couple of early walks. Kirk Gibson tried to surprise him with a bunt but popped the ball straight back to the mound, and the gift seemed to awaken Cone from another disaster. The turnaround, a stubborn five-hitter and a 5–1 victory, which brought the Mets even in the playoffs still ranks high with him, just possibly the best-pitched game of his life. But the Mets played poorly in the finale, losing to Hershiser, 6–0.

The blot of Game Two remains, but Cone did something remarkable that day. "I'd given the Dodgers good grounds," he said to me. "I'd lit that fire and the story was everywhere in the media the next day. ABC even put it on the air during the game telecast. You couldn't get away from it. It was on Johnny Carson—him laughing at me and making a lot of it. It was tough on a young pitcher."

He remembers the Mets clubhouse scene after the loss, with the media pushing in and shoving around him. He'd tried to ask a writer—it was Mike Lupica, the *News* columnist—what he should do now. "And that's when I decided I should stand up to it," David said. "Not say, 'No, I never sat down behind a type-writer and wrote this—Bob Klapisch did it.' Instead I'd say, yes, it was me—I did it and I'm sorry I did."

Jay Horwitz, the Mets' director of media information—he's been in the post almost since Abner Doubleday's time—says, "It was an act of amazing courage. I'll never forget it. There were writers and radio people completely surrounding him, and he took the rap entirely, even though he didn't know what was in that column."

Keith Hernandez remembers seeing Lupica and Klapisch standing together after Cone's clubhouse trial and laughing about what had happened. "I've never forgiven them for that," he said. And Klapisch, for his part, still fumes at Hernandez for blackening him with the other Mets players over the incident. "He killed me," he said. "He told everybody the next spring—this is in '89—don't talk to Bob because of what he did to Coney. He waited all winter."

Cone retired as a columnist after two more efforts, in which the *News* allowed him, late in the day, to try to set things straight. In the farewell, he says that Klapisch had actually writ-ten the tainted lines, but he does not exonerate himself. He apologizes to Howell and says that both he and Klapisch had used poor judgment.

Klapisch told me that he'd filed both the original Cone column and his own full game story from Los Angeles in just over an hour. He was wearing two hats—the beat guy and the Cone columnist—and the deadline rush was a killer.

Klapisch has a lean and dashing look. A former semipro pitcher—he played for Columbia as an undergraduate, and once struck out Ron Darling in a game against Yale—he sustains a murmurous insider's manner with the players. When we talked he admitted to some long thoughts about that night in the clubhouse. "I was rushed, yes," he said, "but I should not have put it in the paper until I'd said, 'David, this is your column—it's got your name on it. Think about what you just said.' I didn't do that and I regret it."

He has not lost his admiration for the way Cone came back and won the sixth game against the Dodgers, really stuck it to them, and the way he has gone on being the ultimate standup guy—the tops in the business. "It's been twelve years now," Klap said, "and I still think how easy it would have been that night for him to say. 'Hey, listen, it wasn't me—'"

Tom Lasorda had the last word. Talking to the reporters in his office after the game, the Dodger skipper said, "That's what makes America great, freedom of the press. . . . My players don't write."

Orel Hershiser won the Most Valuable Player award for the 1988 N.C.L.S., and then took the same award in the World Series for his two wins against the Oakland Athletics. A nice pair of bookends, but then where would he put the Cy Young that came to him a bit later on? Cone finished third in that balloting. In November, both pitchers were members of a touring Major League All-Star squad that made exhibition appearances in Japan, playing several games. These good-will affairs are hard on the weary pitchers, who must actually work through the lineups and get the outs, while the position players dog it a little and have fun. Hershiser skipped the last few games to go home and care for an ailing child of his, and Cone appeared on the field in Hershiser's uniform before a later game, wearing one of those scary Japanese stage-villain masks under his cap. The crowd didn't know what to make of it.

A few nights before this, there was a function at which the American players found themselves lined up along one wall of a ballroom, with an audience of Japanese dignitaries and baseball people on the other. It was an awkward moment. Then one of the hosts came forward and, through an interpreter, announced that he wanted Orel Hershiser to step up and receive an award as the greatest living pitcher in baseball. Hershiser, waving him off, pushed David forward instead. "This is the greatest pitcher in baseball," he said.

11

Night Critters

Second place is hard country. When the Mets finished six games behind the Cubs in 1989 (Gary Carter batted .183 in his fifty games) and four back of the Pirates the next year, the urgency to win became obsessive. "When Doc or Sid or I started, you'd see a weird lineup behind us, because Davey Johnson wanted nothing but offensive bats," Cone said. "Mackey Sasser caught, Jefferies was at second, Howard Johnson at short, and Juan Samuel played center. Jefferies was a third baseman really, and so was Hojo, and Samuel a second baseman—three guys out of position. We weren't opposed to it if it worked but it didn't. The Mets traded away Dykstra and Mookie because someone had the idea that Samuel was a great power hitter, but he was an everyday infielder on the downside of his career. We underachieved. *I* didn't underachieve."

I was there the day David Cone lost it out by first base. It was April 30,1990, but it felt more like April Fool's Day, with me and everyone else in Atlanta-Fulton County Stadium screeching at him "Hey! Wow! Hey, David, look out—yo, down *here!*" as the lead Braves' base runner, Dale Murphy, surprised to find Cone with the ball in his hand and his back turned while he furiously argued a call at first base by umpire Charlie Williams, scurried home all unnoticed. Cone, eyes popping and arms waving, yelled at the ump and pointed down to where he thought he'd just stepped on the bag, and where Williams held that he had not. Another spectator was the Braves' Ernie Whitt, who'd been on first when the play began and scuttled along to third when Murphy scored. While Mets catcher Mackey Sasser jumped up and down helplessly at his post, Whitt now continued edgily down the line like Sylvester Pussycat nipping past a bulldog, and rushed across the plate.

"While you're arguing with me another run just scored," Williams told Cone, but David wouldn't drop the point. Second baseman Gregg Jefferies, grabbing his arm, finally yanked him back to reality. The play had been routine—a fourth-inning bouncer by Mark Lemke that first baseman Mike Marshall couldn't quite reach. Jefferies gloved the ball instead and tossed to Cone, covering, who either stepped on first before Lemke did, or, in the ump's view, missed it. If the call had been protested more reasonably, it would have left the bases loaded with two outs, and the score still 2–1, Atlanta. Now it was 4–1, and that night David was back in the headlines and on the national evening news, big-time.

It made for rich fare in the pressbox, with the Atlanta guys crowing a bit over Cone's mental blackout and New York types saying, "Well, that's David," and enjoying the odd pride that came with it. In the clubhouse, Cone owned up once again. "I'm a human being and an emotional person," he said, tilting toward the obvious. "I snapped emotionally, and it's something I'm going to have to live with. It's an embarrassing moment and it cost our team maybe a ballgame."

Manager Davey Johnson called it vapor lock, and though the Mets lost the game, 7–4, he declined to fine his pitcher. Marty Noble, the *Newsday* beat man, was ravished to learn that the official scorer's ruling attributed the extra bases to "pitcher's indifference"—a variation on the "catcher's indifference" that is invoked when a base runner is allowed to advance unhindered to second or third, usually late in a one-sided game—but when he relayed the news Cone was indignant. "'Indifferent' is the one thing I wasn't!" David cried.

Cone's fugue established him everywhere as a poster boy for intensity. Not until the weird, hotly disputed moment when Roger Clemens flung a broken-off bat head in the path of Mike Piazza in the 2000 World Series were fans given a clearer illustration of the mad focus that these men bring to their work. David's snappage was funnier and less dark than the Rocket's, but they come from the same lobe of the pitcher brain.

Two weeks later, at Shea, with Cone still winless for the season, his last pitch of the day also went into the annals. Leading the Dodgers, 1–0, in the third, he'd waited out an hour-and-a-half rain delay before he could get ready again in the bullpen, but then another deluge put the tarps back on the field. An hour later, warming for the third time that day, he was pleased to find that he still had good stuff, but when play resumed the rains came again, this time for keeps, and David, seething, fired the ball deep into the mezzanine seats—a mythic peg. Mets fans loved this playground rage in Cone, which set him apart from the Nolan Ryans and Greg Madduxes of his era. Pitching requires full effort, no matter who is out there, and while Jack Morris and Kevin Brown and Randy Johnson and David Wells and, yes, Roger Clemens always showed you a vivid personification of the will when in action they lacked Cone's histrionic range: his pallid coldness of concentration, his head shakes and clenched-jaw regroupings when enduring frustration, and these hilarious illustrations of failure in the face of expected success.

The writers loved him. He was quotable and convivial, as much at ease with them in the post-game bars as he was with his teammates, and able to take the talk beyond sports if anyone wanted. Writers are frustrated jocks and Cone was a frustrated writer—he still thought about going into the business someday, once his career came to a close. Now and then the beat writers got into pickup basketball games on the road, and when Cone heard about a scheduled Y.M.C.A. date in St. Louis one day he asked in. Everyone assumed he'd stay on the periphery of the battle, not wanting to risk an ankle or shoulder injury in the tussles under the rim, but he kept driving up the lanes, shoving and elbowing. One of the locals, a larger man, kept shoving back and there was a flareup. "I'll kick your ass you push me like that again, you son of a bitch!" Cone said. Sweating and glaring, they were nose to nose until the writers, who'd been enjoying this, came to their senses and pulled their pitcher away. The Mets front office, when the news of the near-fracas leaked out, was not amused.

Cone was becoming a fixture in New York. In an era when the Mets' lineup had become unstable and their reputation dubious, and their performances ranged from the brilliant to the disappointing to the dreary, he turned up every fifth day and had at the batters like an avenger or an epidemic. Less cherished than the prodigal, self-destructive Doc Gooden and Darryl Strawberry, he became an antidote to their flame-outs and rehabs: the new good guy. One of his pitching confreres, Bobby Ojeda, was animated when he talked recently about Cone's early flowering. "He was so young and intense that you took to him," he said to me. "Rather than anybody looking at him and thinking here's a guy come to take our jobs, we thought here's somebody with a lot of heart and talent, so let's find room for him. He became part of the intensity of that club. He wanted to win but it mattered more to him to do a good job. If the team lost, it was always a dark day for him."

If you were a fan, what you began to appreciate in Cone was that his surface fire and exotic array of pitches—the breaking stuff and the mid-nineties fastball, the plummeting split-finger and the balls that flared crazily wide of the plate and ran up his counts—concealed a steadfast, almost assembly-line regularity of output. He was embarked on a stretch of five years in which he never missed a start. After compiling two hundred and thirty-one innings in his remarkable 1988 season, he threw two hundred and nineteen, two hundred and eleven, and two hundred and thirty-two innings over the next three (I have omitted fractions), while making ninety-nine starts and notching forty-two wins. Only the strikeout totals changed, rising from a hundred and ninety in 1989 to two hundred and thirty-three and then two hundred and forty-one, with the last two leading the National League those seasons. In the final game of the 1991 Mets campaign, he struck out nineteen Phillies batters at Veterans Stadium, tying a league record held by Tom Seaver and Steve Carlton, and one behind Roger Clemens's all-time twenty, established in 1986 and duplicated by him a decade later.

Cone's 14–8, 14–10, and 14–14 won-lost records in those years disappointed him, but not as much as one might expect. To his way of thinking, each of them could easily have become twenty-game seasons, given a few more runs and breaks. Before we look for explanations, including the frail .244 team batting average of the fold-up 1991 club, it helps to remember that in the best baseball circles—within the manager-general-manager-pitching-coach councils, that is—the innings-pitched column carries almost as much weight as the wins. "Gimme a guy who'll take the ball every day" is the way you hear it. Strikeouts matter, too, since they're part of your defense, and take on even more glitter if the pitcher's whiff totals exceed his hits allowed, as Cone's did in most seasons through the eighties and nineties. Cone's records, together with his competitive fire, his appealingly laid-back off-the-field personality, his intelligence, and his flair for the media, qualified him for New York. He had become urbane—the Mets' mayor, once Keith Hernandez left. He took over his No. 17 uniform number, in tribute. Strangely, he belonged also in the center of the Mets' assembly of childish and uncontrollable athletes headed each night for hell or Page Six.

The disbanding of the 1986 World Champions had begun almost from the moment Ray Knight crossed home plate with the go-ahead run in Game Six. The independent Knight and unrestrained Kevin Mitchell were cast away that first winter, then Wally Backman in 1988, and, in a rush, Rick Aguilera, Roger

McDowell, Lenny Dykstra and Mookie Wilson—two wonderfully different center fielders, gone within six weeks of each other in midsummer—Keith Hernandez and Gary Carter in 1989. Then Bobby O. and Straw and Davey Johnson, the manager himself, were gone after another year: the end of the line. Every modern-day ball team is in a state of flux, and though fresh hopes and faces—Kevin McReynolds, Frank Viola, Dave Magadan, and a new manager, Buddy Harrelson—were offered to the Mets' fans after each fresh shock, the departures took on the air of a purge, a progressive Elba that took away the worst and best of that taunting, renegade bunch that other teams and other parts of the country had so feared and disliked. Frank Cashen had built that team and now appeared to take it apart, as well. Ojeda and some other old Mets blame his deputy, Joe McIlvaine (who had once studied for the priesthood), for the way it was done, but alterations on these dimensions could not have come without the consent of the owners.

These Mets had been notorious as well as successful, heavy drinkers and party-goers, prone to babes and drugs (at least some of them), and with a flair for scandal that persisted even as the roster was shuffled. At one point their shenanigans threatened to make Jay Horwitz, the embattled P.R. director, the best known Met of all, thanks to his regular appearance before the microphones, statement in hand, after another midnight outbreak of the unlikely. The news grew grotesque in the early nineties, but none of it was exactly new. Veterans on the Mets beat, Marty Noble and Bob Klapisch among them, hold that the real reason for the Mets' uprooting from their old spring-training center in St. Petersburg and transfer to a new development in Port St. Lucie wasn't the sweetheart real-estate deal that the owners, Nelson Doubleday and Fred Wilpon, were handed at the sleepy, well-gatored East Coast site but a pressing need to keep the club's young girl- and party-chasers away from the Boschian bar scenes along the beach in St. Pete. Another rationale was passed on to me one day by Wilpon himself. "It's been so *inconvenient,*" he said. "With Nelson and his family at

Hobe Sound and mine at West Palm, when our kids come down from school on spring break they have to travel all the way over to the Gulf Coast to see the Mets play. This way, they're going to be right at home."

Not all the Mets were young. Hernandez, the paragon first baseman of his time, suffered a knee injury in 1989, and was signed by the Indians that winter. He was thirty-six and he agrees now that it was time for the Mets to make the move. "I went to Cleveland the next year, but I couldn't run anymore," he said. "I was embarrassed there. I'll always love Frank Cashen. When he called me in to tell me about the trade he had tears in his eyes. I said that I understood his reasons and he said, 'Well, come here and give me a hug.'"

Mex, as the team always called him, is still lean and glittery but there's gray in that gaucho mustache now. He does occasional TV work for Fox Sports and MSG, and is working toward becoming a licensed New York real-estate dealer—"more of a front man," in his words. "I take the clients to restaurants and ballgames and to the Garden. Then my partners take over." He looks back on those jackanapes Mets without regret and only wishes the '86 champs had been a little older. "A whole bunch of them were in their early twenties," he said. "They were young bucks. If they'd been thirty or so nobody would have touched us. We'd have been like the nineteen-seventies Reds—we'd have won everything for five years."

I heard the same thing from Bobby Ojeda, who lives in Rumson, New Jersey. "We were young and pretty loose, and they didn't give us a chance to grow up together," he said. "When we lost in 1988, you could see the second-guessers begin to take over. Joe McIlvaine, with his Jimmy Swaggart mentality, cut the heart out of that team, and Cashen got tired of saying no to him. You could see Keith's role beginning to get less. He had a little wild streak but he always knew how to strap it on and go out there. He had that Gold Glove mind-set. It was a shame."

Hernandez believes that the 1988 team was in decline even while it was winning. Cliques and feuds abounded, with the rapt media in close attendance. He himself had a spectacular public run-in with Darryl Strawberry early the next spring, but it had begun late that winning summer when Marty Noble asked him whether Straw or Kevin McReynolds, the broad-shouldered, semi-silent new slugger in left field—the Stealth Bomber—was the team's most valuable player. The question looked reasonable on its face—Straw had had a great first half, and McReynolds began to hit everything out of sight later on—but it probably called for a pass. "I should have kept my mouth shut," Hernandez said, "but stupid me, I told Marty that I had to go with McReynolds because the second half always means more."

Strawberry had won mention as a strong Most Valuable Player candidate in the National League that fall, and when Kirk Gibson took the honor instead Straw fell to brooding about Hernandez's slight. In Port St. Lucie the next spring, Darryl turned up at the team's Photo Day and offered to take on the captain, there and then.

"I kept saying, 'Darryl, are you sure you want to do this today?'" Hernandez told me. "'Are you sure, with all the cameras here?'" Photographers and writers were agog, but yes, Straw was sure, and when Keith came back with his "I'm tired of your baby shit," Darryl launched a punch that landed mostly on the front pages. The flap was magnificent and didn't exactly abate when Hernandez went on the "Kiner's Korner" broadcast and blamed a couple of writers for fomenting it all—an argument that ultimately had to be sorted out in Davey Johnson's office. Forget the names and shoutings now: Photo Day lives on as the silliest Mets scandal of its time and the most innocent.

David Cone, young and on the loose, eager to fit in with the team's high flyers, and then a carouser and nighthawk with a reputation of his own, was involved to one degree or another in most of the sex scandals that afflicted the Mets of that time. A decade older today, with his maturity and reputation for leadership secure, he is unhappy to have these matters brought up once again. I feel the same uneasiness, and it occurs to me that the youthful excesses of the men and women I know best never come up in our doings and conversations—nor mine with them, I trust. If I appear less discreet or forgetful here it's because these tales are on record and to skip them would become noticeable in its own way and a cause for speculation. When I told Cone about this conclusion, he said, "It's your book—you've got to do what you've got to do." Lynn Cone was equally fair-minded, and less troubled than her husband.

Sex and athletes and the lure of the road are dealt with crisply in Bill Bradley's sports memoir, "Life on the Run," when Knicks coach Red Holzman brings up the subject for the only time. "If you manage to get lucky, don't fall asleep on top of the covers," he tells his veteran players. "I don't want any colds."

Years ago, I asked the celebrated golf writer Herbert Warren Wind, a friend and colleague of mine, about sex and the P.G.A. How many of those tanned, sweet-swinging guys we saw on our television screens each weekend, from Pebble Beach to Augusta to St. Andrews, were fooling around on the road?

"All of them," he said. "Well, all but one"—and he told me his name.

"Do you mean—?" and I mentioned a couple of world-class stars.

"All of them," Herb said. "Except the one."

I've forgotten his name.

Professional athletes live in a night context of total freedom, and we don't need Wilt Chamberlain's boast of twenty thousand women scored, or accounts of the children sired by N.B.A. or N.F.L. players at every road-trip stopover to make the point. Only with baseball does anyone still seem to find this a little shocking, although ballplayers spend more time away from home than the others because of the immense schedule, with half of their season lived out of a suitcase. Young players are almost helplessly vulnerable stumbling into this scene at an age when they're still staring about at the world, and the life that's thrust at them in hotel bars and around the periphery of the game must feel like a Christmas present beyond imagination. Wired after another late-night finish in a strange time zone, they are wakeful and lonely, with chunks of money and empty time on their hands. There is never a shortage of women, and friends on prior visiting teams may have arranged gift dates with the more spectacular or pliant girls in town. All the players, right down to the coaches, are looked upon—except by children and out-of-it parents and geezer fans—as sexual animals and fair game. The same thing applies to rock stars and movie and television people, of course, and to C.E.O.s and authors and other well-travelled, powerful men and women. The road is the road, and everyone carries the same passport. Only in baseball and politics is the anarchic celebrity life looked upon as a moral matter. Parents and voters and baseball owners—some of each group, at least—want ballplayers and Presidents to be good and to set an example. It doesn't come up anywhere else.

Early in October of 1991, in Philadelphia on the Mets' closing road trip, Cone took a telephone call from a bar acquaintance of his, and eventually invited her up to his room. Alone the next morning, he was awakened by a call from Frank Cashen, who told him that he was about to be charged with rape by his night visitor. David was due to pitch that day but Cashen offered him the option of skipping his turn, given the situation. No, Cone said, he'd pitch, even though he was told that an arrest might be imminent during the game itself, at Veterans Stadium.

With the third-place Phillies nineteen games behind the division-leading Pirates, and the fifth-place Mets back by twenty and a half, the game was played before a sparse Sunday turnout. Coming off the field after each half-inning Cone peered into the runway behind home plate, looking for the posse that never came. Cashen, for his part, had agreed to share the game telecast booth with Ralph Kiner and chat about the season that was closing, but he was distracted from the task as he awaited a signal from the team's road secretary that the arrest was at hand. "You'll never guess what's happened," he said to Kiner as he sat down. "And I can't tell you what it is." The high sign

never came—the case was dropped a few days later, with no arrest, after the Philadelphia police had learned the details—but
now Cashen's attention had become riveted by what his pitcher
was doing out on the field. This was Cone's nineteen-strikeout
game.

"I was never more all alone, but I felt calmer there than any-
place else," David said later. "Nothing could touch me—I was
safe as long as I kept throwing. It's no surprise that I did so
well."

He wrapped up the last out and the 7–0 win with regret and
left for the clubhouse, knowing that none of the early questions
to him there would be about the game.

Spring in 1992 at Port St. Lucie was wild. Three Mets players—
Doc Gooden, Vince Coleman, and Daryl Boston—were named
in a rape charge brought by a New York woman who claimed
that they'd met in a bar a year before, then moved along to
Gooden's Port St. Lucie home, where she'd been victimized. The
story went way beyond the sports pages, and the stadium media
room was invaded by city-side tabloid reporters eager for more
of the same. Andrea Peyser, of the *Post*, among others, began
following the players to local bars and writing about what they
did there and whom they left with. There were photographs.
The players howled, indignant over an invasion of privacy and
innuendoes that could be levelled at some of the married players. I was visiting the Mets just then, though not on the trail of
this story, and I remember the new pink media credentials that
Jay Horwitz handed out to us in the middle of this fuss, which
certified us as the real thing—sports guys, not creeps or gossips.
Only the pink cards would be honored now.

It was at this point that two other women got in touch with
Peyser to amplify a harassment charge they and a third woman
had brought against Cone in the fall. There had been a scene in
the stands at Shea, and Cone, coming up from the clubhouse,
had got involved and had called them "groupies." He was there,
in fact, because Lynn, who'd been sitting in the section behind

home reserved for players' wives and friends, had become alarmed on observing the women taunting Sid Fernandez's wife, Noelani, a friend of hers, and had sent word for David to come up and take charge. The women, in any case, didn't look like the kind of baseball follower that normally got into the family section. David appeared and yelled at them, and was slapped with the suit shortly afterward; "groupies," the offending word, had been said to a Page Six reporter after the fact. Now the women told Peyser that they'd amplified the original charge to include another scene, on a different day at Shea, when Cone allegedly exposed himself to them in the bullpen and masturbated—a charge that he has absolutely denied, and which was eventually dismissed. The harassment case never made it to trial; the first two women abandoned the case, and a settlement was reached with the third woman, for the "groupie" word.

The damage was just beginning. A day or two later, the *Post* ran a lurid cartoon on Page Six, depicting Cone, from the back, in an unmistakable posture. Too much, and the angry players, led by John Franco, told club officials they'd had enough. There would be a press boycott for the remainder of the spring and the rest of the season—the Mets were going to dummy up and talk to no one. The beat writers, their days suddenly less onerous, smiled and went along, but after a morning when the *Times* sports section carried nothing from Port St. Lucie but a box score the boycott was doomed. The commissioner's office and the Players Association dispatched emissaries; Cone (as player representative) and Dave Magadan addressed the troops; and the Mets, in Baltimore by now for a last pre-season exhibition at the new Camden Yards, gave voice once again.

David remained preoccupied, and early in April the expected blow fell. Charges in the Port St. Lucie rape case had been dismissed—no jury would decide between the players' versions of the tale as against the plaintiff's—but the end of the investigation allowed the court-withheld names and details to be released. The woman involved, a New York architect, was identified as a friend of Cone's who testified that she had been "dating Dave" at the time of the incident. She and he were sexual intimates, and it was also reported that Cone had told police that there had been a consensual ménage à trois.

Lynn, who was working at MHA, a New York design firm, heard the news in devastating fashion. David had called her earlier and told her not to come down to spring training this year. It was impossible, he said—he'd explain later. Now, with the Port St. Lucie case suddenly on the air and in the papers, she became the target of strange looks and silences in her own office. The complainant, who had not been named, was described as a New York design person, about five feet four, with dark hair. "It fitted me to a T," Lynn told me. "Suddenly I was this woman who'd been raped by three men, and who'd never come forward with the full story. It was unimaginable."

It changed the relationship she and David had made, and for a time almost destroyed it. They had been a couple for five years now, though Lynn had always kept her own apartment, on Second Avenue and Forty-seventh Street, while David had a rental at the Monte Excelsior, in Little Neck, Queens, where he sometimes holed up. They had barely survived the Philadelphia scandal. "Was there something you forgot to tell me at dinner last night?" she'd said to David by telephone when that news came down. They'd patched things up but a cloud remained. This fresh event broke them apart.

"I was young and not ready for something as serious as we'd become" was David's comment to me. "I wasn't happy about it. I made bad decisions. I should never have let it happen."

Lynn said, "I think in those first years David desperately wanted to belong. I told him that for the first time in his life he'd acted like a follower, not a leader. He was very easily swayed. He was taken in by the fame and notoriety of the Mets and by New York. He wanted to become like the Hernandezes and Darlings of the world. I'd begun to feel he was somebody I should stay away from."

I was impressed by Lynn Cone's candor and clarity, and I was surprised in almost the same way when I went to Keith

Hernandez, a Lampwick to many Mets wives, to talk about these matters.

"Women are not part of the team," he said. "A ball team is twenty-five guys with one thing on their minds, which is baseball. Then there are twenty-five wives and girlfriends who have nothing in common. It takes a very special woman to be married to an athlete. She has to be enormously secure within herself, and not many women are. I've been called a misogynist for this but it's what I believe."

He said that Cone hadn't been a leader when he first arrived with the Mets but only a cheerful young guy with a quirky sense of humor—"a Dennis the Menace," in his words. "McDowell was the real joker," he said. "Everybody grew up later on. David grew up and became a great leader. Dwight grew up, after his fashion. Straw almost got his act together for a while. It was a shame about Straw."

Hernandez mentioned at one point what it was like back then when a group of Mets came into a bar together and took over the room, and I recalled that Cone had used almost exactly the same words. "You can't believe what it's like," he said. "All of a sudden you're with a whole bunch of young women, and the men have disappeared, even the ones they'd come with. It's you and them in a minute."

Keith said, "Those Mets in the eighties were a bunch of night critters. I was single and getting a divorce, so I didn't have to worry about who I was seen with. I think I took better care of myself than some. I couldn't sleep after games and I always closed the hotel bar down, on the road. I'd go to bed around three and sleep till noon."

It wasn't just drinking and partying, he said. Some of those Mets—Lennie Dykstra, Wally Backman, Kevin McReynolds—had been serious gamblers, too. They'd waked him up at four-thirty one morning with the sounds of a boisterous poker game in the next room.

"I think what women don't understand is the way men are together," Mex went on. "I enjoyed the companionship of my teammates on the road. It's a precious part of the game to me. I loved the plane trips—playing hearts in the back of the plane. It's sad I don't see those guys anymore—Lenny, Tim Teufel, Hojo, Ojeda, David, Sid, and Gary Carter. I didn't like Gary all that much, come to think of it, but I always thought he called a great game."

Morale was as problematic as morals with these early-nineties Mets. The 1991 array ran off ten straight wins in early July but then quit cold on their manager, Buddy Harrelson, who was fired at the end of the year. He and Cone had got into a shouting, shoving faceoff in the dugout, in June. Shortstop Kevin Elster's wry comment about the Mets' eleven-game losing streak in August, which included ten in a row on the road, summed up the team morale: "We didn't play the last of the ninth most of the time, so we cut about four innings off our season!"

Another loss for David that summer was Ron Darling, who was traded away to the Expos for a lesser (it turned out) pitcher named Tim Burke. Darling and Cone had been tight, drawn together by their brains and cool and success. Listening to them back then, I'd noticed how they both talked baseball with a meticulous passion. Darling, born in Hawaii, was the son of a professional Air Force officer, and had gone to Yale; I'd written a *New Yorker* piece about his smothering eleven innings of no-hit ball against St. John's during a regional N.C.A.A. elimination, at New Haven, in a game he'd lost in the twelfth inning. The winning St. John's pitcher was Frank Viola, who later became a Mets starter, too.

Darling knew the late spots and exciting people. "Our friendship went river to river," Cone said to me. They had another bond: their fathers. Darling was the first player I'd known to express doubt over the enormous new player salaries. After he signed a new Mets contract in 1988, he said that the realization that it would pay him more than his father's lifetime earnings had thrown him into despair: "When I got the news from my agent, I had to call my dad and tell him the news. How do you tell a man who's worked hard all his life and who's a better man than you are—I really, really believe that—that his son is going to be making a million fifty thousand dollars for pitching a baseball? It just blew me away." These were almost exactly the same feelings David later expressed about his salary and Ed's.

The 1992 Mets had a new general manager, Al Harazin, who came from the business side of the game, and a new manager, Jeff Torborg, plus a fresh line of expensive hirelings in Bobby Bonilla, Eddie Murray, and Bret Saberhagen. Cone had become an old-time Met—a condition on this team that did not necessarily endear you to management. He and Steve Fehr had discombobulated the club the winter before when they surprisingly broke off contract negotiations after the Mets had offered a four-year contract for $16.8 million, and won a salary arbitration award worth four and a quarter million. A survivor of the sex wars and the contract wars, Cone was mistrusted by the media-conscious front office for his closeness to the writers. "Every time I pitched that year, I felt I had something to prove," he said to me. Enemy batters must have sensed this in April and May, when he delivered shutouts in four out of six starts.

On July 17th, at Shea, against the Giants, the Mets scored a run in the bottom of the first inning, which Cone protected doggedly, almost crazily, over the full distance, throwing a hundred and sixty-six pitches in the 1–0 shutout. He was all over the map in the early going, putting runners aboard and going to high counts and then somehow wriggling out of each jam. He gave up six hits and four bases on balls in the game, while striking out thirteen. The Mets contributed no double plays, which means that Cone on average went close to the full count on every batter in the game. He got better as he went along, but manager Torborg found no reason to pull him as the extraordinary total mounted. John Franco was sidelined, and Cone, of course, could think only of the next batter and the one after that. "I wanted that game badly," he explained afterward.

The win was part of a stretch of six games in which he averaged a hundred and forty pitches per start—with an inexorable

price paid that showed itself in fifteen earned runs over his next
four starts. The hundred-and-sixty-six-pitch game meant little—
the Giants were in fourth place and on their way to a miserable
finish, twenty-six games behind the Braves—but it perversely
shimmers or pulses in the Cone record, and for me at last settles
the question David had proposed at the beginning of the season:
Who owns the pitcher's arm?

The answer is nobody. A fiery pitcher will always want to
stay out there—it's part of his soul—and if the manager or pitching coach won't take responsibility at this point the arm will pay
the price. Examples abound, the latest of which, for the Mets,
had been Doc Gooden's one hundred and forty-nine pitches
against the Expos on a chilly April, 1991, day at Shea, in a game
I attended and watched with increasing horror. Manager Buddy
Harrelson explained later that Gooden still had full velocity and
wanted to continue, but Doc required labrum and rotator-cuff
surgery that September and was never the same kind of pitcher
again.

Cone's six-year run with the Mets came to an end on August
27, 1992, when he was traded to Toronto for the then little-
known infielder Jeff Kent and outfielder Ryan Thompson. The
move shocked Cone and everyone else in New York, but it could
have been foreseen. That fall, he would be coming up on free
agency in a pitchers' market knocked askew by Greg Maddux's
turndown of a new five-year, $27.5 million deal with the Cubs.
Cone and Fehr's rejection of the Mets' four-year, nearly seven-
teen-million-dollar offer in favor of salary arbitration was taken
as a sign that Cone, too, would be looking for a five-year deal—
something that he has always denied. The Mets, in any case,
were going nowhere—they would finish in last place in their division, twenty-four games behind the division-winning Pirates—
and the Blue Jays had legitimate post-season aspirations. But
there had been no warning for Cone until Frank Cashen, at the
end of a road trip, hinted that something was in the wind—a favor that David still remembers. Only Mike Lupica saw it the
Mets' way, citing Cone's "million innings the last few years" as

evidence that he was a poor bet for a long-term contract. Cone, he wrote, had never been a franchise player.

Departing, David said that the heart and soul of the club had already been bred out of it. "The era of the arrogant Mets is gone," he went on. "They want a more hands-on approach, players of a more conformist nature, and I'm definitely not that." And, later on, "Part of me will be a Met forever."

In Toronto, he joined an old friend, Robby Alomar, and made a quick rapport with manager Cito Gaston. It was exciting but strange to be suddenly back in a pennant race, weeks after the trading deadline had gone by. He still doesn't understand how that all-purpose waivers was arranged. As the Blue Jays played out their schedule, the "hired gun" label became affixed to him in the headlines and kept him on a nervous edge through a four-and-three accounting in those late weeks, with two 1–0 wins and 0–1 and 1–2 losses along the way.

Off the field he felt cast down and acutely alone. He was exiled from New York, playing for another team in another country. He and Lynn were separated—"going through some rough times," in his words—and he was living alone in the soulless SkyDome Hotel, part of the stadium complex. He took a freight elevator from the clubhouse level up to his room, where the window offered a view out over some railroad tracks. Empty beer cans began to pile up and the ashtrays were full of cigarettes—Canadian cigarettes. "It was the lowest I've been," he said to me. "I felt like a derelict. It was time for me to take measure of myself."

Feature stories about him from that day also find him referring glumly to that same SkyDome hotel room, and muttering that New York was still his home, if he had one, but I'd not heard him in this mood before. Now he picked up on an old joke of ours—the moment when my wife, Carol, a Mets fan, had first seen him on the television screen in his new Blue Jay uniform and was startled by his deadly grim expression on the mound. "My God, what happened to David!" she'd cried. "He looks like a serial killer."

Cone understands how fan loyalties can change after a trade, but now he said, "Carol saw something—I knew it the first time you told me the story. I was fighting for my life there."

He moved along to a rough experience he'd had in the sixth game of the American League Championship Series that October—a dead-arm outing when he was hooked up against the Oakland Athletics' redoubtable Dave Stewart, who beat him 6–2. "*God . . .*" he said, shaking his head.

He had better outcomes after this, when the Jays, with Oakland at last dismissed, beat the Atlanta Braves in a wonderful six-game World Series. Cone didn't pick up a decision in either of his starts, but the Jays won them both, and their championship, delivered with an eleventh-inning double by Dave Winfield, was ecstatically welcomed in Canada, which had entertained semi-pathological doubts about its rights to the ancient title. David, edging out the door as a free agent, was happy for his teammates and for Cito Gaston, but I noticed that most of his conversations about that year circle back to his truncated Mets season, and his five shutouts there. His combined season came out at 17–10 (13–7 in New York), and his two hundred and sixty-one strikeouts led all comers in both leagues—his third straight year at the top of that heap, counting a 1991 tie with Clemens. A hell of a year, all in all, but not much noticed in most places. Hired guns got a right to sing the blues.

12

Ticket to Tampa

July, 2000

As fate had it, Cone's rained-out game against the Mets became the cause for a unique baseball holiday a month later. With no open dates available on the calendar, thanks to schedule squeezings, it had to be refashioned as the second part of a home-and-home doubleheader on Saturday, July 8th, with the first game coming, as planned, at Shea that afternoon, followed by the nightcap at Yankee Stadium. Two games for the price of two! It was the first bi-park, one-day doubleheader in New York since September 7, 1903, which came out 6–4 Giants, at the Brooklyn Superbas' Washington Park, in the morning, and then 3–0 Superbas, at the Polo Grounds, later on. I can't claim memory of that date, but the events of the second one will stay with me and the other 109,986 fans who got there, by car or watercraft or subway exploration, for almost as long. The Yankees, to go back a bit, came into the event looking for a lift, after a rocky stretch of injuries and pitching meltdowns and bumbled games—a more distracted time, in Joe Torre's opinion, than anything his other Yankee teams had encountered. Some of the baseball made no sense at all—a 17–4 blasting by the White Sox at the Stadium that was followed by a 22–1 win over the Red Sox at Fenway Park the next evening. The Yankees lost eleven out of fifteen games in the second half of June, dropping three behind the Blue Jays in the A.L. East (for one day they were in third place) during a rumor-haunted Boston-to-Chicago-to-Detroit-to-Tampa road trip. The writers grew short-tempered, chasing down daily trails and denials of an imminent blockbuster deal that would reshuffle the team overnight, and finding themselves frozen out by some players who blamed them for the tabloid fuss given to Chuck Knoblauch's troubles on the field.

Something still had to be done about the sagging power numbers—the Yankees were fourth-worst in the league in runs scored, and ninth in homers—and for a time it appeared that the designated savior would be Juan Gonzalez, a two-time M.V.P. lately and expensively inked by the Tigers, who had played himself into extreme unpopularity in record time. When Gonzalez appeared to turn down the Yankee trade at the last moment, the acquisition of Sammy Sosa became the rumor-du-jour—and, with it, the prospect of a weakened outfield defense, a lot of strikeouts in the middle of the batting order, and a celebrity entourage in the Yanks' once businesslike clubhouse, all in the same package. Other tradees surfaced, almost day by day— Houston's Moises Alou, Baltimore's B. J. Surhoff—but the trophy bat that general manager Brian Cashman actually landed, on the next-to-last day of June, had never been mentioned at all: David Justice, the élite left-swinging Cleveland veteran, with two hundred and fifty-six career homers, and extensive post-season experience compiled with the Indians and Braves. It was a wild bit of luck and opportunism: Cashman had called the Indians on a trifling matter—to arrange for the presentation of a 1999 World Series ring to bullpen catcher Gary Tuck, now a Cleveland scout—and was told almost as an aside that Justice might be available. Justice is lean and suave, with star presence—he was once married to Halle Berry—and the clusters of out-of-town writers trailing after him in his early at-bats appeared to add a little old-time Yankee pizzazz to the WalMart of

the American League East. These celebrated changes of cast
never fail to arouse the skulky hope of a disastrous failure in my
heart, but Justice batted .369, with six homers, in his first month
in pinstripes, and made a better person of me.

Winning is the great antidepressant—it's better than
Prozac—and when the Yankees got better it was hard to remember how low and sad they'd been before. Watching Cone's
miseries had perhaps distracted me from the commonplace day-
to-day unhappiness of slumping and threatened individual players, but that ugly stretch in June felt like a terminal-care ward.
Ricky Ledee, an opening-day outfielder and a fixture in the
team's long-range plans, played unevenly and self-consciously
through the spring, and became the bait in the protracted deal-
ings for a power-hitting outfielder. Intelligent and oversensitive,
his nails bitten down to bleeding, he gloomed and stared from
the bench and in the clubhouse as the days and weeks went by,
asking the writers what they'd heard about where he might be
going, and he gave way to tears when the Justice trade became
fact, and packed him off to Cleveland. (He was there only
briefly, before another transaction ricocheted him to the Texas
Rangers.) Ledee's old rival in left, Shane Spencer, now validated
as the winning heir, made a misstep in left field while on a routine fielding play against the Mets, and felt a stab in his right
knee—a tear of the anterior cruciate ligament that would sideline him for the rest of the year. He wept at the news. Jake Westbrook, that tall newcomer admired by Stottlemyre and Cone in
spring training, failed in two short-order starts in June and became a player-to-be-named-later pawn in the Justice deal, while
the left-hander Ed Yarnall, once the pre-season favorite to take
over as the Yanks' fifth starter, went to Cincinnati as part of the
package that brought in Denny Neagle. But these were agate-
line heartbreaks, remembered only by the departees and for a
day or two by the players on either side of their empty lockers.

Chuck Knoblauch, whose uncertainties in executing the routine throw from second to first had dogged him for more than a
year now, was victimized by a succession of injuries to his left

wrist, including one weirdly knuckling or sailing line drive by Preston Wilson that left a clear imprint of the ball's stitches just below the thumb. Everyone has a breaking point, he'd said, and his came on June 15th, when he committed three ghastly errors in a game against the White Sox, before the wincing Stadium crowd. When the Yankee infield gathered on the mound during a pitching changeover he remained at his position, exiling himself from his teammates. An unforgettable photograph of the moment shows him from a distance—his hands uneasily on his hips and his body tilting oddly—dwarfed by the gigantic illuminated "3" below the "E" on the scoreboard behind. "The beast of baseball"—it's an old line of Kirk Gibson's—had him in its claws. Sitting on the bench a bit later, with a towel held up under his chin, he made a convulsed grimace (watching at home, I said "My God!") and with a gesture to the manager stalked away down the tunnel. Torre sent him home for the night. Talking to the press later, Joe said, "You just want to hug him."

But Knoblauch was back the next day, ready for our questions. An old pro at thirty-one and one of the best lead-off batters of his time, he has kept an engaging youthfulness. With his pointy jaw and horizontal eyes, he has the look of a boy about to be entrusted with a secret mission. He wouldn't go away, he said. He'd called his mother when he got back to his apartment very late the night before. He still loved New York and he expected the intensity of interest from the fans and writers here. "Microscope or no microscope, this was going to happen," he said. "This is what I do." Laughing a little, dazed by the inexplicable, he reminded me of Steve Blass.

The Mets games rocked, starting with El Duque's duelling 2–1 win against Al Leiter in the opener, which set up the following day's extravaganza. That was a double sellout, of course, and early on at Shea you could see the head and shoulders of every single back-row, top-deck patron plain against the blue sky and arrayed from one end of the stands around to the other. Clots of unticketed spectators stayed on, watching from the subway platform out beyond the Mets' bullpen. Scudding clouds threw shadows across the grass and when they went away again the Mets outfielders, in their home whites, glowed in the sunlight like angels. The noise was continuous, with the tension of play appearing to mute the expected taunts. By luck, both sets of fans could cheer for Doc Gooden, plucked from oblivion and given his first start here at Shea, of all places—it was his first time back since 1994—and he delighted himself with a strong, edgy effort, good for a 4–2 win. Starring in a featured role, one could say, was Yankee first-base coach Lee Mazzilli, who had stalked indignantly onto the field in the first inning, crying "Obstruction!" after a near-contact on the base path between his base runner, Chuck Knoblauch, and Mets first baseman Todd Zeile. The first-base umpire, a rookie named Robb Cook, bought the package.

The Yanks prevailed again uptown (and by the same score) in the nightcap, but the joy of the special day was lost when Mike Piazza, batting against Clemens in the second inning, took a fastball to the head that put him down, dazed and blinking, in the dirt of the batter's box. The Mets' star, already the prime hitter in the history of the franchise, and once again a strong candidate for the Most Valuable Player award in his league, had feasted off Clemens in the past, most recently with a grand slam at the Stadium in June, during a humiliating 12–2 rout. Piazza leans comfortably out over the middle of the plate when batting—he moves in furniture, bedding, and lamps—and an admonitory message by Roger was not unexpected. Clemens, moreover, had been under pressure from Joe Torre and his coaches to rely more on his inside heat—to build everything around that early discourager, the way he had once done—and he'd fared better as a result. A fastball at Piazza's belt buckle here or even a fiery brushback at shoulder level would have induced no more than glares, but this was horrifying. Piazza, cringing, threw up his hands in front of his face as the ball took him almost in the forehead, striking the "NY" on his helmet just above the angle of the brim. Clemens walked in a few steps after the event, staring at the trainers and players gathered around the fallen Piazza, but came no closer. Gestures and angry cries came from the visiting-team dugout—the Mets in their club-house after the game were still incensed—and the ritual retali-ation, when Mets starter Glendon Rusch drilled Tino Martinez in the rear end in the bottom of the inning, felt inadequate to the deed. At the press gathering, Mets manager Bobby Valen-tine, his face gnarled with unhappiness, said that what Clemens had done was part of a pattern with him, and that it was terrible.

I don't know. The Rocket has pretty good control, but an in-tention pitch is not an intention to kill. Clemens was disliked by the Yankees when he was pitching for the Red Sox and the Blue Jays—he hit Derek Jeter in the ribs one day at a spring-training game in 1998—and now he was disliked or worse by the team across town. I recall a time when knockdowns were a common-place, and some pitchers—Bob Gibson and Don Drysdale among them—built great careers with repertoires that included fear. I don't believe that Clemens intended injury or even ex-pected to discourage a hitter like Piazza. What he hoped for at best was a fractional hesitation in the next swing. The word that came back to my mind, later on this long day, was "bow tie"—a phrase that Nolan Ryan sometimes used to describe an up-pitch: up by the neck. It was such a trademark that whenever it comes up in conversation you hear it repeated in Ryan's own East Texas accents—a "boww taih." Everyone in baseball says it this way, and then everyone laughs.

We would revisit this day and this issue later on.

The July Yanks took on a new face, as further trade replace-ments found their way into the lineup. There was Jose Vizcaino, an experienced infielder, whose presence would allow Knoblauch to play some games as designated hitter, on furlough from his tortures in the field. Glenallen Hill was a well-travelled right-handed bopper with an electrifying short swing, and for super-fluous muscle here came Jose Canseco, of all people, late in the day via the bargain waivers route. For pitching help there was Denny Neagle, an experienced left-handed starter picked up from the Reds, and Doc Gooden, who had been dropped by two prior clubs this year but came refurbished with a new knuckle-curve picked up after a cram course with the arm guru Billy Connors. Neagle, a control artist with a mature range of speed, has a fondness for off-the-field pranks that would delight a ten-year-old, and I entertained the hope that I'd be in the clubhouse on the day when he first did his Amtrak train-whistle imitation from close behind Paul O'Neill.

The Yankees' payroll, with the new additions (including the nine hundred thousand dollars they would be paying Canseco), came to about a hundred and ten million dollars, the most in the majors, and, while agreeing that the fiscal bullying imposed by the major-market team is unconscionable, I will take a pass this time on the tilted-playing-field, unfairness-of-it-all editorial and point out instead that preservation has been a central theme in the Bronx. Bernie Williams, Paul O'Neill, Derek Jeter, Mariano Rivera, Andy Pettitte, and David Cone have been together on the Yankees since 1995, and, along with manager Torre, who arrived in 1996, have set that uniquely preoccupied, senior-executive tone that has characterized the team's inexorable six trips to the post-season and four World Championships.

Through these Yankee sags and surges of fortune, Cone's line never took an upturn. A solid start in Boston went for nothing when the bullpen gave up five runs in the seventh. At Detroit's new Comerica Park, he gave up a homer to Tony Clark and then a grand slam to Dean Palmer, on a hanger. Against Baltimore on the Fourth of July, he was battered for four more home runs—solos by Mike Bordick and Harold Baines, a two-run blow by Brady Anderson, and a first-pitch three-run shot by the unthreatening Mark Lewis. "I was stunned," Cone said. "I'm killing us."

Scheduled to pitch against the Mets in the last game before the All-Star break, he was told that Andy Pettitte would start in his place, a day short of his full rest. David would go to the bullpen, just this once. "I felt badly that my poor pitching put Joe in this position," he said to the writers.

Irony had come aboard, clanking, when Cone's old Mets side-kick Doc Gooden, freshly signed after that reclamation project in Tampa, won the first game of the Saturday double-parked doubleheader, at Shea. None of the columnists or call-in fans could leave this alone: Cone, the twelve-million-dollar starter had become low man in the bullpen, his place taken by another old hero. David, happy for Doc, told me how strange it felt to be out there in the left-field pen, with its faded pitcher graffiti on the walls, and to find himself an outsider in the secret fraternity of relievers. Mike Stanton and Jeff Nelson ran the Yankee pen, and he got some friendly heat out there as an intruder and wannabe. "I would have died to get into that game, but the call never came," David said. "I've been waiting eight years to pitch at Shea."

Chatting earlier with some columnists and broadcasters in the visiting clubhouse there, he suddenly asked, "Who are the five best Mets starters, all-time?" We looked at each other, and he answered, "Seaver, Doc, Koosman, me, and Ronny Darling. Got to be, although Al Leiter's making a late run at it."

This was a different tone for him—the detached, bitterly amused observer. I'd had a glimpse of it a few days earlier, in the Yankee clubhouse, when Cone got out a tattered old Alfred E. Neuman poster that a fan had sent him, for luck—that goofy hayseed, and the famous tag line below. "'What, Me Worry?'" he said. "That's me now. This is going up here on the side of my locker." But he rolled it up and tucked it away.

Help was pouring in from all sides. The nonpareil Tom Seaver, now a Mets broadcaster, stood face to face with David near the batting cage at Shea (fans were yelling and pointing) and said, "I look right here"—he was pointing at his hip, a bat-ter's hip—"that's where my brain is. If you move your focal point to your catcher, you feel you gotta pull it over there, and you end up opening your front side. My brain is connected to my arm and the only time I ever look at the catcher's glove is the fastball down to a right-hander. You gotta keep your fingers on top of the fuckin' ball. You go to the side, you start throwing spirals. We all do it."

That same day, the iconic Jim Palmer, relaying what he'd just imparted to Cone, said, "You look at the radar guys and you know you're thirty-seven or however old you are now and people are saying, 'Well, he can't do it anymore. He's lost velocity.' So you're trying to throw harder, when it's counterproductive to what you've got to do as a pitcher. If you're tense and your body gets out in front of your slider, you're always going to be underneath it. Stay over the pitching rubber as long as you can and get your arm out! My first roommate was Robin Roberts and he said, 'Jim, you have a great fastball. Just rock back and get your arm out in front. I hope you're smart enough to understand this.' I was nineteen and he was thirty-eight. The same thing applies to David. I have no doubt that it'll be fine, but only if he can relax."

Palmer is a broadcaster, and so are Bert Blyleven and Rick Sutcliffe, who weighed in similarly when they got to town within the next few days. Sutcliffe said that Cone should start making little adjustments, like an older batter shortening up on his bat.

"How much of this was news to you?" I asked Cone later.

"It's all well meant and it's helpful," he said.

"But how much of it did you know before?"

"All of it," he said.

What was going on with him, he went on after a minute or two, was a loss of concentration. "This long hard dry spell is kind of beating me down," he said. "Even when I've pitched well, it didn't come out right. I tend to get overcreative when things aren't going well. I've tried all those different grips— some I've never used before—and somewhere in the middle I lose my way. Too much tinkering, too much Young Tom Edison. I'm a victim of my own style."

And I remembered what Tim McCarver had ventured one day back in April, before the nature of Cone's season had become clear. "Most pitchers are obsessed with 'release-points'—

not him," he said. "The most refreshing, intelligent thing about David is that he allows his animal instinct to dictate what he's thinking. He's told me that even when he's at the top, with the balance on his back leg, he has no idea where he's going to release the ball. He has immense knowledge built in to those pitches but it's not by the numbers—it's not 'I'll do this, I'll do that.' This is what the hitters find so confusing about him—there doesn't seem to be a pattern.

"When batters step out against Cone, they may not shake their heads but you can see doubt inside their heads. Andy Van Slyke"—a vivid outfielder with the Pirates in the eighties and early nineties—"once said, 'I can't figure that son of a bitch out. He's got great stuff but it's more than that.' What he sensed was that demonic, instinctive part of David. Jim Lonborg had that, too—at his best he was pitching on instinct."

Not much of this instinct was available to Cone now—a performer whose miserable season had placed him in a constant state of self-examination. And McCarver, in that same conversation, wondered what would happen if Cone continued to struggle. "In an odd way, when David starts explaining to himself what he's doing out there it's almost time to retire," he said. "It's his abandon that's served him so well. That's what batters fear but don't know why they fear it. And I don't know if that's something you can get back, once it's gone."

Another form of self-consciousness was squeezing David as well. Losing in New York in front of his old and loyal fans had always been a fear of his, and now it was staring him in the face. "It's almost my worst nightmare," he said. "You want to go out the right way. I've talked with Paulie"—O'Neill—"and David Wells about this. I told Boomer he'd done it exactly right, getting out of here after a great year. His legend is safe now. That's not going to happen for me. I haven't given up hope, but the important thing for me now is to show some dignity and grace in the face of bad pitching and a lot of people speculating."

I had come to expect these eloquent summaries from Cone by now, but they didn't turn up every day. There were times when he would say little beyond what he'd proffered for the cameras and the waiting writers after another workout or hard game. He was tired of seeing me there, with my notebook and concerned face. He'd walk away and I would hear little from him for days on end. He didn't return my phone calls. More than battered pride was at stake here, I sensed. He was open to everyone but cautious about his feelings, which he needed to keep in hand in the midst of this evolving disaster. Perhaps all pitchers are control freaks in the end. Though he didn't bluster or evade—there are world-class practitioners of these arts in every clubhouse—sharing wasn't his style. Lynn Cone said, "David's been on an island for thirty-seven years. He doesn't want people to know what he doesn't know until he's come to an emotional conclusion about it. He doesn't trust people to understand his feelings, except when he's out on the mound. He's a contemplator. He's his own worst enemy."

Suzyn Waldman, of MSG, has won almost perpetual access to most of the Yankee players in their worst and best moments, and I was taken aback when I overheard a little aside of hers, in a conversation with someone else: "I wonder if I've ever heard David Cone say an honest word."

I waited for days before I came back and asked what she'd meant.

"Well, 'honest' isn't the right word," she said. "David would never lie. But he's emotional—he's the most emotional player I've ever seen—and he doesn't want you to see that head-on. What you get from him is the real thing but it's from up here"— she tapped her head—"by the time you hear it. But I've seen feelings, too. I was there when he came off the field after those no-hit seven innings out in Oakland, after his operation, and there were tears."

Cone's talk with me about his misgivings on the mound and his envy of the Boomer came on a quiet afternoon in the Yankee clubhouse—it was right after the All-Star break—and he went on to say that there had been more to the tense moment, a week before, when Joe Torre had called him in to his office (Mel was there, too) to tell him that he'd be going to the bullpen for the Mets games. David said O.K., he could accept that, the way he'd been going. But he wanted Joe to promise that he wouldn't bury him in the bullpen now. Tell me the truth, he asked, we've been through too much together. If Joe got to the point where he didn't like what he saw, or when enough was enough, just let him know and they'd work something out. He'd move on. And Joe had said no, that had never been in their plans. He looked closely at David and said, "Yes, and I promise you if that ever changes I'll let you know." Mel had said the same: they weren't about to give up on him.

"It was a very serious, candid conversation between three men who've been together a long time," David reported. "Then Brian Cashman came by, a little later, and said no, don't think that way—they counted on me. So that talk with Joe and Mel and me had gone up the Yankee organization, which was good with me."

Moving on could almost have been an option. Realistically, he had no trade value now, if the Yankees wanted to get rid of him. But what if the club tried to unload him and he'd cleared waivers, here in the middle of the season? Were there any teams out there who'd want him for half of twelve million, for half a season? What if he could buy back his freedom and begin to bargain? "Anybody out there who wants me for three hundred thousand?" he said to me, sounding like an auctioneer. "Two hundred thousand? Do I hear an offer? I told Mel I could even go out to Arizona and pitch with Todd again." Todd Stottlemyre, Mel's second son, was a starter with the Diamondbacks and an old teammate of David's. "Anything is possible now."

This was kid stuff and it died away, and, much more quietly, David said, "There's been a difference for me this year, in the middle of everything else. A kind of contentment." The other night, he'd been cruising the late tube when he came on an interview with the swimmer Mark Spitz, the old Olympian who'd won all those gold medals. There comes a time, Spitz said, when champions have to get ready to lose. "That's stayed with me," Cone said. "Listen, I haven't given up hope by any means. But this season is what it is."

Cone's age and the true state of his arm were always on my mind by now but I felt that he had enough troubles without my always pushing such questions at him. I'd also begun to hope he wasn't noticing stuff like this when it came up in the news. Orel Hershiser, abruptly terminating a comeback bid with the Dodgers, had just hung up his spikes, with the words "The best thing that happened to me is I got hit with a sharp knife, not a dull knife." He meant that suddenly he couldn't pitch at all.

Doubts about Cone's fastball came up with increasing frequency—the writers with each new visiting team asked about it, without putting the question to Cone himself. His catchers were diplomatic, but there was a story going around that Posada and Girardi had talked about this at the All-Star Game. Posada said that Cone's fastball had been levelling out at about eighty-six or eighty-seven miles per hour, and Joe sighed and said, "Well, then, he can't win."

And a writer, Allen St. John, in an arresting *Village Voice* piece, had compiled frightening descriptions from gerontologists and neurologists and orthopedists of what happens to older pitchers, sooner or later: a loss of muscle mass in the tendons, a decline in connective-tissue flexibility, a deterioration of neurons in the nerve-muscle interface, and so on. Age is hell on pitchers. Age or maybe just the hitters. Facing the visiting Phillies on a Monday—it was July 17th, a day short of the anniversary of his perfect game—Cone gave up a two-run homer to Mike Lieberthal in the second inning and then, in the fourth, a double, an infield single, a little bloop to right, and, to Pat Burrell, a three-run homer, hit off a slider down by his ankles. "Everything that could happen bad happened bad," Joe Torre said.

Cone tried to be offhand with the writers—"Any suggestions? I'm willing to try anything"—but the laughter was thin. What had come to him after the second home run, he admitted, was *My night is ruined again.*

When the crowd thinned out, Marty Noble, an old friend from the Mets days, dropped by and said, "I know you're the last in the world who'd want anyone to be sorry for him, but I'm entitled. I'm sorry you're going through all this."

Cone's games were becoming operatic in their emotions. Working next against the Tampa Bay Devil Rays, in the fourth week of July, he gave up a solo first-inning home run to Greg Vaughn, but was still in the game in the sixth, tied at 2–2. He'd pitched well, perhaps finding a tiny boost to his psyche from his latest new look on the mound: his pants shortened up to knee level and now and then a funny lift to his lead leg when throwing. Yes, he said after the game—a tribute to his "semi-idol," El Duque.

With a man on second and two outs, he ran the count full to Jose Canseco (this was before Canseco's change of colors) and then threw a fastball that appeared to cut the bottom line of the strike zone. Home-plate ump Terry Craft failed to punch it up, allowing Canseco the base on balls, and Cone came down the mound raging and gesturing. The next batter, Steve Cox, stroked a single, putting the visitors ahead in the game—and for the day, it turned out. Cone finished the inning, but he was done, after ninety-four pitches. A loser again—his record had gone to 1–9—he was red-faced and terse with the reporters afterward. He kept his hands oddly tucked behind his back, and that vein in the middle of his forehead was bulging. "Nothing encouraged me," he said. "I wasn't good enough."

The next morning, another Sunday in the clubhouse, David came in wearing a getaway-day shirt and tie—the team was going off that evening on a road trip to Baltimore and then Minnesota—and a different look. He seemed boyish, almost lighthearted. He beckoned me over to tell me something that had happened the night before. None of the media and none of the players knew about it. Almost certain that he'd not be allowed to go back out for the seventh inning against the Devil

Rays, he had come into the clubhouse, where he set himself up in a comfortable chair in front of the television set in the manager's office. He lit a cigarette. He was cool, but when Mel came in and told him that Joe had decided to go to the bullpen, he lost it. "What fucking difference does it make?" he screamed, and he picked up a ceramic ashtray and fired it across the room. "It was a big hand-painted thing," David said now, "and it hit that photograph of Joe DiMaggio and Mickey Mantle on the far wall there—you know the one—and smashed it all to pieces. Glass everywhere. It was bad—I apologized to Mel right away. He said he understood—he's always that way—but I'd shook him up. Clubhouse boys came in and began sweeping up the glass, so no one would find out. I'm going to have to apologize to Joe. I don't know what got into me."

But he didn't look apologetic, he looked free. "Listen," he said, "there's nothing wrong with my arm. I made a good pitch there."

At batting practice one weekend afternoon, a boy with an autograph book called out from behind the dugout, "Mr. Jeter! Mr. Jeter! I'm looking for someone."

Barely turning his head, Jeter said, "Who you looking for?"

"David Cone," the kid said.

"We're all looking for David Cone," Derek answered, almost to himself.

I never could tell how much flack or chilliness Cone got from his teammates during his travails. Not much, I think, but direct expressions of sympathy weren't forthcoming, either. When I asked Paul O'Neill if he'd said anything lately to comfort his old colleague, he looked uncomfortable—he *always* looks uncomfortable—and murmured, "Well, he's a pitcher. They don't say much to us, and us everyday guys kind of stay to ourselves. It's always been like that."

And the friendly Chris Turner, Cone's regular catcher now, when asked if he'd tried to cheer up David about his long slump, said, "What good would that do? Everybody here has got problems. Just look around."

Roger Clemens, speaking to me directly from Planet Roger, was full of praise for Cone—"One of the best pitching buddies I've ever known"—but left his colleague's torments pretty much alone. "He seems to pitch his best games when he's backed up a tree" was about the size of it.

They were right, of course. This was midseason and everybody was struggling with something. Chris Turner had had a little run of hits late in June but then resumed his habitual placidity at the plate. His Yankee year was running down on him, and at thirty-one, with a lifetime .238, he could not escape knowledge that this, his fourth different posting as a backup catcher, would be a short stopover. Tino Martinez, whom David had envisioned as a road buddy this year, had his own vanished batting stroke to think about. Ramiro Mendoza, who'd been tremendous in June, was facing a potentially career-ending injury to his shoulder. The normally effervescent El Duque had something on his mind—perhaps it was just his back spasms and elbow pains—and the Rocket himself had only lately come off the fifteen-day D.L. with a groin pull. Toil and trouble. Only Bernie Williams had room for Cone in his thoughts. "He has no idea how much everyone on this club is pulling for him," he said, looking carefully at me, as he does with everyone in a conversation. "David tries to be the same guy out there, but you can see this situation is eating at him. Everyone in this game has to go through hard times in order to enjoy the good parts, but this is too hard for anybody."

There'd been another significant change for Cone—something I didn't pick up at first. But on the day Chuck Knoblauch took himself out of the lineup I noticed that the writers went clustering to Derek Jeter for the team view. He was calm and diplomatic—"If we're gong to win we're going to need Chuck"—and seemed not surprised that he had become the quote captain now. David's reign was over. When I mentioned this shift to him, he shrugged and said, "You lose credibility."

Back on the road again, Cone took on the Twins in the Metrodome and was helpless—five walks in five innings, nine hits, eight runs. There was another killer double down the line: almost a specialty of his now. David looked pale, almost ill out there, nothing like himself. The Yankee announcers (I was far away) kept talking about his body language, which was submissive and pleading. When it was over, he stood at 1–10, with a 6.88 earned-run average. Not counting the 1999 post-season, he'd won three games in his past thirty-two starts, going back to the perfect game.

When I reached him by telephone the next morning it was clear that I'd waked him up, but he seemed to want company. "I'm a little shell-shocked," he said. "It's hard to say what will happen. Stuff kept running through my mind. I remembered that I'd started my first game as a Yankee right here in the Humphrey Dome in '95, and wouldn't it be ironic if this turned out to be my last game as a Yankee. I have a no-trade clause, but there are these wild scenarios. Could I end up pitching in the Olympics?"

The scenario—the real one—took Cone out of the lineup that day and away from the team. Dispatched to the Yankee complex in Tampa—El Duque was down there already, on the D.L., as were Allen Watson and Ramiro Mendoza—he reported to Billy Connors, the vice-president for player personnel, who put him out on a mound and started him back toward some basics. Only later in the year did David learn that George Steinbrenner had said, "Oh, why don't we just cut him loose?" after one of his recent disasters. At about the same time, he'd vented his anger and impatience with Cone's season to some executives from the *News* who were visiting his box one night. The Boss appeared willing to give him his unconditional release and eat his salary for the rest of the year. But Torre had argued against it, and so had Cashman and scouting V.P. Gene Michael. They'd won the day.

Connors, who looks like Tweedledum or Tweedledee in a warmup jacket, is a pitching guru. He remained in conversation with Mel, up north, but this sort of remake wasn't an argument about styles. Pitchers were always getting themselves screwed up. Back in 1995, Jimmy Key had gone on the disabled list and came to Tampa to find his motion again. Here Connors kept David throwing while he made small suggestions. A shorter back step at the beginning of his motion would keep it crisper. He needed to work on his balance. Keep it up—it'll all come together.

Cone wasn't so sure. Throwing in live batting practice to a Class A batter, he watched a line shot whistle past his ribs, and walked off the mound. "This isn't working," he said to Connors. "I'm done." This was his fourth straight day of pitching off a mound, going back to the Minnesota game, and suddenly it was all too much. He dressed quickly and drove to his house in Cheval, on the north side of town. And here Connors came and found him at the end of the day and—in David's words—"talked me off the ledge." The Yankees still wanted him, Billy said. He was already on the way back.

That night they went out to dinner with George Steinbrenner, who told him he was a warrior.

13

Style

The refurbished Yankees had been winning in July, even while Cone had gone south (in both ways), and they maintained a cruise-control pace now as the midsummer weeks went by, holding a divisional lead over the Red Sox that stayed stuck between three and five games. More S.U.V. than juggernaut, they rarely won more than three in a row and never lost more, but you could look out the windows, so to speak, and begin to enjoy the ride. Shortly after David got back from Tampa—he was there for a little over a week—the clubhouse was delighted by the arrival of the amiable all-purpose infielder Luis Sojo, an old friend and teammate who had been in temporary residence with the Pirates. He'd been let go after the 1999 campaign—according to one story because George Steinbrenner didn't like his habit of leaving the top button of his uniform unbuttoned. Sojo, a Venezuelan, is thirty-four but looks as if he'd put on a much older guy's body that morning by mistake. Seamed and saggy, forever smiling, he could sit uncomplaining on the bench by the hour or day or week, then deliver solid innings at almost any infield position, plus (as the Mets will not forget) the big base hit.

Later in this season, there was speculation that Sojo might actually be older than his announced age, but the players liked the idea that he'd *added* a year or two to his data somewhere along the line, the better to fit his face.

The Yankee tone—no hangers-on, no TV in the main part of the clubhouse, no blasting CD portables—was working on the new personnel. Canseco, a grownup Bash Brother with a lifetime four hundred and forty homers, became a part-timer or d.h. without a murmur, and Justice, never known for his immodesty when he played with the Indians and Braves, was finding that attitude was not a requirement here. Playing every day in left or right or as a left-handed d.h., uncoiling on the inside pitch from his upright, shoulder-pointing stance and lacing it long, he led the Yankee offense for the rest of the distance, with twenty homers by the end and sixty runs batted in. He had a couple of two-homer days, and supplied the afterpiece in the team's most electrifying finish of the year, at the Stadium on August 8th—a lead-off, first-pitch ninth-inning homer by Bernie Williams, against the Oakland closer Jason Isringhausen, which tied the game at 3–3, and then Justice's shot into the right-center-field bleachers on the very next delivery, which won it. You could see it again via the late-night replays, or, almost better, on Isringhausen's line in the box score the next day: "(L)" for loser, "0" for innings or parts of innings pitched, and the same "2" five times over—hits, runs, earned runs, home runs, and pitches delivered and disbelieved.

Almost as unlikely for Bronxian fans was the arrival onstage of Glenallen Hill. If you were writing a baseball novel or musical you'd throw away a passage like this, while congratulating yourself for your characters' vibrant names. *David Justice*, tah-dah! . . . *Glenallen Hill*, sounds like a single malt! Hill, who joined the Yankees after service with five different teams in his twelve-year career, startled his teammates with the shortest batting stroke since Mike Tyson. A righty hitter, he took an almost open stance, with the bat poised somewhat forward, then completed his brusque business with a cut that used no more than a third of the available distance. It was like someone idly banging shut a closet door while walking down the hall. "I've never seen anyone hit like Glenallen," Joe Torre said. Hill announced himself with a first-at-bat homer, then a pinch-hit, ninth-inning grand slam against the Twins, at the Metrodome, and later sent a poke into the rarely visited center-field black seats at the Stadium. His .411 and ten dingers made him the American League Player of the Month for August, and toward the end of that run you'd see his teammates edging up toward the front of the dugout for each of his plate appearances, and then whooping and falling about with laughter whenever another shot—*Bonkk: elsewhere!*— went out.

Indoors, Hill would return from shower to locker with a towel enfolding his middle in the style of an Egyptian pharaoh and a modish pigskin ditty bag slung from one shoulder. His torso cuts down dramatically from his enormous shoulders to a mini-waist and tyke's tokus—a nice top-level sample, in an era of player bods unimaginable to Babe Ruth or Johnny Mize. Hill affected short tangerine-colored dreadlocks when he first arrived with the Yanks, but after a conversation with the manager quickly converted to the low-upkeep David Justice–Yul Brynner pate mode. Joe admitted later that this was his first do-consultation.

Justice is high-style, too. Leaving work one afternoon after a day game, he wore yellowish mini-shades, a round canvas hat pulled down to his ears, knee-length baggy shorts, and a silky outer shirt, untucked and unbuttoned, of a sensational orange. Outstanding, but when Glenallen walked out, a few minutes later, he was less dramatic in similarly oversized shorts and shirt, but ahead, I'd say, by 3.7 points in the critical Not Really Trying division. This battle, like the R.B.I. and dinger stats, went on all summer.

Stuff like this reminds you how young the players really are. Weekends now, there were little kids rocketing around in the clubhouse—Jason Grimsley's three towheaded sons always led the pack—and the fathers, dropping a soft word or gesture into the action, became playground dads, a role for them that we writers never imagine. I got the same reminder whenever I came by a couple of players heading off for the weight room or the batting cage, hours before game time, in their gym shorts and sneakers and cutoff tops—Jorge Posada with a bat, Mike Stanton with a weight bar in one hand. "Morning," they offered, going by, fresher and more hopeful than they'd looked late last night: inbound commuters now. Another day, Derek Jeter brought over a letter from his thick daily stack and asked Scott Brosius for help with the handwriting. Then Chris Turner read it, too—there's a lot of interest in Derek's mail. "I am a sixty-eight-year-old widow," they made out, line by line, "and I would like you to accompany my eighteen-year-old great-niece to her graduation dance. She is a good person and so are you." And Brosius recalled a letter he'd had, maybe last year, from a woman who'd wanted him to fix up a date for her daughter with Derek. "Who am I in there, the grandpa?" he said indignantly.

Later on, a batboy, Luigi Castillo, stopped by Cone's locker for a minute, to talk about his cut fastball—Luigi's, not David's. He's seventeen but looks younger—a five-foot-something pitcher in the Jaws Division of the Bronx Little League, who plays at Roberto Clemente Field, in Crotona Park. When I asked what "Jaws" stood for, he said he didn't know. Before this, he pitched on a team called Lola's All Stars. The last time I heard, Luigi's E.R.A. was 2.38. A year ago, after he and Cone began to throw together in the outfield, David showed him how to hold his curveball loosely, with a little gap showing between the thumb and forefinger. When Luigi took it into a game, the first batter said, "Jesus, where did *that* come from?" On that hot Sunday when David had to sit out a rain delay in the middle of his perfect game, he grabbed Luigi the moment the sky began to lighten and threw with him, out beside the tarps, to stay loose. "He's my idol and my role model," Castillo said to me. "He's given me a little of his talent to go with my talent."

Another day, and the writers—George King; Larry Rocca, of *Newsday;* Ken Davidoff, of the *Record;* Anthony McCarron, of

the *News*; the *Post's* Ursula Reel; Bill Madden, the *News* columnist, among others—are standing around in the middle of the
clubhouse once again, facing in different directions like gulls on
a beach. They know this place better than their own living
rooms, and their eyes roam across the ranged player cubicles in
search of an unwary occupant—or, worse, a player talking to
another writer. But this is midsummer, and there isn't enough
news to keep the mutual nuclear deterrence on full alert. Most
of the players hang in their lounge or the training room, which
are off limits, but we all know their slots here: Cone and Chuck
Knoblauch on opposite sides of the short hallway that leads to
Joe's office and the coaches' room beyond, and the agreeable
Mike Stanton and the useful Jorge Posada farther up on the
right-hand side. (Cone's locker faces a column, affording an illu-
sory sense of privacy, and it feels as if much of my summer has
been spent there, with my back against the fake-stucco column-
façade, while Cone sits and talks and I stand and write.) Bernie
Williams has the élite corner space, back near the front door—
the suite once occupied by Mattingly—and Paul O'Neill super-
vises us all from the head of the room, on the same flank with
Roger Clemens and Mariano Rivera. To the left side, near the
showers, is El Duque country, while Derek Jeter's spot, farther
up, is getting so crowded after games that he'll probably be
moved next year.

Just now I overhear Michael Kay, the broadcaster, discussing
the stock market with a clubhouse attendant named Joe Lee and
Jason Zillo, the assistant director of media relations and public-
ity. Lee, who has a terrific smile, is a senior at Fordham major-
ing in finance. "Give me two million at a quarter below prime
and I'll—" he says, but I turn away, swooning.

Don Zimmer is in the big leather chair just inside the door of
Joe's office, an upright bat in his pink hands. The top button of
his uniform pants is comfortably unbuttoned. He's been talking
about the dog tracks, as usual, and about friends of his in cities
all around the country. "St. Pete?" he says at one point. "I'm *huge*
in St. Pete." Then he gets back to baseball, where he's got fifty-

three years in. We've been wondering whether David Cone's problems come down to his age in the end, and Zim says, "Age is a crazy thing—I never paid no attention to it. If you're twenty-two and can't pitch you're no use to me. If you're forty and can't pitch it's the same. I've seen pitchers who were done at thirty-two and others just getting going. Some get a little age and they start changing what they do every time out, but that don't mean anything. Yaz and Cal Ripken changed their swings every week for their whole career, and Will Clark's never changed his. Don't worry about it—show me what you got."

Up in the pressbox, every night ends the same way. Herb Steier, a retired *Times* sports copy editor, comes to every game and sits motionless in the third row, his hands in front of him on the long table. He doesn't keep score but watches the action intently, with bright, dark eyes. When the ninth inning comes, he gets up and stands by the railing behind the last row of writers, near the exit, and after the potential final batter of the game has been announced, Bob Sheppard, the ancient and elegant Hall of Fame announcer, comes out of his booth and stands next to him, with a book under his arm. (He reads novels or works of history between announcements.) Eddie Layton, the Stadium organist, is there, too, wearing a little skipper's cap. Eddie has a private yacht—well, it's a mini-tug, called Impulse—that he keeps on the Hudson, up near Tarrytown. He gets a limo ride to the Stadium most days from his apartment in Queens—it's in his contract—and a nice lift home with Bob Sheppard and Herb Steier at night. Eddie and Bob Sheppard make a bet on every single Yankee game—the time of the game, the total number of base runners, number of pitches by bullpen pitchers, whatever—but won't tell you which one of them is ahead. The stakes are steady: a penny a game.

Steier is Sheppard's neighbor, out in Baldwin, Long Island, and he drives him to work every day and home again at its end; they're old friends. Sheppard, a stylish fellow, is wearing an Argyle sweater and espadrilles tonight. This is his fiftieth year on the job at Yankee Stadium, and once in a while I ask him to enunciate a player's name for me, just for the thrill of it. "'Shi-ge-to-shi Ha-se-ga-wa,'" he'll respond, ringing the vowels. It sounds like an airport.

The instant the last batter strikes out or pops up or grounds out Sheppard and Steier and Layton do an about-face and depart at a slow sprint. Out the door they go and turn right in the loge-level corridor, still running. A few kids out there are already rocketing down the tilted runways. "Start spreadin' the noooss . . ." comes blaring out from everywhere (the Yanks have won again), but Bob and Herb and Eddie have turned right again, into the quiet elevator lobby, where the nearer car awaits them, its door open. Down they go and out at street level, still at a careful run. Herb's car, a beige 1995 Maxima, is in its regular slot in the team parking lot, just across the alley—the second car on the right. They're in, they're out, a left turn up the street, where they grab a right, jumping onto the Deegan, heading home. The cops there have the eastbound traffic stopped dead, waiting for Bob Sheppard: no one else in New York is allowed to make this turn. Two minutes, maybe two-twenty, after the game has ended and they're gone, home free, the first of fifty thousand out of the building, every night.

Cone's first start after Tampa—Saturday afternoon, August 5th, against the Mariners—came in two parts. Working with a pared-down, tauter motion, he threw early strikes to the tough Seattle batters but kept running up his pitch counts thereafter, straining for the K. At one stretch he went to the full count against eight straight batters. Much was at stake, and there was something like a groan or a sigh in the press rows when Alex Rodriguez pounced on a fastball that had drifted over the plate and drove it into the right-field stands for the second and third runs of the inning.

Down by 3–2, Cone now persevered, perhaps recalling the look on Joe Torre's face when he'd taken him up the tunnel between innings for a talk about body language. But Torre kept him in the game for a full six—no more runs, six strikeouts, and a startling hundred and thirty-seven pitches. When Cone fanned Mike Cameron in the fifth, the announcement came that it had been his twenty-five-hundredth career strikeout—a level he shares only with Clemens and Randy Johnson, among all active pitchers—and the fans delivered a sustained full minute of applause: an ovation, of all things. They'd been waiting weeks for the chance. The Yanks lost the game in the end, going down in the ninth, 6–5 (Doc took the loss), and leaving David's horrible W–L record intact. "It's frustrating," he said. "I feel as if I'm this far from locking in a good groove." He held up his fingers, barely apart.

Cone looked thinner than he had in the spring, and I suspected that his season was getting to him away from the park now, too. Always an insomniac, he'd been short of sleep for weeks. It wasn't like the old days, when pain in his arm or shoulder woke him up every night, and when painkillers bothered his stomach, and sleeping pills left him down and dopey. He had no pain at all this year—he felt great—and that, in turn, added to his broodings in the dark. Maybe he needed pain in order to throw right . . . Some nights now, he'd pop an Ambien, which was good for four hours' sleep, but then he'd find himself awake again at dawn and still thinking about this year and his record. His mind would go over the places where a couple of Yankee runs would have turned things his way and made his miserable season look a bit more respectable; he knew these games and innings and pitches by heart. On a similar performance record that I'd been keeping, I found nine games, out of his twenty-two starts from April 12th to August 20th, in which fortune had dealt him a chilly hand. He'd lost two of those games, departing behind by one and two runs. The Yanks won three games and lost two in which he'd also pitched well but did not gain the decision, and, more painfully, they'd lost two in which he left with a lead that was then squandered. In these nine selected games—which do not include far worse outings of his, let's be clear—Cone was an official 0–2 over fifty-seven innings, with fifty-four hits surrendered and an earned-run average of

3.15. In that spell, the Yanks had scored nineteen runs on his behalf, or 3.0 per game. This built-in unfairness is a commonplace
in baseball, to be sure, brooded over by guys who are becalmed
in a season or only suffering through brief slumps. Bert
Blyleven, talking to David in July, reminded him that it wasn't
how you pitched but which games you pitched that mattered.
This is Nembutal backward: a guaranteed formula for sleepless-
ness.

Luck turns bad for hitters, too, of course. Paul O'Neill, bat-
tling a midsummer hip injury and a Gobi-like aridity at the plate,
hit some predictable scorchers straight into the glove of a waiting infielder. "Never mind, Paulie," David said in the dugout after one such setback. "Next time, that's a chinker that falls in."
But the following day he came by O'Neill's locker and said, "Remember what I said last night? Well, fuck that—you're never going to get that hit back again."

David told me now that he'd return next year, no matter
what. He didn't know where—probably it wouldn't be with the
Yankees—but he wasn't going to go out on this note. But Lynn
said that he was considering retirement: it was on his mind all
the time. "He's a basket case," she said one day. "I tell him he's
got to put stuff like this away until the end of the season. Nobody can deal with everything at the same time this way, night
after night. But you know David."

Lynn had been there through the hard games. I couldn't count
the times I'd found her, well after midnight, standing amid a scattering of relatives and cops and Stadium attendants just inside
the press gate—looking thin and beautiful in a stylish leather
jacket, with perfect makeup and her shining hair slicked back—
as she waited for her husband to appear at the top of the stairs
after another horrible day at the plant. One night there, she
waved me over to say that she'd called Chili Davis and asked him
to call David back—he needed a lift. Chili came through, but
when David asked where he was headed next he said, "Maui—
living the life." When David got off the phone he said, "Why am I
doing this? Why am I still killing myself like this?"

Cone asked me now and then what I thought about retirement, and I'd said I just hoped he wasn't going to be one of those guys who go through life after baseball with the conviction that they can still strike out the side. The great Steve Carlton, who is fifty-six now, was famously rumored to believe this, and Jim Palmer, when we'd talked at Shea, said that only a little hamstring injury had kept him from a longer career. He had retired in 1984 but later changed his mind, and when he started up again in spring training, seven years later, he'd found that he still had his great stuff. "I could still get batters out, except that I got hurt," he said. But guys who'd been at the Orioles' camp in Sarasota that spring—Tom Boswell, the Washington *Post* columnist was one of them—said this wasn't true at all: Palmer had been atrocious.

Mark Gubicza, David's long-term friend and teammate with the Royals, quit baseball in 1998, and is a budding sports TV star, making regular appearances on Fox's "Baseball Today" show, on the West Coast. He believes that David would find the transition tougher than he can imagine. "Maybe you never get over it," Gubie told me. "If somebody came to me tomorrow and said, 'Listen, we need you to pitch this one big game on Sunday,' I'd be there in a heartbeat. It's in your blood."

I kept trying to think of something useful to say to David, to help him make up his mind, but I couldn't come up with the right examples. Dreams and pride suffused the field. Jim Bouton, still pitching in a semi-amateur circuit at the age of fifty-eight, had told me that he'd stopped just lately when batters at that level began to take him deep. One doofus who'd just hit a home run off a knuckler of his actually produced the ball after the game and asked for a certifying autograph. Bouton obliged but felt compelled to add "aluminum bat" in parentheses under his name.

It must be torture to give up something tough and demanding that you once did extremely well, I finally said to David. If butchers and lawyers and schoolteachers felt this way, how could pitchers and tenors and Presidents be expected to pull it off—people who lived off the crowds and thrilling repeated challenges, and weren't old yet except within their professions? How would you ever get used to that? I said I could remember Dennis Eckersley talking about this, at the moment after he'd hung them up at the close of a twenty-four-year career. When I went back to some old notes of mine to hunt out Eck's lines, I could almost see his long legs propped up on his locker in the grottolike clubhouse at Fenway Park that Sunday, and his eyes burning like flashlights as he spoke: "I've thought about it a lot—I mean a lot. There's no getting around the fact that it's going to be devastating. It's like dying—you know it's inevitable but no matter how you get ready for it you're not ready."

But Cone surprised me once again. He didn't believe that illusions about his strikeouts or sliders would haunt him, once he decided to retire. It was the other way around. "I've always been a super-realist," he said. "I go over things in my mind—I can't let them alone. It's how bad I've been that gets me. I could use a little fantasy right now. Guys who can kid themselves are much better off."

David had been smoking more. He smoked Marlboro Lights. I almost never saw him light up, even when he was at home, but Lynn said he'd stopped inviting me to drive up to the Stadium with him or back home after a game, as he sometimes had, because he smoked in the car and didn't want me to know. When I asked him how many cigarettes a day he smoked, he said more lately but less than a pack; Lynn said he was way up over that by now. Cone did tell me that his doctor, John Olichney, had recently prescribed Zyban, a mild anti-depressant that would help you get off nicotine when you were ready. One of its side effects was powerful dreams, and then, here in August, David said that only the night before he'd found himself pitching for the Red Sox, in a dream. It was all perfectly clear—the green wall behind him and the red letters on the uniform. "It wouldn't be bad there, at that," he said musingly. "*That* would be a change—pitching with those fans on my side. And I like Jimy Williams as a manager. I've always wondered what living in New England would be like . . ." The dream had become an option for him. He was there already, pitching with better luck in a year when he could win.

And then he won. Next time out, handed a welcome seven-run lead against the A's, he gave up two runs over six innings, with eight strikeouts. He had tempo, he had poise. With two on in the fifth, he fanned the side. The 12–6 victory took him off the schneid—his first win in sixteen starts. On the road after this, he beat the Texas Rangers, 10–2, on a sweltering night in Arlington—with strikeouts of Rafael Palmeiro, on a first-class slider, and Frank Catalanotto, on the split, as Whiffs of the Day.

On the phone—I was in Maine, writing and worrying—he no longer sounded puzzled or haunted. Lynn had come along on this trip. They'd gotten in some nice pool time at Anaheim, and they were looking forward to a family dinner with an uncle of hers who lived in San Dimas.

Great, I said, but what was going on? How come he suddenly looked so workmanlike, so suave? What kind of body language was this?

"I'm national news," he said. "'Cone Ends Slump!' It's been one hell of a dry spell."

He said that what excited him right now was the fastball, which had more life to it, even though the numbers were still mostly in the eighties. It didn't show on the gun but there was late movement to it at last.

Did Billy Connors do all this? I asked.

"He was certainly part of it," David said. "He'd asked me to visualize the way it felt back when I was throwing good and winning games. He particularly wanted me to keep my hands farther away from my body in the middle of the delivery."

I said this sounded like the opposite of what Tony Ferreira had been telling him, a million years ago in Florida, and David laughed and said, "Yeah, this always happens." The new, trimmed-down delivery wasn't quite second nature to him so far, he went on. It was almost as if he'd had to learn a whole new muscle memory.

Ed Cone had come to New York before this swing west, and the two of them had gone over some videos from 1986 and 1987, which reminded them how deliberate he'd once been on the rubber, and how vital it was for him not to rush things when he was ahead in the count. This was going to become part of his new pattern now, too, he hoped.

While his dad was still in the city, he and Ed had gone up to Columbia-Presbyterian to visit Darryl Strawberry, who'd had to come up from Tampa for more cancer surgery. This time, a tumor near one of his kidneys had been taken out. Straw's room, in McKeen Pavilion, was just down the hall from the room where David had been after his aneurysm operation, and where he'd listened to Doc Gooden pitch his no-hitter. Charisse Strawberry was there with her husband; it was like a Mets family reunion. Darryl kept talking about David's problems.

Sunday, August 20th, Yankee Stadium:

Whitey Ford, my favorite Yankee alumnus, came back to the Stadium this afternoon for a Day in his honor and told George Steinbrenner that it was really nice of him to have one of these affairs for a guy who wasn't Italian. The occasion felt like a rain check for an Old Timers' Day, but without the geezers to embarrass us by creaking through the motions of a game. Whitey was a bit pale—he's seventy-one and had recently undergone chemotherapy for recurring skin cancer—but hadn't lost his sparkle. His celebrated smile hangs around the corners of his mouth, always at the ready, and his wife, Joan, looks like someone who's heard laughter every day for forty years.

"I've been a Yankee for fifty years, and I'll be a Yankee forever," Whitey told the enchanted crowd, but I thought he summed himself up better at a pre-game mini press conference, when he said, "I was never nervous out there"—out there pitching, he meant. His sixteen-year, 236–106 won-lost record comes out at .690, which is the best percentage in baseball for pitchers with more than two hundred wins. He's the winningest Yankee pitcher of all. Answering our then-vs.-now questions, Ford agreed that the smaller modern ballparks and shrunken millennial strike zone would have raised his 2.75 lifetime E.R.A. but—one-beat pause—"but I'd have won as many."

Whitey was born in Manhattan and grew up on the sandlots of Astoria, and witnessed his first major-league game from the Stadium bleachers in 1938, at the age of nine. "You had to come to the park to see the players then," he reminded us. One of his boyhood teams was called the 34th Avenue Boys, and I remember his telling me one day that playing unsupervised, parent-free ball in those summers he often got in fifty innings over the course of a Friday-to-Sunday weekend—twenty or so as a pitcher and the rest wherever he could jump in. Equally dated and flavorful, I realized during this reunion, is Ford's accent—the pure I.R.T., which has almost gone out of earshot nowadays, thanks to the flattening and duhing of television.

Cone pitched against the Anaheim Angels on Whitey Day, and I wasn't the only writer there who sensed a connection. Ford agreed. "I've thought that sometimes, watching him," he said. "He's from the other side"—a righty, that is—"but he has a good curveball and fastball like I did, and he comes from all different angles. He stays on top, the same way, and brings his shoulder out over his front foot."

Cone, told about the compliment, was flattered but wary. "I'm no Whitey Ford, that's for sure," he said. He told me that he'd consulted with Ford during the difficult days before the aneurysm operation, because Ford in his day had also suffered puzzling vascular problems in his shoulder, and had undergone corrective surgery. When Whitey resumed pitching he noticed that he'd stopped sweating on his left, or soupbone, side. Explaining the medical oddity to the press back then, he cited a popular toiletry of the day and said, "With me, a 5-Day Deodorant Pad lasts ten days."

Cone, at six-one, and Ford, at five-ten, share a graceful, put-together look that makes them appear a little smaller than their

size, and they have both been famously businesslike at their
place of work. Comparisons stop there, I guess. Prodigal with
his pitch counts, Cone strikes out more batters per game than
Ford did—he's averaged close to one K per inning in his career—and walks more, too. This takes time, while with Whitey
you'd look up from your scorecard or peanut and find that the
inning was already over. On this day, though, Coney got on with
it. The Ford press conference overlapped a bit with the first inning, and I missed him striking out the side, after going to three-
and-two on all three batters. I was back when he wrapped up
the second by fanning Troy Glaus on the slider away—the genuine sailer, which left the batter tilting awkwardly to starboard
and Cone already headed toward the dugout. He pitched six
shutout innings, striking out six—it was nice to see the ice-
cream-cone "K" symbols flapping from the upper-deck facings
again—and departed the scene most reluctantly, ahead by 3–0.
Only the bullpen, which had lately taken on the texture of a
damp hot-dog roll, could spoil the day: five runs in, and the
game and Cone's win gone.

Three in a row would have been nice, but, never mind, Cone
was back, and this game against the Angels on Whitey's Day was
of a higher order. In full form, he'd pitched like a house afire,
suddenly performing in relation to nothing but the last pitch and
the one that came next. Fastball, slider in, sinker, fastball up,
curveball down, fastball inside—he called on each without musing, picking up the sign and swinging into his motion in almost
the same breath, and correcting a pitch away from the plate or
too low with something sharper and better that kept him level in
the count or ahead. There were no pauses for forehead-wiping
with his glove-tip, no irritated shakeoffs of his catcher's signs,
and none of the puzzled, slack-jawed starings that had accompanied his unaccountable earlier efforts. Watching him at work
like this, you could compare him to nobody but himself, and
wonder why it had taken him so long to find the model that had
once been so reliably at hand. Pitching is style, and when you
have it it appears innate and untouchable: yes, this is me. When

it's gone, you must think and grope—it's more a psychic loss than something mechanical—and you feel bereft and clunky even before you've been punished by another defeat. Now the key had been turned, and style, from wherever it had been, came whispering back, perhaps to stay a bit and to make it all feel so easy.

14

The Four-Forty

September 1st, Yankee Stadium:

I first heard the question put at supper one July night in the Stadium press dining room, and it was so trifling and conversational that I forgot who'd said it—the founder. Too bad, because the thing went on for weeks in its own quiet way and made for a lot of pleasure. Well, not exactly *pleasure*. Killing time is what it was, and it brought us media people together, because nobody could produce the full answer right away. Some might call it a baseball trivia question but, as an old Tigers fan I knew always said, nothing about baseball is trivial. Anyway: *Name eleven players with four letters or less in their names who hit forty or more home runs in a single season.*

Nothing to it, I decided. Let's see . . . Ruth, Mays, and, yes, *three* letters: Mel Ott. And Jimmie Foxx.

Easy stuff, but now the people at my table fell into an unaccustomed silence while they scrabbled around upstairs. What made us happy, I think, was that no one could instantly rip out all eleven names, making the rest of us feel like dolts or baseball impostors, and that there probably wouldn't be an outside entry into the list—Bingo Putz, of the old Red Stockings—when we finally filled it out. We'd know the eleven in good time.

Someone said "Mize" at this point, and we all said yes, of course, Johnny Mize, and I had a little flash of the melon-faced Hall of Famer, late in his career, leaning out over the plate from his left-handed stance—he's in pinstripes, a Yankee now, no longer a Cardinals or Giants thumper—and stroking the ball sweetly into left field, the wrong way, for another pinch-hit double. Mize, who lived all his life in his birthplace, Demorest, Georgia, was called the Big Cat long before Andrés Galarraga came along. By chance I came to know a writer named Frank Gannon, who also hailed from around Demorest, and now and then I'd get a postcard from him, keeping me up to date: "Saw the Big Cat downtown today and hailed him—'Hey, Cat, how you doin'?'—and won a nod back. Semi-friendly. Didn't have to remove his cigar."

An old New York Giants teammate of Mize's once told me that the Big Cat liked his whiskey but always claimed he could sweat it out of his system during his batting-practice workout the next morning. There was a footbath in the Polo Grounds clubhouse that you stepped into on the way to the showers, and one day a jokester laced its fungicidal waters with lighter fluid, which he touched off a moment after the Big Cat, naked and streaming perspiration, arrived: *Ka-poof!* The laughter went on almost up to the first pitch that afternoon, and guys noticed that Mize switched over to beer—mostly, anyway—for the next couple of weeks.

Foxx, Ruth, Mays, Mize, and then on the way up to the press-box someone said how come all these names were so old, from way back. Surely there was a four-letter guy playing today who could hit the ball out, and in chorus we came to Sosa, how could we be so dumb?

That night, I woke up in the dark and said "Cash!" out loud, pleasing myself. Norm Cash, of the Tigers, in that one year when he began to hit homers in bunches. The year he corked his bat.

I went off to Maine for a while at this juncture, but when I got back, the Four-Forty—as I'd begun to think of it—was still alive. The Tigers had come to town, and when I chatted with Ernie Harwell, the perennial Detroit broadcaster, behind the cage during batting practice, he joined in with alacrity. Carlton Fisk and George Bell, the former Blue Jay slugger, had lately found their way onto the list, but Ernie said no, he was pretty sure Fisk hadn't pulled it off. Did we have Norm Cash? Feeling like a curator, I said yes but thank you.

Ernie wanted to know who had thought up this teaser, and it came back to me that it must have been the amiable Cormac Gordon, of the Staten Island *Advance*, who proposed it at that supper in early July. A neighbor of his, a fan, had started it or heard about it from somebody else. Then, while Harwell and I were talking, we asked ourselves how could we have dared to think about Fisk and not remember his Red Sox teammate Jim Rice. Rice—*of course*, Rice. And, nah, forget Fisk.

No one wanted this to end. There were a dozen-odd writers and front-office guys involved by now, including Rick Cerrone, the Yanks P.R. pasha, and Red Foley, the once red-headed *News* writer who still served as scorekeeper for a lot of Yankee games. It would have taken only five minutes for somebody to settle the thing by consulting *The Baseball Encyclopedia*, not forgetting to track down the rush of round-trippers in the past few seasons. We wanted to gnaw on this a little longer, just for fun.

It was *Newsday's* Joe Gergen who tipped me off to the surprise entrant—I was wrong in thinking there wouldn't be one—who was Wally Post, of the 1955 Cincinnati Reds. I'd thought of that club but believed its candidate might be Gus Bell, which would give us two Bells, but no way. Meantime, I'd been roaming around with Rudy York, but forty home runs was a ton of dingers back then. Some flighty visiting writer had also proposed Rob Deer, who'd been known to hit a long ball for the Brewers and Tigers a decade or two ago, and this won a horse laugh. Then I remembered Jimmy Wynn—Jimmy Wynn, the Astros' Toy Cannon—at about the same moment that everyone else did, and our list was complete. Eleven blurts with forty round-trippers. Good for us.

Not so. The next morning, a late participant, Lee Lowenfish, of WNYC, came around with the news that Jimmy Wynn had never done it—his best total was thirty-seven homers, in 1967. That meant there were only ten players, not eleven, with four or less letters in their names who ever parked forty in a season. Ten? Oh, O.K.—ten is neater. And it was over.

Here they are, with their top-year totals:

Babe Ruth	60
Mel Ott	42
Willie Mays	52
Jimmie Foxx	58
Johnny Mize	51
Sammy Sosa	66
George Bell	47
Jim Rice	46
Norm Cash	41
Wally Post	40

I mentioned the Four-Forty to Cone one day in the clubhouse but found him minimally responsive. Wary was more like it. "Mel Ott—that's history to me," he said. He brought it up again a few days later, though, and after I'd showed him the final list, scrawled in my notebook, he looked more cheerful and perhaps even managed a "Wow!" He'd only wanted to be sure that none of the four-letter homers had been smacked against him. These guys were the enemy.

15

Families

This is Cone's turf, and he's agreed to drive my rental car on our trips around town or out to the ballpark and back; this leaves me free to catch the sights and the shape of his season. After Whitey Ford Day, he'd lost in a poor outing at Oakland, but came back strongly at Seattle in his next turn, giving up a lone run to the Mariners in a winning 5–4 outcome, saved by Mariano Rivera. Things are looking up. With their batters delivering seventy-five homers since the All-Star break, the Yankees hold the second-best won-lost record in the league, and their lead in the A.L. East has just climbed to six games. Offense is a Power-Bar for pitchers. Hernandez has won three in a row, aided no little by the Yankees' twenty-six runs, and Pettitte's loss to the Mariners the other day broke his streak of nine straight winning starts, during which the batters contributed a hundred runs. Cone, after his Tampa exile at the end of July, has restored himself in impressive fashion. His three-and-one record for August, with a 3.98 E.R.A., is second only to Pettitte's. What pleases him most is that a men-on-base situation often ends with a strikeout now instead of a double or a three-run homer. This is good for a pitcher's disposition, and I notice that he is calmer about the umpires. A rookie ump named Chris Guccione had worked behind the plate in the Mariners game, where he failed to ring up a third-strike slider to lead-off batter Rickey Henderson but appeared awed by it at the same time. Posada, coming out to the mound, reported that Guccione had gone "Whoo!" after the ball bent over the plate after all. "He did that all through the game," David says now. " 'Ball—whoo!' . . . 'Ball two—whoo!' A least he was admitting this was all new for him."

Cone tells me that these Kansas City homecomings on the schedule bring him close not only to his beginnings but to his stay here with the Royals in 1993 and '94, a young team he still remembered with fondness and frustration. His hired-gun stint with the 1992 Blue Jays had ended with a World Series ring and an enhanced status as a free agent at the December winter meetings in Louisville. The Yankees, who were also pursuing the Cubs' Greg Maddux, evinced a serious interest, but David and Steve Fehr had also been hearing from Ewing M. Kauffman, the owner of the Royals, who wanted to redress the disaster of losing him to the Mets. Kauffman, a pharmaceutical billionaire, had founded the club as an expansion franchise in 1969, and built Royals Stadium, on the east side of town, with its golden-crowned scoreboard, pulsing fountains, and broiling Astroturf carpet. He had put together the compelling Kansas City clubs— the Royals of young David Cone's dreams—that battled the Yankees through the late seventies, and made it at last into the World Series in 1980 (where they lost to the Phillies). Kauffman, an old-style baseball magnate, came to every home game and took a fatherly interest in his players. This is not a metaphor. In 1984 and 1985, a Royals partner of his, Avron B. Fogelman, offered forty-million-dollar "lifetime contracts" to three still active Royals icons—George Brett, Dan Quisenberry, and center fielder Willie Wilson. Forty million apiece. The gifts gave the players a long-term interest in the Fogelman real-estate holdings, and when that market fizzled spectacularly, in the late eighties, so did the recipients' share. The thought had been there, one could say, and no one blamed Kauffman, who eventually assumed responsibility for the guaranteed contracts.

The contract that brought Cone back to Kansas City in 1993 matched a Yankee bid of eighteen million dollars over three years, but packaged it to include an up-front signing payment of nine million dollars (eleven million in all, for the first year). This tactical front-loading anticipated the players' strike—it was less than two years away—which would shut down player salaries for its duration. The deal briefly established Cone as the highest-paid pitcher in baseball (Barry Bonds, that same week, became the highest-paid player, with a six-year, $43.75-million contract from the Giants), but David and Lynn and Steve Fehr believe that the chance for him to put in some baseball time away from New York just then may have been its greatest value.

"The first year here, '93, was extremely difficult," Cone said in the car. "I loved the team and the manager, Hal McRae, but we started bad and struggled for runs all year. Never got out of the pack. I just could not *buy* a run. I finished eleven and fourteen, which looks like a lost season, but all my other numbers were solid. In my last seven losses I think we scored six runs. Mr. Kauffman was sick with bone cancer, but before he died in August he called me in and said he could see how I was pitching and not to change because it was going to turn out all right. A remarkable man."

The next summer was more like it. David was staying in suburban Leawood, in a house he had bought from Bret Saberhagen. He was living more cautiously, and it was on his mind that late nights here posed a greater risk than in New York, where there were always plenty of cabs to take you home. His parents were in Florida, but a family illness brought Ed back to Kansas City for extended stretches, and he stayed with David when he was there. Lynn was coming for visits as well. The year before, hearing about his return to Kansas City, she'd sent David a letter to say what a great move it was for him. "New York has eaten you up," she wrote. While David was still in spring training, down in Baseball City, Florida, she came out and, with his brother Chris, bought some furniture and rugs and curtains for the place, to fix it up for his return.

"That was a really enjoyable summer," Cone said, back in 1994 now. "That was when some of the dark clouds from the Mets first began to lift for me. I spent a lot of time with my family—my dad was actually there for most of the year—and I was seeing Lynn again. I had a great year going—some of the best work I've ever done as a pitcher."

Encouraged by Hal McRae and pitching coach Bruce Kison to be more economical on the mound—to get more outs on fewer pitches—Cone solved the low-run-support problem by firing three consecutive shutouts in May. "Other times he was so competitive that he'd pitch himself out of games," McRae told me. "He'd be there in the seventh with over a hundred and twenty pitches, fighting to stay in the game, and I'd be in the position of having to bring in what we both knew was a less talented pitcher in his place. David's arm was still tender from his days with the Mets, so we wanted to look after him. But he set the example for us. He was never afraid to go out there and fail."

The '94 Royals numbered Mark Gubicza and Kevin Appier among the other starters and Jeff Montgomery as closer. Rookie of the Year Bob Hamelin was the designated hitter, Brian McRae (the manager's son) played center field, and the veterans Jose Lind, Greg Gagne, and Gary Gaetti steadied the infield—a lineup not exactly highlighted in the annals but full of itself just then. A fourteen-game midsummer winning streak, largely played at home, brought out the fans in unaccustomed numbers and took the young Royals within a game of the tied, division-leading White Sox and Indians, on Monday, August 6th—six days before the strike and the end of all that.

"Really an overachieving team," David said. "We all still talk about it, everyone who was there, as one of the most disappointing parts of our careers—not knowing what might have been."

This note—*if only, couldn't buy a run, what might have been*—surfaced so often in Cone's conversations that I sometimes found myself impatient with him. That '94 season was Cone's Cy Young year, in fact, but I perversely wanted something even better than its shining 16–5 won-and-lost and 2.94 earned-run average, and wished that it might have brought a championship. This is the Sisyphean burden we fans lay on the pros at all times, priding ourselves in assessing blame for anything short of a triumphant outcome. The normal year-to-year swings—a batting average down twenty points from the season before, a loss or a couple of no-decisions that take away a twenty-win record—are not quite countenanced. There is always someone up there ahead of our team in the standings or our man among the league leaders, so why weren't they better? What we don't want to accept, in truth, is the sovereign nature of sports, which works in this implacable fashion to sort out the one team or player at the top of the lists. Only the best—the Madduxes and Pedros, and the Yankees—stay up there for long, and when they, too, fail and are replaced, we are impatient again. The players are more merciful, but I sense that their explanations of anything short of a dominating performance are only a shield against the chilling realities of their profession, and a spur to go back and do better next year.

Driving back from Kauffman Stadium (as it's now named) on Labor Day night, after Andy Pettitte's opening 4–3 win, David told me that he'd been bringing a Spanish-language CD with him on road trips, as a means of improving his friendship with the ravishingly interesting but monolingual El Duque. Another free spirit on the team was Glenallen Hill, it turned out, and it was terrific having Luis Sojo back. "It's much funner than it was," he said. Watching the oncoming car lights cross his face as we went along, I had the notion that at long last he was able to put his pitching worries aside for a time and free the moment from the next day's burden of fortune.

"I've felt disconnected from this team," he went on. "I know I should have made more of an effort to make a bond with Jorge. Other years, you know, I used to organize team dinners—take guys out and give them a chance to know each other—but not now. I'm not a team leader. It's classic hindsight, but all I could think for a long time was that if I pitched well I didn't win, and if I pitched badly the team didn't win. I got caught up in that and I wish it hadn't happened."

He was out there pitching again the next evening, matched up against the Royals' right-hander Jeff Suppan. The weather had eased, after a stretch when the temperature had got up into the hundreds for days on end, and a small crowd had come out to see their old Royals or Rockhurst leading man, or perhaps just to catch a breeze. It was strange not to be in a mass of fans, the way I always was at Yankee Stadium, and to be able to hear what people were saying from a few seats or rows away. The fountains out in center field did their plashy stuff between innings, and a little whiff of summer came off the infield turf, which is a merciful grass now. I was sitting with Ed and Joan Cone in the family section, up the sloping stands from home. Ed, quiet as always, had his David-game face on, but I think we were all convinced that we were off the hook now and ready for some easy outs.

Cone walked the tough Mike Sweeney in the first, who came around to score on a double, but then he struck out Mark Quinn to end the inning. By the third, ahead 4–1, he had found his poise, or almost. With one out, Johnny Damon walked on four pitches, and the next batter, Rey Sanchez, squaring on the first pitch, popped a feeble infield looper to the left side, not quite in reach of Scott Brosius at third. Cone whirled and sprinted after the ball and made a half-turning last-minute grab, falling heavily on his left side as he came down—a great play but one that you wanted back at the same instant. Splayed face down on the grass, with his arm awkwardly under his body, he writhed in pain, then twisted his head in a scream I couldn't hear—the Greek-mask cry that made such a horrifying picture in the next day's sports pages. Tended by trainer Gene Monahan and surrounded by his shocked teammates, he lay there for long minutes, and when he got up at last and made his way off the field and up the dugout, with his left arm held at an odd angle, he was still in shocking distress.

Ed, leaning forward in disbelief, said nothing, while Joan slowly brought her hands up to her face. I was less admirable. Gaping, I stared and pointed, repeating "He's hurt! He's hurt!" His season had turned again, and now perhaps his career as well. I had seen other baseball injuries—beanings, broken ankles, outfielders crashing into fences, a third baseman and a left fielder running into each other at full tilt and knocking each other unconscious—but nothing like this skulking little disaster.

A Cone entourage assembled quickly in the hallway between the two clubhouses—his parents, his brother Chris, Christal's daughter Justine, Steve Fehr, and others—but I hung back when we were beckoned inside. Two Royals attendants left with me in the hall exchanged a joke about the kind of following that only a Yankee player could whip up when things went bad, and I held back from muttering "Plus a biographer." The casualty party emerged at last, with David, white-faced, in their midst, heading off to St. Luke's Hospital for the precautionary X-rays. I went up to the pressbox, where George King came over and put his hand on my shoulder. "Typical Cone play," he said.

The news was better than anyone expected. David had fallen in a position that threw his full weight onto his left elbow, driving his arm up out of the shoulder, but the Royals' doctor, Steve Joyce (a friend from Cone's days with the team), had been able to reduce the injury—put the arm back in its socket—after a struggle in the training room. X-rays were negative—no tears or tissue damage—and they'd take another look with an M.R.I. in the morning.

Doc Gooden was pitching now, and Scott Brosius blew the game open with a grand slam in the eighth. In the clubhouse, the Yankee players told us how it had looked to them: and then David was there, too, amazingly, slowly getting dressed and talking to the writers. Back again, he was suddenly just another Yankee with a problem, not all that different from Bernie Williams, who'd been walking around with an icebag bandaged around his middle after pulling a rib-cage muscle, or Paul O'Neill, with his hip-pointer, or Chuck Knoblauch, with his wrist, or Ramiro Mendoza, who was just coming off his second stay on the D.L. with a bum shoulder (and would go back again shortly, this time for surgery). The end of Cone's career hadn't lasted out the evening. I asked Gene Monahan what he'd thought about David's crash, but he's a secret agent when it comes to his training room. "What we'll see now," he said, "is his bulldogness."

David told us, in any case. "My shoulder was in my neck," he said. "My first thought was fear. My second was that this was a fitting ending to a miserable season. My third thought was maybe I could come back."

I drove this time, heading back to the hotel, with Cone sitting up straight beside me, his arm in a sling. He was O.K., he kept saying—not too bad. He wanted to know if I'd been in there when Steve Joyce and Geno and some others had been hauling and tugging on his arm, trying to pull him back together. I said I'd taken a pass, and he laughed and said good move.

"For twenty minutes there it was about as bad as I could stand," he said. "I knew it was serious when I saw Knoblauch peeking over and he does this 'Let me out of here' move like he's going to be sick, and backs out of the room. Couldn't take it. They began to think they'd have to take me to the hospital that way and do it under an anesthetic. I can't remember anything as bad as that—not for a long time. Then it went back in—you could hear this double sound: *Pop-pop!*—and I felt better right away."

Torre had been there, of course. David, seeing his face upside down above him on the table, said he was glad he'd been able to clear up Joe's thinking about the post-season rotation this way.

"But why didn't you make the double play?" Joe said.

So many of David's friends and relatives had turned up at Kauffman Stadium to see him pitch against the Royals that evening that he'd told the ticket lady just to let everyone in who'd used his name and send him the bill. After the game—after his shocking fall and the vision of him rolling on the grass with his face twisted and his mouth open; and, later, after his return from St. Luke's Hospital and the reassuring X-rays—the best and closest of these pals have moved along to the lounge at the Fairmont hotel, where the Yankees are staying, to have a drink with him and cut him down to size. Here, late in the shadowy, comfortable room, David sits on a couch, with his left arm still in the sling that was gently slipped on by Gene Monahan in the clubhouse—a more modest affair than the Velcroed mummy-wrapping he'd picked up at St. Luke's. He holds himself a little stiffly, but relief has turned him cheerful. Sipping a double Glenlivet, he recounts the scene in the training room when he lay on the table, while Steve Joyce and the others tried to pull him together. His mother and father and his brother Chris— where is Chris now, anyway—were there, along with Steve Fehr and the rest. They'd come to the park for another ballgame, and now they're all in "E.R."

"I was pretty miserable," David says lightly. "I'm going *'Arghh, arghh!'*"—he bares his teeth and rolls his head about, in boyish imitation—"and I'm nauseated and thinking I'm going throw up and then it suddenly, wow, it goes into place—*pop-pop!'*—you can hear it. Instant relief, and the whole room goes 'Aaah!'"

His friends laugh with him—they can't get enough of this— and David reminds them that his mother was in there in the training room all this time, when terrible things were coming out of his mouth. "Dr. Joyce asks me, 'Does this hurt? Does *this* hurt?' and I'm yelling 'Fuck yes, man!'"

The friends around him on the big chairs and sofas at the Fairmont are in sweats and message-bearing T-shirts and big sneakers; they look like a neighborhood softball team. Most of them are wearing caps—Yankee caps, of course—and when I ask Steve Doherty about this celebratory loyalty he says, "Yeah—right! David has cost me a fortune. I've got a whole closetful of caps and jackets back home—Yankee caps, Blue

Jays caps, Mets caps. Why can't the guy stay in one place? You begin to think he's getting a cut."

Steve is David's closest friend—he's a lawyer now—and like the others here he goes back to Little League ballgames at Budd Park or at one of the diamonds down behind the Ward's plant, and to basketball games at Holy Cross parochial (the court in the church auditorium, only a block or two from the Cones' house) and Wiffle-ball games in the Cones' yard, and to other days and times of year at the park swimming pool or on Sunday family picnics up over the hill there. Steve and his brother Danny and a few of the others went to Holy Cross, but Craig (Birdman) McQuillen and his brother were public-school kids and met these others when they played against them in tournaments. Families are big tonight. Chris Cone doesn't turn up, but Jeff and Brian Hertzog are here, and Steve Doherty's Danny, who's the older brother, and Birdman McQuillen's younger brother Ricky and his kid sister Tara. She's pretty, and so young that she's never met David; Birdman points her out, and she gets up and leans across the table and shakes his hand, a little embarrassed but tickled. There are a couple of other younger-looking guys and their dates or wives in the circle who don't get introduced and don't say much, but never mind—everyone here tonight is home folks.

Birdman, who's wearing a backward-facing Yankee cap, is tall and gangly, with a pale-blond mustache and chin whiskers and an athlete's easy way of moving. These are neighborhood jocks, some of whom went on and made names for themselves on school basketball or football or baseball teams, and in college, too. Danny Miller was a pole vaulter. Steve Doherty played football at William Jewell College, and Birdman McQuillen played basketball at Missouri Valley College. It's hard to know whether the rush of nicknames here began with the sports scrimmages or just from neighborhood kids' hanging out together for so long, but the handles are a big help to a newcomer trying to sort out the party. Danny Miller is Flyguy, and Danny Doherty is Dode. That makes his kid brother Steve Little Dode, even though he's bigger. The Hertzogs, Jeff and Brian, are Zog and Little Zog.

Flyguy is quiet here, holding himself strangely erect in a tall chair in the corner; it turns out he's a warehouseman who recently suffered a serious back injury. When he asks Cone if he can see what kind of painkillers the Yankee trainer has given him for his shoulder David hands over a little glassine packet of them, and says to keep them, he's got plenty. Flyguy holds them up to the light—they're a dark red—and says, "Do you want to *autograph* these for me, maybe? Maybe one by one, with a tiny pen?"

The talk and the ribbing are continuous now. David gets taken down for his fashionable, squared-off New York shoes, and somebody tells him, hey, Mel Gibson gets about three separated shoulders and stuff in every picture without all this yelling and rolling around. Someone else notices that David has a tiny circle of gray hair on the top of his head, and David says yeah, it's sad—it used to be red. Another round of beers and drinks arrives and David fires up a Marlboro Light, to go with the double Glenlivet. "I'm taking Zyban for these," he says, holding up the cigarette. "I'm going to beat this." But everyone is listening to Brian Hertzog now, next to David on the couch, who has us squirming with laughter as he tells how he rolled over a ladder truck a month or so ago, on the way to a fire—no shit, he really did. He was driving—he's a Kansas City fireman, as his father was before him—and when he came bombing down this avenue, out by Seventy-second Street, there was a badly marked construction barrier and he had to extemporize a sliding hard right and a last-minute cutback into a driveway, which brought the whole rig teetering slowly left, up onto the vertical and barely over, and crashing tremendously and finally down onto its side. Brian is a small guy, with an eager, precise way of telling a story, and we're cheering as he imitates himself clawing his way up the cab and out the top at last.

"What's that costing the taxpayers—half a mill?" his brother asks, and Brian says no, he and the department have been cleared and the people who put up the barrier wrong might be looking at a lawsuit. But whenever he goes into another fire station now, all the guys there are looking at him with their heads bent over sideways. He's a celebrity.

David is a lot better by the time we begin to break up. "I'll just finish this brewski," Little Dode says to me. "I'm working tomorrow but not in court." There's a late rush of autographing before the friends part. Birdman gets David to ink a message inside his Yankee cap—he whispers it into David's ear—and when he gets it back he puts the cap on backward again, carefully smoothing it into place with both hands. Cone picks up the unopened envelope of painkillers and muscle relaxants that Gene Monahan has given him and slips them into a pocket. His arm still hurts—he will sit up all night in a chair, only dozing a bit now and then—but a night like this is better than a prescription, anytime.

I ended up going to St. John Avenue and around the old neighborhood with Ed as my guide, instead of David—he'd gone off for his M.R.I. (which turned out the right way, too)—but we had a great tour, with a stopover at the Negro Leagues Baseball Museum at the end. I had a meal with Chris, too, who unexpectedly said, "When I was young, I was the one and he was the runt. That's totally turned around but it doesn't embitter me. I love to brag about David—I do it by the hour." He mentioned that David had come to a wedding of one of his, Chris's, old friends, Timmy Presko, a while back, and when the guests and old friends there kept clustering around he'd said, "Hey, wait— you guys were *my* idols!"

The next day, David and Chris and Ed and I had lunch at the hotel—a strange, silent affair. Christal was working, and the other brother, Danny, was living in Arizona now. David was going back to New York the following morning for some further examinations and the start of his rehab programs, while the Yankees would catch the post-game team plane to Boston for their last big series of the regular season. The mood at our table was like late Thanksgiving afternoon or the end of another family weekend, where everybody is thinking about the car keys and where the kids are, as their lives close in around them.

That night, sitting with Steve Fehr in his regular seat behind the third-base-side dugout, I remembered what a family game this is, away from New York. We were in a little section of older fans who had been early supporters of the club when Ewing Kauffman was starting up the franchise, in 1969; their privileged seating was a carryover from the reserved seats they'd held at Municipal Stadium, before the Kansas City Athletics eloped to Oakland. After I'd met some of Steve's parents' friends sitting around us—Sharon and Howard Levitan, Irene and Sherman Dreisezun, and Helen and Marty Brown—I got the impression that they were watching the game and their young, semi-talented team with an almost botanical detachment. Helen Brown was deep in a book; she'd never been a fan, she said, but she came to every game to be with her husband. A little later, offering me a bag of delicious grapes, she asked what I thought of Al Gore.

Steve told me he thought Cone would be all right—we'd see in a week or so. I asked him if he thought David might seize the injury as a chance to retire, once the season ended. "We'll see," he said again (he is a lawyer). "I suspect he's going to want to be very deliberate. On the other hand, he might be pitching for another team somewhere, to test a change of scene. But if I was convinced he couldn't be himself again I wouldn't recommend it."

Like where, I asked.

He paused, considering my reliability and pub date. "The Cardinals?" he offered. "Boston? The Giants? There are some good teams out there looking for pitching."

Steve Fehr is tall and shy, and when he speaks you can get the idea that he's just mounted a little step stool to look for something up over your head. He's also a fan. When I told him about him the Four-Forty he lapsed into a musing half-inning's silence, then asked, "Can I have until tomorrow on this?"

He told me that the scattering of David's last team here had come as a shock. Days after Cone reported to the Royals' spring-training camp at the end of the strike he was told he'd been traded back to the Blue Jays. (It wasn't until late July in that same 1995 summer that he was dealt along to the Yankees, to begin his eventful stay in the Bronx.) Many Kansas City fans suspected that David's prominence in the union during the strike had been behind the sudden dismissal, but of course nothing could be proved. Brian McRae was traded, too, and his manager-father, Hal, was long gone, fired the previous autumn. "We've been in a wilderness here ever since then," Steve said.

Hal McRae, a prominent figure on the tough Kansas City teams of the seventies, never left any doubt about his baseball emotions—I hold a vivid memory of the notorious street-sweeper block he threw on Yankee second baseman Willie Randolph when breaking up a double play in a league-championship game in 1977—and he may have lacked the diplomatic touch as a manager. In 1994, he'd indulged himself in a spectacular rant against the media in his office one day, in the midst of which a tape recorder or an ashtray slipped out of his hand and clocked a local writer, Alan (Scoop) Eskew, of the Topeka *Capital-Journal*, right in the face. Other writers caught the moment on tape, with McRae cursing and railing and then turning pussycat in mid-sentence: ". . . teach you fucking bastards a— Oh my God, Scoop, I'm so sorry! Jesus, man, are you all right? Are you O.K. there, guy?" Eskew, holding his notebook or handkerchief up to his bleeding noggin, says sure, Hal, I'm O.K., and the chewing-out goes on unabated, exactly as before. When I asked McRae about the moment he burst out laughing. "Oh, that's just what happened! And it couldn't have been worse—Scoop was the nicest guy there, by far!"

The Royals put on a ninth-inning rally against the Yankees that night, when an R.B.I. single by Johnny Damon completed a comeback win against Mike Stanton—there's nothing sweeter than that moment when a home-team guy comes flying across the plate to shut down the day—and I was delighted for my new friends, who stood up during the action and exclaimed happily when it came out right, for a change: 3–2, K.C. Too good to last, of course, and the following evening—this was Thursday—things went the other way when the Yanks, shut out for eight innings, brought home seven runs in the top of the ninth, to win the game and this four-game series, too.

A couple of hours later, after midnight, David and I walked through a labyrinth of tunnels in the depths of Kauffman Stadium and up some stairs to a door that opened out into the middle of the team parking lot. A few older cops and maintenance people along the way said hello to him and reminded him of their names. Ed was with us. He'd been at all the games, of course, and his car was not far from mine in the almost empty lot. A dozen or so fans were gathered along a waist-level chainlink fence here, and when they called David's name he walked over. He'd taken off his sling and stuffed it into his windbreaker pocket. Earlier, he'd said that his shoulder was already much better. He rotated it for me in gingerly fashion. He wanted to start throwing again soon, he said—maybe tomorrow. You couldn't let a pitching arm get slack because of a little bad luck. You never knew—he might get back in the rotation after missing just one turn. You could make do with limited movement on that left side for a while—it wasn't like you were a tight end reaching for passes.

He was talking himself back into the game.

There was a little night breeze moving across the empty lot, and some stars waiting overhead. One of the figures at the fence was Birdman McQuillen, who'd brought his daughters, Niki and Madi, to the game to meet his famous friend. Cone shook hands and signed a program for them, and then he signed a ball for a man with a small son at his side, a sleepy kid of about four. When his dad gave him the ball with David's name on it I could see that it wasn't the autograph that mattered with the boy but the ball itself. He kept staring at it and turning it around in his hands.

David said, "Gotta go," and thanked the fans, and they waved and wished him luck with his sore arm.

Ed took David aside, out behind our car, and I could hear him murmuring, "Wear the sling while you toss," in his low, flat voice. "Get someone else to catch the ball for you. Don't take any shocks with that arm. Don't rush things."

"Sure, Dad," David said. "Sure thing—I'll be careful, you know me. Thanks, Dad." He hugged him goodbye.

16

This Statesman

Months before this—it was late in May—David was revisiting various stretches in his tale with me when he began to talk about his part in the players' strike of 1994 and 1995. He was slumped down on a couch in his East Side apartment, with a half-empty can of Pepsi in his hand. The lowering sun was coming from behind him, so I saw him only as a shape, a shadow. He would be facing the Oakland Athletics at the Stadium in a couple of days—another shocker for him, as it happened—but his mind wasn't on that game yet. He had a touch of flu or something, and in a halting way said that lately he'd been going back over his bad times with the Mets and what it had been like getting up each morning to see his name in another batch of lurid headlines. I offered that those days were long gone, and after a silence he unexpectedly said how startling it had been to find himself in Washington, D.C., in the early winter of 1995, as a representative for the Players Association. Another difficult time, to be sure, but a very different atmosphere. Baseball was in the midst of the numbing, all-encompassing two-hundred-and-thirty-four-day players' strike, and here he was talking strategy with Donald Fehr, and the union assistant general counsel, Lauren Rich, and the associate general counsel, Gene Orza; or plan-

ning how he would testify before Orrin Hatch and Strom Thurmond in an antitrust hearing the next afternoon; or meeting with
players somewhere to catch them up on the latest issues and
maneuverings; or huddling with lobbyists to decide which players would be wheeled in next to bend the ear of a key congressman. Those were strange, almost hallucinatory times—baseball
was in limbo, with no pennant races and no World Series—and
David was busier than he'd ever been in his life, flying back and
forth between Washington and New York, then to Pittsburgh or
Tampa or Atlanta, listening to player groups and lobbyists and
union tacticians and owners' lawyers, living out of a travel bag.
It had happened in a hurry.

This leaping about over the years is hard on readers, and I offer it in this form, the way it came out that afternoon, only because it is exactly like Cone—so much the way he thinks and
operates, and deals with things inside. Not much is forgotten or
put away, particularly the bad games and harsh stretches, and if
they come rolling out together it's because he has connected
them in his mind and is trying to find a pattern or solution. He is
rarely confessional but always in process, and although you
don't always pick up the trailside markings right away, you learn
to pay attention.

Cone was one of two union player representatives with the
Royals in '94 but, according to Steve Fehr, not a particularly avid
or attentive one. Steve, as we know, lived in Kansas City, but he
had served the union as *consigliere* and had tried a number of
successful court cases on its behalf. Summoned East now, he invited David to come along and get involved. "He was bright and
articulate, and it didn't hurt us that he was suddenly a Cy Young
winner, too," Steve told me. "He was known and he understood
the issues. Of course we had no idea that he'd turn into this
statesman."

Cone said that he'd found his new role almost overnight. "I'd
had experience with the media in New York and I could talk in
complete sentences, and now suddenly everyone was saying
'You can do it. You've got the balls and you don't care—*you* be

our front guy.' And there I was, being interviewed by the national reporters or going on TV after another one of those deadlocked meetings. Talk about an education—I couldn't believe it."

Donald Fehr, Steve's older brother and the union's main man, saw something more. "You have to have people like David Cone in this work," he said. "Players are strongly individualistic but also look for leaders. Players lead players. You must be respected by them first as a player, then as a leader. The players will find someone and think, This guy could make it in the world even if he wasn't a player. That was David."

The strike had begun on August 12, 1994, after the owners, ignoring the players' declaration of a strike deadline if their demands were not met, had made evident their plans to institute a salary cap like the ones in effect in the National Football League and the National Basketball Association. The average player salary had just gone to $1.2 million per year—and the owners, though rarely unified, yearned for a rein on this apparently inexorable rise. And they wanted much more, in truth, including the elimination of the existing salary-arbitration procedure, one of the rocks on which the union stood. When I asked David to define the basic issues of the strike for me, I was poised for a lengthy explication of the positions taken by each side, the successive proposals and counter-proposals that clotted the news each week through that long fall and winter, and an anatomy of the hard-liners and accommodators within the owners' ranks. I'd heard him talk along these lines with an insider's avidity, but this time he said, "The main issue in the strike was clear. This was a major effort by the owners to break the union. Some of them had been waiting years for the chance, and right after the first negotiating sessions we all knew it was here. They were coming after us. This was war, and we had to dig in and fight."

Cone, elected by his peers as a representative for the American League (his opposite number was Tom Glavine, of the Atlanta Braves), had played in both leagues and now he took a place in the association's front-line roster: Scott Sanderson,

Kevin Brown, Jay Bell, Cecil Fielder, and B. J. Surhoff, among others. "It was an extremely difficult time for us," David said. "We were getting hammered as greedy, overpaid ballplayers. We got ripped every day in the media and by the public. On the other hand, we stayed together. We fought it out. I spent the entire off-season on these issues—I never picked up a ball—in Washington and Miami and all over, in and out of hotels. The Doral Arrowwood, in Rye Brook, New York—we camped out there for days on end."

I remember the bitterness of those times, too, and the daily arguments from fed-up friends of mine who wanted the players to remain as they had always been in their imaginations—lucky guys who were being paid, after all, to play a game. I didn't see it that way, and I found confidence in the way someone like Cone could put it for me. And it was after the strike when he'd said, "We'd be more popular if we'd won a lottery."

The strike grew harsher as 1995 arrived and the owners made preparations to open a new season without a settlement—to enlist "replacement players," as they delicately put it, in place of the striking regulars. Meantime, in a parallel but separate movement, the Players Association was lobbying Congress to vote out a bill that would do away with parts of baseball's antique exemption from the antitrust laws, thus making team owners more vulnerable to court actions. The Clinton Administration summoned both sides to an early-February round-the-clock bargaining session at the White House that might wring out an agreement—a political coup, if it happened. But the move came too late in the day. Cone, there at the nightlong session in the Roosevelt Room, met chief of staff Leon Panetta, George Stephanopoulos, Vice-President Gore, and President Clinton, among others—he was particularly impressed by Gore's knowledge of the issues, from both sides—and saw the shock with which they and their aides and lawyers, one by one, began to understand the nature of the owners' objectives and the hopelessness of finding a solution.

Cone knew most of the principals by now, from other days and meetings: acting commissioner (and Milwaukee owner) Bud Selig, federal mediator Bill Usery (a disaster, in the opinion of almost everyone), Phillies' executive Dave Montgomery, opposition lawyers Chuck O'Connor and Rob Manfred, and owners Jerry Reinsdorf, of the White Sox; Drayton McLane, Jr., of Houston; John Harrington, of the Red Sox; and Jerry McMorris, a powerhouse who'd recently bought the Colorado Rockies. Meantime, Cone was testifying before Senators Joseph Biden, Arlen Specter, and Strom Thurmond, and calling on Ted Kennedy, Bob Dole, and Orrin Hatch to enlist support. Hatch was sympathetic to the players' cause (he was a friend of the old Pirates pitcher Vern Law and his son Vance, who'd gone to play in Japan after being victimized in the collusion wars), while others in Congress, it became clear, felt a rapport but had to remain silent because of the major campaign contributions they'd received from the owners and their corporations down the years.

The union, for its part, exploited the players' obvious celebrity value on the Hill, knowing also how the legislators would be moved by the young pros' seriousness and insight. Some believed that Representative Henry Hyde, of Illinois, became a secret sympathizer, although he remained bound hand and foot by Reinsdorf and the Chicago *Tribune*, which owns the Cubs. Baseball, of course, makes for odd politics, with the owner-capitalists relying heavily on the support of government and its antitrust exemption, while the well-compensated worker-players represent traditional open-market capitalism at a glorious extreme. The market share for the owners is not guaranteed, and replacement workers, by whatever name, are a more than symbolic threat. Meanwhile, the fans and to some extent the public itself continue to think of themselves as the spiritual owners of the ancient industry, which lends passion and error to each new development in a crisis.

"David at this time was extraordinary," Fehr told me. "He'd come up to me before a meeting and say, 'You need to talk to—' or 'These guys want to hear more about—' whatever it was. He seemed to reach these judgments intuitively, and in every case he was right. He was thoughtful—deliberate in all matters. He managed to do all this while carrying the look of a kid—but not as much so near the end as he once did."

The strike didn't stop everything. On November 12, 1994, David got away from meetings and hearings and shuttle flights long enough to attend his wedding. He and Lynn had been together again since he'd come back to Kansas City but had begun to feel that a resumption wasn't enough. The Mets trauma was over, and it was time for them to move along. A hundred and twenty people—"just the families and our closest friends," as Lynn puts it—turned up at the executive dining space on top of the Equitable Center, in New York, for the celebrations. Steve Doherty was David's best man, more or less returning the favor. David had agreed to be *his* best man two years before but had had to cancel out because of a last-minute business appointment. The moment the Dohertys tied the knot, the wedding party gathered around a TV set and watched the best man pitch the sixth game against the Braves in the World Series. The bride's family was not wholly entranced to see that many guests had turned up wearing Blue Jays caps.

The strike was grim but the strikers youthful; Tom Glavine, the National League player rep, had to absent himself in the middle because his wife was giving birth to their first baby. Marianne McGettigan, a Portland, Maine, lawyer who headed the lobbying efforts in Washington, thinks back to the fun of it all, as well as the hard work. Selecting teams of players from the Players Association to lobby specific congressional groups was like some children's indoor game. One typical team, "Eddie and the Reds"—Eddie Murray, of the Indians, and Barry Larkin and some others from the Cincinnati club—went after Ohio congressmen. Cone remembers Cecil Fielder, with his bright suits, dazzling smile, and baton-sized cigar, making jaws drop when they pressed a call on still another congressman's or senator's office. Kevin McGuiness, a Washington lawyer who was also a lobbyist with the union's team, was walking down a corridor under the House office building one evening with Fielder, and asked him if there was one pitcher in all baseball who'd given him real trouble—someone who could always get him out.

"Yeah, him," Fielder replied, jerking a thumb at Cone, who was a few paces ahead. "Never could *touch* him—except this one time, when I took him deep. Got all of it, just that once—that ball is still travellin'."

"That was in the minors," Cone said, eavesdropping. "Minors don't count."

McGettigan, like Fehr, recognizing the celebrity appeal of the major-leaguers, organized a gigantic party at Union Station, where staff members from the congressional offices could meet the guys. Rushing about to put it together, she hurried back to her office at the end of the day with the realization that invitations to all five hundred and thirty-five members of Congress still needed to be signed by some star player and then shoved in the mail. But it was already done—Cone had signed them all, not just one or two, which could have been photocopied. "My God," she said to her staff, "you can't do that to a pitcher!"

Great party, it turned out—a 10.

"He was a workhorse," McGettigan went on. "He and Orel Hershiser and Tom Glavine were the intellectual leaders. They understood the relationship between the antitrust laws and the labor laws, and how they'd affect the negotiations, and at the same time they could explain why the players' position wasn't just monetary."

Senator Jim Bunning, a Republican from Kentucky—the same Jim Bunning who pitched seventeen years in the majors from the fifties to the seventies, mostly with the Tigers and Phillies, and who threw a perfect game for the latter club against the Mets on June 21, 1964—remembers being visited by a players' delegation that included Greg Maddux and Cone, who'd come to lobby him about the owners' antitrust exemption."I was extremely impressed to see players of this caliber standing forth on issues of importance," he said. "That didn't happen so much in my day. Of course I was an easy mark—I'd been on their side all along."

When it became clear one day that the vote of Senator Spencer Abraham, a Michigan Republican, would be needed to vote the antitrust-exemption bill out of the Senate Judiciary Committee, David was entrusted with the call. Abraham was believed to oppose the players' position, and Cone helped win him over. When the vote came—it was years before the matter was actually voted upon in the Senate and the law went into the books—Abraham sided with the players, and the vote went the right way.

"David will tell you that was a ten-minute phone call," Don Fehr said, "but it was an hour, easily. He was very persistent."

Cone believes that one of his real contributions to the Players Association's cause came near the end, when spring training was about to open with scab teams on the field—those replacement players, who were mostly young minor-leaguers under heavy pressure from their parent organizations to sign on or face the end of their careers. The picture was looking bleak for the striking major-leaguers, and word began to seep out that some superstars might be on the point of defection. Barry Bonds had been mentioned by the press and, before that, the White Sox' Frank Thomas. Now some prominent Philadelphia players—Darren Daulton, Lenny Dykstra—might be wavering, with others waiting only for someone else to take the first step. Strategists in the Players Association were extremely anxious, but Cone saw the situation differently. "I didn't think we were in real trouble yet," he said. "I didn't believe that any owner—Jerry Reinsdorf or the Phillies' Bill Giles, or anyone thinking about their team's future standing with the fans—would allow one of their top stars to step forward at this point and declare himself a strikebreaker. It just wasn't going to happen. They'd have to come in groups, almost full teams, and no club was close to that moment. Our strike fund was still strong, and I didn't think the danger point for us was as near as some others did."

A full crisis—baseball back, with non-union players on the field—was averted at the last moment, when Federal District Court Judge Sonia Sotomayor issued an injunction against the implementation of the owners' new working rules, and the owners, in need of a season now and a restoration of their game, caved in. Play began three weeks later, on a hundred-and-forty-four-game schedule. (Low-level negotiations over the basic agreement resumed in June, and the document was eventually signed in November of 1996.) Before all this, though—late in February, in a time of rumor and fear among the players—there had been a meeting at the Hyatt Regency, in Tampa, where numbers of replacement players had been summoned to meet the striking big-leaguers. Almost five hundred people turned up, filling the room, and stayed on for nearly five hours. It was a passionate, crisis-tinged scene, with animosity rampant. There were yells, face-to-face shouts and curses, fingers jabbed in the air. Some of the old-line union guys—Steve Bedrosian, Todd Stottlemyre, Turner Ward—seemed possessed by a blue-collar righteousness.

Tom Glavine and Scott Sanderson spoke for the union, but came off as being too analytical or technical to suit the particular mood of the day. When David's turn came, he moved to one side of the long table at the head of the room, where he could be seen in full, then turned his back and grabbed his ankles, so his rear end was in the air. Back at the mike, his face alight, he said, "The owners are trying to stick it up your ass without Vaseline. That's what this strike is about. This is about your rights, not your money. They want to get rid of what Curt Flood did for us. They want to kill free agency. They want to put the genie back in the bottle. Don't let it happen!" Sensation.

He turned toward the minor-leaguers and changed his tone. No one here failed to understand their dilemma, he said. Everyone in here had been a young player at one time, hoping some day to make it into the majors. Everyone understood that wives and families were waiting on their decision. Old players knew that you younger guys were afraid that if you said no and stood up to the owners your careers could be over. But others here, Cone went on, some of their own minor-league teammates, had already faced these decisions and had said no. All of them were under huge pressure. Managers and coaches had been heard from, telling the kids to join up and save their careers. Pete Rose, according to one story, had told his own son, Pete, Jr., a low-level White Sox prospect, to go along and become a re- placement player.

If they chose to play, David went on, chances were that when the strike ended they'd just be thrown away. Those same own- ers would turn their backs. Don't let it happen. Think of Curt Flood. Think of us. Talk to us.

"That was one of my better moments," David said now. "The mood at the meeting changed, and people there said I'd made a difference. We hung together better after that. That whole union involvement was one of the best things I ever did. It wasn't just baseball—it meant that baseball wasn't all that I could do. I was glad I took the chance."

His tone had changed, and after I'd left him that afternoon I saw, of course, where the unplanned, twisting path of his talk had taken us. He'd begun with the Mets scandals—those spring weeks almost a decade ago when his name was connected again and again to some ungodly embarrassment, and he'd have to face up to more grilling and demands for explanations from the grinning big-city media. He'd learned to handle things back then, under brutal conditions, and when the chance came later he'd been able to put his self-possession in the public eye and his hard-won skills to a better end. He'd turned himself around.

A sense of reprieve and possibility hung around the sport that spring and summer. David hadn't picked up a ball during the long siege, but everyone had to make do with a short spring training this time. Traded back to his old Blue Jays, he pitched well in Toronto, even while the two-time defending World Champions ran into disappointments and slid to the bottom of the division. At the SkyDome one day, he retired twenty-five bat-

ters before giving up his first hit—a single to the Rangers' Benji
Gil, with one out in the ninth. He won nine games and lost six
while with the Jays, and was 18–8, over all, in the shortened season. He also led the league in innings pitched.

The Cones were living in the Four Seasons, in Toronto—a big
step up from the SkyDome. While he was away on the road trips,
she was back in New York, changing her career from office design to the redesign and restoration of private houses. David and
Lynn enjoyed Toronto, with its closely adjoining ethnic districts
and lively restaurants, but as the midsummer trading deadlines
drew closer there was a sense that they wouldn't be there for
long. Cone believes that some other contending clubs (the Angels, for one) made better offers for his services, but he'd made
it known how much he wanted to be back in New York, and in
the end the Blue Jays' C.E.O., Paul Beeston, obliged him, ac-
cepting three young pitchers—Marty Janzen, Jason Jarvis, and
Mike Gordon—from George Steinbrenner in return for David's
ticket to the Yankees.

The next day, July 29, 1995, he reported to the Hubert H.
Humphrey Metrodome, in Minneapolis, in time to beat the
Twins, 4–2, for his first Yankee victory. He looked a little funny
out there, because the Yankee equipment manager, out of uniforms in his size, gave him Billy Connors's extremely capacious
gray shirt, with No. 36 on the back—his number from then on.
Reporting that afternoon for duty, Cone staged his own press
conference while still in his street clothes—a move that just
about floored Buck Showalter. A closemouthed, full-plan sort of
manager, Showalter had scheduled a meeting for his new
pitcher to go over the Twins' batting order with the scouts and
coaches, but David passed it up. "I'd pitched against them two
weeks before," he told me. "I knew New York, so I thought I'd
get the press conference over with, first thing. I knew what
those media guys wanted." He was home.

17

When You Reach September

Every season has its own story, and this has been the strangest one for us in five years—don't you think?" Thus Joe Torre toward the end of September, when his team, comfortably approaching its sixth straight entry into the post-season, found itself enmeshed in a slump of grotesque dimensions. Holding a nine-game divisional lead over the next-nearest Red Sox on September 13th—those three games at Fenway Park had been swept, with an opening blanking by Clemens and then a big 5–3 Pettitte win over Pedro Martinez in a battle of the Cy Young candidates—the team lost fifteen of its next eighteen, including the final seven in a row. The Yankees' subsequent triumphs in the divisional and league championships, along with the buzz and hoopla of a subway series, and the implacable fashion in which they did away with the Mets and took their third successive World Championship, have rubbed away the memory of what came just before, but it would be too bad to miss it altogether. Those losses were spectacular in their awfulness. At mid-month, the downside scores of two games against Cleveland and one in Toronto came out at 11–1, 15–4, and 16–3. And then 11–1 and 11–3 pastings by the Tampa Bay Devil Rays, plus a 13–2 loss in Baltimore the following night, became part of a gruesome finish in which the pitchers coughed up sixty-eight runs in that last winless week.

What was this about? What conclusion can be drawn? I have no idea. Yes, these proud Yankees finished at a measly 87–74, in the process losing home-field advantage to the Oakland Athletics in the divisional playoffs, and subjecting themselves to a soul-bending four transcontinental flights in seven days, but then they won. They swept the board. Was this a conservation of energy? Nope. Was it a semi-unconscious tune-up by this veteran-loaded troupe for the trials to come? Don't be silly. This was Loony Toons—a patch of baseball history that had no meaning at all. The Yanks were Wile E. Coyote plunging downward, clawing the air and becoming a tiny puff of dust on the desert floor below—and then back on the mesa again in the next frame, eyebrows waggling, ready for action.

Torre, mournful but unjittery as the losses mounted, dwelt on the bright incidentals—Pettitte's one-hundredth lifetime win, Jeter's one-thousandth lifetime hit. At twenty-six, Derek was the second-youngest Yankee (to Mickey Mantle) to reach this level. "Some kids haven't even made the majors at twenty-six," Joe said. When columnists came by, he could join their recollections of the epochal late losing streak that always comes up in these circumstances—the Phillies' irreversible ten straight in 1964, which horribly cost them a pennant on the last day and put a permanent kink in the psyche of their manager, Gene Mauch. It was the Cardinals who slipped past them and into the World Series, while Torre, then a catcher with the Braves, went nine for fifteen against the Phillies pitchers that final weekend.

When Joe's numbed Yankees sidled into their divisional title after a 13–2 whaling in Baltimore on the final Friday—a Red Sox loss in Tampa had erased the team's last possibility—the first players into the clubhouse walked right past the iced and waiting champagne. Derek Jeter checked protocol with the manager before Joe gave his O.K.—it was what they'd accomplished, not how they looked—and the corks were popped.

Cone's September had no parties in it. As I'd expected, he had talked his way back onto the mound again after a single missed turn, but lost to the Indians on September 15th, giving up six runs in six innings (it was one of those 11–1 embarrassments in the end). He'd thrown some useful sliders, and he told the writers that the shoulder wasn't a problem except now and then. Maybe the pain would keep him from opening up in his delivery. But he was less upbeat with me after they'd gone off toward their deadlines. He was taking Darvocet for the pain, and sleep was still a big problem. He'd just remembered what his teammate Bobby Ojeda had told him late in 1988—the year Bobby O. finished by almost cutting off the top of a finger on his pitching hand with a hedge clipper: "Kid, the year is going to come when you're going to have to take it up the ass every day out there. Don't forget I said so." We managed a laugh.

I hated what was happening. Seeing performers struggle through an injury is a commonplace in the sport, of course, but being forced to watch a damaged player endure repeated humiliation is barbarous. Back again, this time in Toronto, David gave up seven runs over three and two-thirds innings, with a lone strikeout. He looked helpless. There wasn't a vestige of a fastball, and the Toronto batters simply fouled off his breaking stuff until they'd worked out a hit or a walk. Only five pitches were swung at and missed.

There was nothing left of the season now, no space in which to turn something around, and comments from people in the Yankee family had begun to take on a valedictory tinge. Third-base coach Willie Randolph said, "He reminds me of Catfish Hunter near the end of his career. David used to throw harder once, the way Catfish did when he was with the A's, but he's always been a guy who knew how to challenge you when he had to. A consummate pitcher."

General manager Brian Cashman said, "He's been carrying us for a long time and maybe it's time for us to pick up a bit of the slack. He's been a big piece here. Maybe because of his experiences in the strike, he has a unique ability to see things from the management point of view—we've consulted him before some of our trades. He's something special."

And George Steinbrenner: "This will be the deal I'll never regret in my life. Everything about him is tremendous. David Cone is a leader, and whatever he does in life is going to be successful because he knows the price—he'll give you every ounce he has." The Boss was in sneakers and bright-blue satin warmups. Soon he was talking about one of his racehorses, Granting, who was running in an upcoming stakes event.

The people closest to David could no longer summon up a bright side. "You could see he had nothing," Posada told me after the Toronto game. "There was zero up here"—he gestured across his shoulders. "He knew it but he didn't say anything in the dugout."

Mel Stottlemyre wasn't around—he'd gone to Sloan-Kettering for stem-cell transplants, the toughest part of his regimen—but Billy Connors, the pitching coach pro tem, knew David, too. "He's opening up," he told me. "He can't help it, with that front shoulder. When you do that there's nothing left and you try to make up for it with your arm." He shook his head.

Cone would be going to the bullpen, Torre told us. He and David had talked casually and candidly. "He was as easy on me as he could be," Joe put it. David wasn't himself, he said. The shoulder grabbed him in certain situations—it wasn't anything he could defend against. It was sad, because his starts just before the dislocation had been so strong—he'd been striking guys out.

"There's never been an easy decision about him, given what he means in a game and to the team, and to me," Torre continued. "He's got such an enormous heart. Gibby"—Bob Gibson—"and some others had that competitive fire but it's hard to burn hotter than David."

Doc Gooden started against the Tigers at the Stadium on the final Monday and was gone in less than three, down by 5–1. Cone walked in from the bullpen at the top of the next inning, making his first relief appearance in eight years, and got a nice hello from the fans. They understood the awkwardness here. Almost predictably, there came a bad umpire's call—a walk instead of a strikeout—then a double to left, poorly played by Justice, and in the next inning a single, a broken-bat single, a double, a walk, and some boos at last as Joe came out to get him. Five hits, four runs, three walks (one intentional) in an inning and a third. No one in the pressbox had anything to say.

In the standup, very late that night—the Tigers had won by 15–4—Cone was asked if it wasn't almost cruel to be expected to go on pitching this way, with so little to call upon and so many people there as witnesses to another bad performance. "Everyone is always watching," he said, his hands in his pockets. And, "It didn't go well tonight, I wasn't good enough." He was soon gone.

Everyone is always watching. Yes, but why was I still watching? I had that argument with myself many times. Friends of mine and people at my office and some of the beat writers, surely (though they didn't say so), believed that the book was done for by now, pushed aside by Cone's hard season and his age and the way he was pitching. This tent should be folded, out of respect. Cone must have felt this, too, at times, but he would never say it. There was so little of his pride and skill left out on the mound that a waiting, persistent sideline watcher and interviewer must have felt like a paparazzo. His situation was torture, and almost worse because it was to some degree predictable: this was what happened to old pitchers. Even if he didn't agree with that verdict, the unspoken rules required him to walk back out there every five days and take what came. My book was nothing compared to his reputation and his record, of course, but he'd see it through, too, at whatever cost.

One night in Baltimore, where I'd come for the last weekend of the regular season, he and I sat at a table in the lobby bar of the Yankees' hotel, the Marriott Inner Harbor. It was a tawdry scene. An island of tables had been roped off for the players in one corner of the smoky room, and the drinking, ogling fans—

men and women in their thirties, most of them, in Yankee re-
galia—clustered close by, a bare six or eight feet away.

"This is a zoo," I said to Cone.

"It's a petting zoo," he came back. He wasn't smiling.

Chris Turner, sitting with a beer across from us, asked about
the book, and David said, "It isn't the book that was planned.
That was going to be a different kind of sports book—technical
things about what pitchers do and how they take care of themselves, and who owns the pitcher's arm. But it changed."

I was startled by his tone but said nothing. I didn't want to
say that his struggles this year had slowly made that book irrel-
evant: you couldn't devote many chapters to techniques that had
stopped working. His defeats and his stubborn energy and
courage had become the story—a reversal that neither of us had
imagined. We had never quite negotiated this shift, but the new
plot had become engrossing and it swept us along.

I could never come to an easy answer to these uncertainties,
but I wanted this resolved somehow—a better ending, not for
the book but for him. And if aging and disappointment were as
much a part of the story for a great athlete as the repeated glo-
ries of his peak years—a more human and elucidating part, at
that—then this last lurch of events, with his injury and near-
helplessness, couldn't be left out, either.

Tom Boswell, the Washington *Post* columnist, asked whether
it had occurred to me that Cone's crash in Kansas City and semi-
disablement afterward might not have been psychologically predictable. He meant that some part of David's makeup could have
spurred him into a sudden high-risk play in an ordinary game—
a dive after a trifling infield out—at a moment when it was not
yet certain that his return to form could be sustained. An injury
would take him off the hook, so to speak, if the comeback had
to be aborted. I'd have been as good as ever, he could tell himself, if only—

I rejected the notion—I don't think the unconscious is that
cynical or that good an athlete—and in its place propose simply
that older and younger players get injured every day, but the

damage goes deeper when you're thirty-seven, with collateral wounds that include the popular instant assumption that the end of a career must be at hand.

David had one more start, after all—his last in a Yankee uniform, it would turn out—in an insignificant Saturday-afternoon game at Camden Yards. The Yanks had clinched the night before. Torre had already given him the news he'd been anxiously awaiting: he would be on the twenty-five-man post-season roster but only in the bullpen. When I heard from Torre that Cone had made the cut, I said, "Well, I'm relieved."

"So am I," Joe said.

No game is trifling to Cone, but here again he could produce nothing: eight hits and six runs in four innings plus, with home runs by Cal Ripken and Brady Anderson. His season was over. Since his accident on September 5th, he'd pitched in four games and lost three, with twenty-eight hits, twenty-three runs (all earned), twelve bases on balls, and two home runs: an earned-run average of 14.11. His final pitching line, the one that went into the books, was 4–14, with an earned-run average of 6.91.

When the year-end statistics were published, Cone's name appeared only in the "Longest losing streak" category, where his eight straight was shared with Jason Johnson, of the Orioles. On the 2000 lists, Pedro Martinez's 18–6 and 1.74 again led all comers—and brought his second consecutive Cy Young Award. Roger Clemens's 13–8 and 3.70 placed him a distant second in the league, while Cone's old sidekick David Wells wound up at 20–8 for the Blue Jays—one of four twenty-game winners in all of baseball this year.

There had been four strikeouts for David in the Orioles game, with the last one, a called K on the catcher Brook Fordyce, coming on a sidearm fastball. For some reason, I mentioned it when Cone and I sat down together in the half-empty visitors' clubhouse at Camden Yards. "Not a bad pitch," he said. We had no idea, but it would become his last strikeout for the Yankees.

He looked tired and sad—or perhaps just relieved. He said

he'd been taking oil of cortisone for the pain in his shoulder, along with the Darvocet—not a good regimen for your disposition. The sleep problem was no better. Down in Tampa, where the Yankees had just been, he'd been up each morning when the sun rose. He got dressed and went on down to the ballpark for his therapy—the first player there.

"It beats you down, trying to pitch through an injury," he said now. "I've done it so much the past few years. I need to catch some rest."

But not quite yet. "Playoff games are so different," he murmured in the next breath. "There's such a premium on outs. One game can really change everything."

Whenever things were at a low ebb with Cone, I tried to get in some time with Lynn, looking for a lift. Here in September— David was down in Tampa with the team, a couple of days before Baltimore—I'd found her at their house in Greenwich, Connecticut, in a gated community called Conyers Farm. They were living in a tiny apartment over the garage—a couple of rooms. Max was there, the sleepy old shih tzu, and Lynn and I were alone for a couple of hours—alone except for twenty-odd electricians and wood panellers and plasterers and kitchen-fixture workmen and stonemasons and landscape gardeners who were remodelling the house. This had been going on all year, under Lynn's supervision, and wouldn't be done until well into the next. The house is a large gray fieldstone affair with English Tudor touches and towers, set on a handsome wooded hillside above Converse Lake. Not a big house, Lynn said, and if she meant Manderley-big or Shaquille-big I might agree. Or perhaps it looked huge because it rose so magisterially above its tilted green hillside. Most of the front, or lakeside, face of the house had been opened for Lynn's redesign, and she walked me confidently through a succession of plasterboarded, plywood-floor spaces—a family room, a couple of bars, a billiard room, a smoking room, a library, a wine cellar, four or five bedrooms and baths, two children's rooms with a shared overhead loft, a

sizable upstairs guest area, and a main living room with an indoor stonework pool and spa at its center, opening onto the sky
and nearby woods. Most of these were built to the Cones' own
design, and made cozier and more sensible use of what had
been a sprawl of lofty, cathedral-style spaces. Outside, there
were flagstone paths and walkways, and terraces with handsome limestone walls: a setting for a wedding or a movie shoot.

Lynn once said that when David retired it would be up to her
to bring in a seven-figure income, and if I'd doubted her I took it
back now. She was a talented professional mansion-redesigner,
working in a luxury real-estate market, here in Greenwich, that
was international in its clientele and price levels. David had
spoken of her work with admiration, adding that once in a while
he'd had to say, "Lynn, are we going to have lunch or talk about
doorknobs?" I'd seen photographs of the Cones' first house in
Greenwich, which they'd built for close to four million dollars
and flipped for close to seven. This more ambitious place had
been bought in 1998 for $5.1 million, and in April they had re-
ceived an offer for more than eleven. Every single thing in the
first house—furniture, rugs, bedding, kitchen stuff, paintings,
raincoats—had been included in the sale, and later on this afternoon Lynn would be driving over to New Jersey to look at fab-
rics and wall coverings, the first decorating purchases for this
new place, which would be sold, too, in due course. For now it
was home.

Cone has made stacks of money—more than sixty-six million dollars in baseball salaries and bonuses alone—and while
it's fair to guess that his net worth is not far from that level, this
Greenwich house was the first real suggestion for me of the size
of his fortune. He and Lynn have high-performance leased cars
at their disposal—the Porsche Carrera, a BMW 740-I sedan, and
an Audi A/8—but because the two are always informal and low
key I'd never had the impression that they took undue pride in
their wealth. Their sense of privacy is equally impressive. I'd
spent many hours with them over the course of this summer,
talking about complicated and sometimes intimate things, but

there was never an assumption between us of palship, or a slip into the compulsive modern confessional mode. I didn't meet their friends. Late one night, inside the Stadium press gate, Lynn did introduce me to three or four people who'd gone to the game with her and were waiting now for David to emerge; we talked a bit, and after I'd taken my leave I wondered what Lynn was doing with these young people, couples barely in their thirties. Then I remembered: Oh, yes, the Cones are young, too. They're just starting.

David and Lynn also had the house in Tampa and a small rented apartment in New York. A larger one in the same building in the East Fifties had been let go after they moved to Greenwich, and in April they'd got a place in Tribeca. But their new duplex apartment there had had to be vacated in May, just at the time of David's first pitching troubles, after a major leak from the roof destroyed some closets and left a mold infection in the walls and ceilings. They'd moved back to the smaller East Side place, which had been intended only as a pied-à-terre for Ed and Joan and other visiting family.

Charity work is always mentioned the minute a ballplayer's latest contract level becomes known but all I knew about David's causes—the David Cone Kids Clinic, the David Cone Charity Softball Tournament, and the rest—was that children's care was a recurring theme for him. He was also a contributor to the New York chapter of the ALS Association, where he had worked seriously enough within groups and boards to become close to doctors and patients, and to understand some of the conflicting directions and strategies in the pressing biomedical research. Perhaps a philanthropist's brains matter as much as his heart. Mel Stottlemyre said that David had stayed intensely informed about leukemia because he'd known about his son Jason, who'd died of the disease. There is a member of my own family who suffers from ALS—Lou Gehrig's disease—but it wasn't until I'd spent some months with David this year that I discovered that he was knowledgeable about it. He was close to Chris Pendergast, a Long Island teacher and iconic ALS fundraiser who suffers from the condition himself. Some years ago, David had made friends with a five-year-old leukemia patient named Michael Jacobs at Sloan-Kettering Institute, and after the boy went into remission the two established an E-mail friendship that continues to this day. Talking with me once about visits he'd made to juvenile cancer victims, David said, "It's usually the parents who are most in need of help."

He and Lynn have helped raise capital to break ground for the new Maria Fareri Children's Hospital at the Westchester Medical Center—a state-of-the-art juvenile hospital for long-term-care patients. The project was conceived about three years ago, after a friend of theirs, a developer, lost a child to rabies. Marianne McGettigan, the labor lawyer, told me that David was the kind of person who never mentioned his charity work, and, more to the point, who seemed entirely at home when with the most seriously stricken patients. She suffers from multiple sclerosis, and as she observed, "You get to notice stuff like that."

Sitting on a low limestone wall with me beside the Palazzo Cone, Lynn said, "David and Paul O'Neill can't let themselves leave this team. It's never been easy for them carrying that responsibility, and with David it's turning into burnout. Ever since he came to the Yankees I've heard him say, 'It's up to me to talk to the media. It's up to me to lead by example.'"

What the burden meant to him had come out in August, when Roger Clemens signed that huge contract, Lynn went on. "That week I heard him say, 'I'm going to pass the torch. Let Roger deal with it all,'" she said. "It was pride with him, not the money. He sensed something had changed but he'd felt all along that the responsibility for the club was on him. For five years now—ever since the game in Seattle when he walked in the tying run—it's been like that. It's been pitching and pain and finding some way to get through. He loves to reinvent himself but the price is much too high sometimes."

She said that David's health was a real concern now. He'd given up the Zyban—the dreams were unbearable—and his cigarette cough bent him double in the mornings. He'd been told he had an incipient ulcer, from stress and maybe the painkillers. "He'll never say how much pain he's in," she said. "All I hear is 'I wish I could shut myself down.' But he'd never do that. Athletes take themselves for granted. He's on the same regimen he's followed since he was thirty."

Lynn has the habit of referring to David as "my husband" in conversation, and I ventured to ask what she called him when they were together.

"What do I *call* him?" she said.

"Yes, when it's just you two."

" 'Dave,' 'Honey,' 'Schmuck'—it depends."

When I asked the main question, what was ahead for them now—next year and after that—she said David had no idea. He'd see what the Yankees said—he'd be a free agent in a few weeks—and if he ended up pitching somewhere else, she'd go there, too. "We live by his schedule," she said, "but there's a balance between us. He doesn't control my comings and goings—he's very relaxed that way. He chose to have a strong wife."

Lynn looked more calm than strong, facing me as we sat on the wall, with her arms folded around her middle. She is small-boned, with large, deep-brown eyes, and she speaks in low, unironic tones. She is relentlessly matter-of-fact.

"What about the baby thing?" I asked now, using a phrase of hers. She and David had agreed to put off having children until the end of his career—she didn't want to find herself raising kids by herself, as so many baseball wives did, with their husbands forever going on the road.

"It's getting to that time," she said. "Family life after baseball is going to be good for David. All he has to do is look at George Brett."

Brett, David's old avatar and nighttime companion on the Royals, had married at the age of thirty-eight, astounding barkeepers and party pals across Middle America, and had produced three sons in close to record time. As it happened, I spoke to him by phone only a week or so after this visit with Lynn, and when I passed her compliment along to him he said, "David is going to get a different idea about things. I was in Home Depot for two and a half hours this morning, getting stuff for something my guys want to build. Halloween is coming up, and they're up to their ears in sports."

But there was another question ahead for David, Lynn said now—one that she couldn't answer for him. "His greatest fear is that he'll never find something to replace what pitching has meant for him," she said. "This is on his mind all the time. It never goes away. He wants to wait awhile before he decides on his next work. He's in no hurry. He amazes me. He can do nothing—sit watching CNN all day or lose himself on the Net. I'm in awe of his freedom with the computer and his thirst for knowledge. If he only wanted to manage our money for us I wouldn't doubt his competence. He's good at things. Or he could go into politics."

I was almost startled. Back in April, I'd heard the same idea mentioned by an old colleague and admirer of David's, Dr. Allan Lans, who is the team psychiatrist with the Mets. Lans, without suggesting that David had ever been in treatment with him, said that Cone had the capacity to win instant respect. "There's a loving-kindness to him that you don't often find in sports," he'd said. "He has bigger fish to fry than the Players Association. I see him as a representative of some sort, with a career in politics ahead."

Lynn told me she'd brought this up with David from time to time, but he recoiled and said, "What—with my past?" But he knew better. "He's independent and reliable, and he has charisma," she said. "He draws people in and he always knows what to say. It's a real gift. A friend of ours says we're the First Couple. We're Hillary and Bill."

18

Late Wars

I'd been watching Joe Torre gearing up for the post-season tournaments for weeks now, but I never got the impression that carrying an injured and demoted 4–14 pitcher on his twenty-five-man roster was a difficult decision for him. Anti-sentimentalists can put the move down to sentiment—Torre and Cone go back a long way together—and anti-royalists will mutter that only the Yankees, with their supporting cast of expensive, well-experienced starting and relieving and closing specialists, can afford to be kindly or strategic in this particular way. Few other teams, for that matter, would have stuck with a pitcher in Cone's straits. As he remarked, if you took his games away from the Yankees' total and put a .500 pitcher in his place they'd have finished at their old mid-nineties games-won level. But Torre took the risk. One way or another, he wanted Cone there at the end.

Torre's weighty and balanced résumé and his smoothness in shifting from the now to the then, to tomorrow and back again in his conversations among writers and players, with references to his own emotions and ideas thrown in along the way, tends to diminish speculation about his motives. He will speculate right along with you, I mean. Players read his media-interview stories to get news about the club, and he claims to pick up information about his players from the writers and their questions. He doesn't hide much, himself least of all, which adds an aura of compliment and continuity to his work.

There is also the thrown-in pleasure of anecdote. One evening Joe was talking about the waning days of the 1967 season, when he came up to the plate against the Cincinnati Reds in the doldrums, desperate for a hit that might push his extremely ordinary .279 average up to .280. The Reds' catcher took pity on Torre and said he'd tell him each pitch he'd be calling, in advance—fastball, curveball, whatever. No use: Torre went oh-for-four and wound up the year at .277.

Almost in the same breath, he took us back to an earlier season's wind-down, in the early sixties, when the Milwaukee Braves (as they still were then) would face the Giants over the final weekend. Joe, a young Braves catcher, was going over their lineup with his pitcher, Lew Burdette, when they came to the slugging Orlando Cepeda, who had held a perennial hot hand against Burdette, wearing him out with line drives and shots off the wall. "The hell with it," Burdette announced now. "Let's tip him every pitch in advance and see how he likes that. It can't be worse than what he's been doing."

Torre took him at his word. "This is your big day," he announced to Cepeda as he stepped in. "First pitch is a slider—you gotta trust me." And he put down his fingers for the slider. On the next pitch the declared fastball arrived as promised, and so on. "Here's a wet one, Cha-Cha. Bottom's going to fall out but you're ready, man. I wouldn't lie to you." On he went—full disclosure with each pitch. Cepeda, one need hardly say, was helpless against Burdette that afternoon and by the third or fourth at-bat was pleading for mercy. "No, Joe—don't tell me. Shut up, I don't want to know!" When it was over Burdette said, "Damn, we should have pitched him this way all along."

The Cone-Torre bond, with that fabled mound confab in Game Three of the 1996 World Series, has already been set forth. "In my five years here, that's the best decision I ever made," Torre says. "Cone is the easiest guy in the world to manage and the toughest to read, because he always expects to do well. He makes the commitment."

But a different Cone-Torre connection can be plugged in, if we go back one more year, to the end of the 1995 American League divisional series, when David delivers the last of his hundred and forty-seven pitches against the Mariners in Game Five—that scarifying ball four to Doug Strange, which forces in the tying run and sets up the series-ending Seattle win in the eleventh inning. The Yankees are gone and, with them, their manager, Buck Showalter, who was allowed to walk when the season ended. Torre was hired in his place. But what if Cone strikes out Strange and the Yankees win? We'll never know, but at the very least Showalter stays—he would not be cut loose even if the Yankees lost the league championships. Taking his team to the second stage in October saves his job.

This puts us straight into "Back to the Future" land. With no Joe Torre, do the Yankees still become four-time World Champions over the next five years? Does Buck allow David to stay in and pitch to McGriff? Does Leyritz get to bat? Does Paul O'Neill flower and El Duque emigrate? *Quien sabe.* Joe Torre, managing the Red Sox now, almost marries Michael J. Fox's mother as a teen-ager, while David Cone, re-signed by the Mets for a bundle in 1996, beans Bernie Williams in the interleague subway series. . . . No, too much: let's put it all back. But Cone-Torre is *mystical*, man. It had to happen.

The deeper weavings and interconnections on the Yankee team derive not simply from the World Series sweeps and shared trophies and dynastic history but from the run of life experiences and hard news that came along with the good stuff: Frank Torre's heart-replacement surgery in the middle of the '96 post-season, the shocks of Straw, the departures of Chili and Joe Girardi and the Boomer, Joe's prostate-cancer operation last year, and the loss of the fathers of Scott Brosius and Paul O'Neill and Luis Sojo in that same season. Less known, perhaps, are the vanishing of Chuck Knoblauch's father into Alzheimer's, and the sudden death this spring of Cindy Lloyd, the wife of the reliever

Graeme Lloyd, an absentee from the Yankee circle after his trade in 1999 but family for all that. Baseball doesn't always come down to the stats.

The sweet rush of post-season ball, with all those expectant and excited teams—the White Sox and the Mariners, the Braves and the Cardinals, the Mets and the Giants—facing off, day after day, can't quite be fitted into this story, but the fans know what happened, including the instant disappearance of the bemused Braves and sore-armed White Sox, swept in three straight games each. Some other time we could think about Rick Ankiel, the phenomenal Cardinals' rookie left-hander (whom I'd been tracking all the way up from the early minors), who fell victim here to the Mets and to his string of wild post-season pitches—stuff fired breathtakingly into the screen and away outside the foul lines, while manager Tony LaRussa gazed on aghast.

The Yankees, still uncertain about themselves after their free fall into October, managed a split of the first divisional games out on the coast against the Oakland Athletics—a young and exuberantly talented bunch who took their spirit from the thick-armed first baseman Jason Giambi (.333 at the plate this year, with forty-three home runs, a hundred and thirty-seven runs driven in, and an eventual M.V.P.). Home again, the Yanks won behind El Duque's four-hitter, and stood at the brink of the next stage and a rare couple of days off, only to drop the chance in shocking style with an 11–1 Saturday pasting by the A's, who jumped all over Clemens and Gooden. Now the team would have to rush back to the other coast for a deciding game at four o'clock the following afternoon, on the A's' home turf. The Mets, meantime, playing across town on this same Saturday, had staged another of their extra-inning heartwarmers, beating the Giants, 3–2, on Benny Agbayani's thirteenth-inning homer, in a game that had arrived in odd scraps on the press-box screens.

The Yankees had gone belly-up once again, with their old

offensive and pitching weaknesses so evident that this lost chance felt terminal. Clubhouse boys hurried about in the untidy, semi-silent clubhouse, collecting "NY"-emblazoned trip bags, and stay-at-home media types eyed the depressed players, in their expensive shirts and ties, heading out to meet their wives and board the bus for that six-hour trip back to the coast, and made private note of those we might not find in this room again: the haggard Paul O'Neill, Doc Gooden (in his golden necklace), and David Cone.

I'd seen little of him lately. He hadn't returned phone calls, and when I'd approached him, moments earlier, while he got dressed in front of his locker, he murmured a few words and dismissed me in a barking, impatient way.

A postscript came only three nights later, after another blur of games and flights and remade hopes. The Yankees, fed up with themselves, delivered six runs against Gil Heredia in the first inning in Oakland and held on for a 7–5 win, to gain the championship round once again, against the Mariners. The wearisome, critical game against the A's was a managerial coup for Torre, who started Pettitte on three days' rest, then spliced in Stanton and Nelson and even Orlando Hernandez for bits and pieces until he could get to Rivera, with one out in the eighth, for the save. The flight back was better, and David, drinking beer in the back of the plane, shouted, "Let's hear it for Joe! A little noise for the skipper!" As he said later, he'd become the team joker.

Back at the Stadium on Tuesday, the Yankees dropped the first A.L.C.S. game to the Mariners, 2–0, with Neagle losing to the Seattle right-hander Freddy Garcia. Cone was the last to emerge from the shower that night. It was past one in the morning, and except for the yawning clubhouse boys going about their laundry we were the only ones there. He looked wan—he can never sleep on planes—but he wanted to take back our last meeting. "I was still in that game that we'd just lost," he said. "They had me warming up in the bullpen in the ninth, in a game that we're losing 11–1. It was the most embarrassed I've ever been. A year ago, I'm a starter in that game"—he meant the second A.L.C.S. game in 1999, when he'd whipped the Red Sox, 3–2, at Yankee Stadium—"and I couldn't get that out of my head. That's what this season has come down to for me. I'm sorry I took it out on you."

The baseball was running out. The Yankees scored no runs at all against the Mariners in the first sixteen innings of those A.L.C.S. playoffs, then brought home seven in the eighth inning of the second game. Waiting for the Yankees to become the Yankees again was the edgiest fun of the year, with the jammed-in Stadium mobs groaning and sighing and by inches dying as their torpid Pinstripes hit thirty-foot grounders and stranded base runners and got picked off base (well, once), and only at last recalled themselves, down only by 1–0, and got the job done. It was El Duque's somethingth birthday, and after he'd finished off his night's work in the eighth by striking out Alex Rodriguez and Edgar Martinez in succession, Justice, in the bottom half, whanged a double just under the cusp of the left-field wall. While Bernie Williams worked out a lengthy, masters-thesis at-bat against Arthur Rhodes and delivered the tying run with a single, the stands came burstingly alive—"BERN-*EE!* . . . BERN-*EE!* . . . BERN-*EE!*" The familiar cries reverberated and met themselves coming back, while the wavelike exhortations in the bleachers and the thick noise of the scoreboard music and the clapping and jiving of the fans grew into a dark and deeper sound, startling us a little when the seats behind our knees and the floors under our feet and the upper-stand facings seemed to tremble and thrum in time to the din. This had been a while coming, and the home crowd enjoyed an extended release here, with hits from Tino and Jorge, and the needed sacrifice fly ball by O'Neill, and then—goodbye, Arthur Rhodes: c'mon in, Jose Mesa—the hit-and-run deftly done by Sojo, and a Vizcaino double, and the capping two-run homer by, who else, Derek Jeter. As sports entertainment goes, this is an old turn by now, with mostly the same names being floated into the night air by Bob

Sheppard ("now batting for the Yan-kees: Der-ek JEET-uh") and pretty much the same hokey looks and mannerisms up and down the order—Tino's heads-up bright gaze; Knoblauch's flattened bat and twiddling fingers up behind his head; and Paul O'Neill's crazy moth-slashings before he bats—accompanied more or less the same results around the bases and up the alleys, all seconded by the menacing and comical Stadium chorus. There's no measuring how much longer the celebrated act will run or how badly the rest of the country wants it gone, but I don't care. Eat your heart out, America—this is ours. And I'm a Mets fan.

That catch-up evening stays with me, even while I admit that Game Six of this A.L.C.S., back at the Stadium again, was a better event, perhaps a classic, with the lead changing hands and home runs flying about, before the curtain came down at last on the Mariners, 9–7. Lou Piniella, who had cajoled and inspired this excellent Seattle club and would not soon see its like again—not with A-Rod gone, at a king's ransom—offered a touching farewell in the interview room. Smiling and shaking his head, with thoughts of his players still almost visible in his eyes, he said, "And now the Mets fans and the Yankee fans can go spill beer on each other and get raucous with each other, and I can watch it from afar."

Before this, out at Seattle's new Safeco Field, with its locomotives and stage-scenery backdrop, the Yankees had furthered themselves with a pair of essential wins—the second one a full-Roger, fifteen-strikeout effort by Clemens. I didn't mind the Mariners' getting their turn the next day, and I was watching with heavy-lidded eyes when the fifth Yankee pitcher of the evening came on in the bottom of the eighth, with the M's ahead by 6–2, and got them out one, two, three. It was Cone.

I stood up and paced about for the short time he required for the job—thirteen pitches, with two ground-ball outs to second base and a foul fly by Mike Cameron to Brosius. Cone looked matter-of-fact, but I thought I saw a less pained or constricted action from him on the mound, and some down-moving pitches at the other end—a splitter to Raul Ibañez and a swing-and-miss slider to Cameron. He'd reopened his case.

The Yankees went two-up in the World Series after Clemens pitched shutout ball for eight innings in Game Two, giving up two hits and striking out nine, while the Mets, rebounding with two homers and five runs in the top of the ninth, fell just short, 6–5. But forget all that: nothing will survive of this game except Clemens's inability to distinguish between a bat and a ball in the first inning, and a mass failure of the players and the media and fifty-six thousand witnesses to agree on what the hell happened after that. The event itself remains clear—clearly weird. Mike Piazza, up at bat with two out in the first, takes two called strikes and a ball, and then, sawed off by a burning inside pitch, hits a foul to the right but sees the head of his broken-off bat go spinning out toward Clemens. Piazza has lost track of the ball and makes a half-hearted trot for first, still carrying the busted-off handle in his left hand. A few steps up the line he is startled by the same pronged and splintered top of the bat, which helicopters past him on a new trajectory and bounces across the grass toward the Yankee dugout. Clemens finishes his motion—he has thrown the thing, flung it hard in this direction—and he and Piazza stop and stare at each other with something like awe.

In reality, the bat doesn't come close to hitting Piazza, though he makes an instinctive little flinch as it comes by, nor do Piazza and Clemens react much. Run the Zapruder footage back, and you'll see Clemens stoop down, with his glove low and his other hand poised above it, to make a picture-book two-handed grab, right out of the manual, and come up with—the bat. Goggling at what's in his hand, he fires the lumber irritably toward the Yankee dugout or batboys. Only at the last moment does Piazza appear, trotting in from the right-hand edge of the frame, where Clemens spots him in mid-throw and even does a little double-take at the last moment. Who says there's nothing new in baseball?

No exception to these facts can be offered, but the moment

was inflammatory and confusing, touching off emotions that had hung around in the city ever since July and that scary Piazza at-bat at Yankee Stadium, when Clemens hit him on the helmet with a fastball and put him on the ground. Sports TV shows had been rerunning the scene ever since this second Mets-Yanks subway series—the real one, this time—became fact, but the fresh event was beyond hype. You could hear the startled roar of the fans scale down to the staticky, intense-interest hum of fifty thousand people saying "Holy shit!" and "I don't *believe*—" and "Didja see—" over and over. Great theatre.

As with so many New York street encounters, the closer you got to this one the milder the offense became, dwindling off at last into mere bonkerdom. Piazza, approaching Roger, asked what his problem was, and Clemens responded with the gnomic "I thought it was the ball." Players and coaches swarmed to the field, without much fire except for the Mets' bench coach John Stearns, whom Torre described as wanting to "choke everybody."

Interviewed later, Piazza said, "I was taken aback. It was bizarre." The umpire, Ed Montague, said, "It was an emotional reaction. I didn't think he, Clemens, threw the bat at Piazza. There was no intent." But many of the writers refused to see it this way, and their grilling of Joe Torre about Clemens's motives caused him at last to lose his cool and stalk out of the press conference. He came right back, but the fire wouldn't go out of this. Torre had expressed unhappiness about the repeated showings of the beaning, earlier in the week, and the argument grew harsh when Joe wouldn't agree now that throwing a bat was part of Roger's arsenal.

The interview room felt jittery and worn down that night. Some of the columnists and beat writers here hadn't been home for weeks. Meeting deadlines at the final pennant-race games, filing their late stuff from the divisional games and then the championship eliminations, often flying coast to coast and back again in a short span of days, they had convened for the World Series opener, the game before this one, which became an ogre—a twelve-inning, 4–3 win for the Yankees, played out over four hours and fifty-one minutes and ending at 1:04 A.M. It was the longest Series game ever. Pete Hamill, a member of the *News*' Series platoon, said that the toiling journalists crammed haunch to haunch in the low-ceilinged Stadium press room that night reminded him of haggard, white-bearded lifers cast away in the bowels of Dumas's Chateau d'If.

Clemens's dangerous bat sling, it seemed to me, showed not evil intention but only a suddenly opened little window into the dark convolutions of a starter's cortex. No pitcher prepares as fervently and ritualistically as he does, and I've noticed more than once that his post-game summaries lean toward the incomprehensible, since they refer almost mystically to the intention of each pitch and the ideas that launched it, rather than to what happened afterward, out where we could see it. The batty bat throw was no different, and when the Rocket took his place before us his first effort was to convey a state of mind. He'd been extremely emotional, and after the events of the first inning had to leave the dugout and sit alone in a room for six or seven minutes, trying to refocus. "I really, really had to calm down," he said. "I mean, I was just extremely fired up."

His problems centered on having to pitch to Piazza once again, after what had happened months ago, but without hitting him, without doing the unimaginable. "It's bad enough when you're out there and you know you want to pitch him in, but you know you can't afford to miss up and in," he said. With this burning in his mind, a sudden ground bat in front of him was startling but he knew what to do with it. "It was just a reaction all of a sudden," he said. "I thought it might have been the ball at that time, I was so locked in."

Locked in is the right Roger trope. Counting this outing and his previous shutout against the Mariners in Game Four of the American League championships, he'd given up three hits and no runs over seventeen innings, with twenty-four strikeouts. Perhaps inevitably, he was fined fifty thousand dollars by the commissioner's office, later that week, for "inappropriate behavior," but this gesture may have been more for our benefit than his. I was tired in the interview room, too, and nearly ready to join the popular view about Clemens, in spite of all. It's easier to conclude that the Rocketman is nutzoid and dangerous than to start getting into his head. Forget his problems. What the hell, he's making fifteen million a year: let him watch his step a little out there.

Moments after the Yankees had eliminated the Mariners from the championship series and gained passage into their third straight World Series and thirty-seventh over all, Joe Torre came up to Cone in the midst of the on-the-field celebrations at the Stadium and said, "I may have a nice little surprise for you next week."

Cone might just start a Series game, he meant—it would be Game Four, at Shea Stadium. Andy Pettitte would go in the opener and then Clemens and El Duque, and if those games went reasonably well Torre would be in no hurry to bring Andy back on short rest, in spite of the scheduled off day between parks. He'd watched Cone for that one inning in Seattle, and re- alized that he was throwing with more freedom at last and that the shoulder injury might have run its course. David had also been surprised when he warmed up that night, but then it came to him that six weeks had gone by since the crash in Kansas City—the earliest period predicted by the doctors when he could look for signs of a recovery.

Torre gave the news to the writers about Cone's possible start, and David told them that this was what he'd been waiting for—a little shot at redemption, something to take the edge off his horrible season. His tone was subdued—events up the line are never assured—but you could see the excitement in him. He'd tried to stay upbeat before this, pointing out to everyone that his E.R.A. had gone from 6.91 to 0.00 the instant the regular season ended, but no one could envision a role for him. Now the media revelled in the ironies and overtones: Cone's six bygone seasons with the Mets, his miserable 2000 record as against his five lifetime Series starts, with two wins and a 2.15 E.R.A. He'd be going back to Shea, the showplace of his early brilliance and celebrity, and doing so, moreover, in the middle of a Subway Series. He hadn't played in a game there in eight years.

Torre had another option, however, which was to appoint his fourth starter, Denny Neagle, for the job. He was a left-hander, which didn't match up well against the Mets' righty-tinged batting order, but he'd started twice against the Mariners in the A.L.C.S., pitching well in the opener and hesitantly the next time. Both Yankee losses in that series were his. There the matter hung for a couple of days, while the Series took its vivid course, with the Yanks capturing the opener on a twelfth-inning Vizcaino single, and the second amid the distraction and brilliance of Clemens's hectic evening.

Torre couldn't make up his mind, and eventually David decided for him. When Joe called both pitchers into his office on Monday—the off day—he told them he'd been leaning toward Cone because of his major-game cool and experience, but he was concerned about how many innings he'd be good for, given his injury and limited service over the past weeks. Cone, out in the corridor a few minutes later, said, "If it helps you make up your mind I have no trouble getting loose, and I could probably pitch two days in a row out of the bullpen."

And so it came to pass. "That did help me in determining Neagle," Joe said. He'd thanked Cone, and David told the press that he was grateful to be of use in any form, considering his season.

I didn't catch up with him that day or the next, and maybe it was just as well. I wanted to shake his hand—and to throttle him, too. That hadn't been an empty gesture of his—it was entirely like him—but he was overdue for a break. Why didn't he ask for the spot? But I knew the answer. Torre, it had become clear, didn't care for Denny Neagle, who had pitched so well on his arrival in July but so haltingly and cautiously thereafter. His record had been at 8–2 when he came over from the Reds, but he'd become a lesser pitcher in the Bronx, with a 7–7 record and

a 5.81 E.R.A. A potential multi-year contract with the Yankees
had been postponed—he'd be a free agent at the end of the season. Neagle acutely didn't want to lose, and pitched that way at
times. Joe hated a nibbler—you could see it on his face during
the hitters' lengthy at-bats against Neagle. Denny could use a
chance, here in his last days with the club, and in Cone's long
view it might as well come from him.

Afterward, he told me how much he'd wanted that start, and
quietly amplified on this to his old friend Jack O'Connell, the
Hartford *Courant* national writer. He'd have loved the chance,
he said. He almost wished Torre had decided the matter on his
own, instead of leaving it up to him. That was the way things
went sometimes.

My Series seat at Shea was in left field, in an auxiliary pressbox at the mezzanine level adjoining the left-field foul pole,
where overflow writers and columnists were stacked (I am an
overflow writer)—or, on another day, in a box seat one level up,
by the outer rim of the loges. I know this faraway perch from
previous seasons, and have come to appreciate its sweeping
views of the slovenly, appealing old garden, with the pennants
and airliners just overhead, the left fielder's cap and shoulders
directly below, and its pleasing, surveyor's-eye view of doubles
or homers, when the ball takes off from the minuscule environs
of the plate and grows in size and vigor as it rapidly approaches,
eating the air from right to left. A good place, this time, to take
in the rival-fan faces and affiliations and noise apparatuses. The
Mets-folks were fiercer though more apprehensive than one
would expect (a pair of whistle-tweeting, thirtyish sisters
nearby had clung together in wild anxiety through one of the divisional games, against the Cards), and the Yankee-types less
raucous. The decibel level at the Subway Series was a fraction
down, to my ear, which I attributed to higher ticket prices—a
hundred and sixty dollars a pop, even out there—and a toned-up
clientele. But then the whole lid over Queens ripped loose in the
eighth inning on Tuesday night, when Benny Agbayani's tie-

breaking double off El Duque went all the way to the wall below, and the Mets, with a 4–2 decision, put an end to the Yanks' string of fourteen straight World Series wins.

The Mets played this Series with confidence and zing, and even while I smiled and exclaimed to myself over their extreme willingness I sensed a psychic overmatch. Their young out-fielders—Timo Perez, Jay Payton, and Benny Agbayani—began to look younger and smaller as Paul O'Neill and Bernie Williams and David Justice succeeded them out there, inning after inning. And if pitching experience counted, comparisons became cruel. Among the Mets, only Dennis Cook and Al Leiter had appeared in a World Series before this one, compiling twenty-one and a third innings' worth between them, while the ten Yankee pitchers had fifty games among them, with a hundred and thirty-nine Series innings pitched, a cumulative 9–3 won-lost mark, and a 2.53 E.R.A. Or else you could just put down Rivera's numbers: one run given up in ten Series games, for 0.61. Call the cops.

This is the stuff that makes Yankee-haters flush and sway— and no doubt accounted for the lowest Series TV ratings ever— but what one thinks of the Yankees' performance this time challenges many assumptions about sports, I think. The Yankee old-timers who came through once again—O'Neill (who batted .474) and Martinez and Brosius—had looked creaky and joyless in the summer but not here, while Jeter, who is a veteran, too, had saved his best of the year for this little run of games and his deserved M.V.P. Not everyone draws pleasure from this. One columnist, a thoughtful weekly journalist, gave way to an epochal snit when the Series was over, writing that these Yan-kees left one with a cold shudder. With a little luck, the games could have gone the other way, he insisted, and he urged fans to hope that the old Yankees would be kept together for another season as their skills continue to erode. This year, he con-cluded, had been the one when "new heroes could and should have been cast."

Sports renew us because they're about youth and the

thrilling things the species is capable of at its early best. But I believe that its other face has to do with a harder, more complicated side of our experience. Nellie King, a former pitcher and broadcaster with the Pirates, once said to me, "Being good up here is so tough—people have no idea. It gets much worse when you have to repeat it: 'We know you're great. Now go and do that again for me.'" If these words didn't come into my mind during this World Series, it was because they'd been there all summer long.

Derek Jeter smashed a homer on the first pitch of Game Four, against the Mets' Bobby J. Jones, with the ball burying itself in the bleachers just to the east of me. In the bottom half Mike Piazza missed another dinger, directly overhead, when his shot passed above the left-field pole, barely foul, with a thousand nearby umps craning and complaining. I was in my pressbox seat this time and not in a position to make my own call, but Piazza's next shot, in the third, was both far and fair, and brought the Mets to within a run, at 3–2.

Neagle, pitching well enough, had two outs and no one aboard in the fifth when Piazza's turn came up again, and during a pause or stir in the proceedings I saw Joe Torre slowly emerge from the Yankee dugout and head toward the mound. Understanding flooded over me. In a flurry, I gathered up my printed game notes and notebook, my scorecard, binoculars, and shoulder bag, and departed the premises like a commuter dashing for the 8:18. I was on the same level as the main pressbox but a considerable curving distance away, and when I got there, gasping, David Cone was digging at the mound just below me, in preparation for his warmup tosses. A sector of New York writers in the third row burst into laughter at the sight of me, and managed a small hand.

Torre had said that David would come in after Neagle, if needed, but Joe's move took everyone by surprise. Cone said later that he hadn't expected to be summoned in mid-inning this way. I'd been watching for him, but the Yankee bullpen was tucked away beneath my auxiliary pressbox, with its occupants out of sight. Whatever Cone or anyone felt now, the surprise was small, an atom, compared to Neagle's. Ahead in the game and with no one aboard, he was one out away from the full five innings that could qualify him in the scorebook as an official World Series winner. With less than five he was expunged. Staring, he'd handed the ball to Torre and made a swift exit. His father and brother, seated in a family section, got up at the same moment and walked out on the game.

Torre's reasoning came down to one word: Piazza. Mike had already delivered the two Mets runs of the game with his homer into the bleachers, and had poked that farther, higher blow in the first—the shot that went foul above the pole. He had Neagle, a lefty, within his sights, but Joe wasn't going to let him squeeze off another round.

The moment was over quickly. Cone, pitching from the stretch—he'd wanted to keep himself in check, he said later—threw Piazza a fastball inside for a ball, a fastball away for a called strike, two sliders away, for a strike and a foul, and came back inside with another fastball that he popped up weakly to Luis Sojo at second. Cone went back to the dugout expecting more work, but when Brosius singled with two out in the top of the sixth Torre was obliged to dispatch a pinch-hitter, Jose Canseco, in the pitcher's slot in the batting order. Canseco struck out. The Yankees won the game (Jeff Nelson, the next Yankee pitcher, got the decision) and, the next day, in a thrilling, exalting game that matched Andy Pettitte against the indomitable and emotional Al Leiter, won the Series and their third straight World Championship. The end came on a little Sojo single, rolled up the middle in the ninth and dived for simultaneously by the shortstop Abbott and second baseman Alfonzo, who went flat in the same despairing moment, like sheaves cut down, as the ball went through.

Cone, walking onto the scene the night before, had noticed Piazza notice him and then look back at his teammates in the Mets' dugout in surprise at the move. Yes, it was a big out, David

told the writers in the interview room—a huge out. He appreciated it, pitching at Shea again after all these years. He'd listened
for the fans' reaction as he'd come in from the pen—"a pretty
firm boo." He joined in the laughter.

He didn't say that as soon as he was officially out of the game
he'd gone into the Yankees clubhouse, looking for Neagle, and
found him in the tunnel—a retreat near the visiting manager's
office there. Denny was raging. David agreed that coming out of
the game that way was tough to take and said he was sorry he'd
been the one to deprive him of his win. But it was time to get a
grip, he said. The media would be around in no time. It wouldn't
do for him to let fly with his rage or to show up Torre. It wasn't
professional. Neagle listened and began to cool off.

Cone went back in the bullpen the next day but wasn't
needed. His work for the Yankees was done.

We'd spoken briefly at Shea, after he pitched, but I only saw
him in the distance at the champagne baths the next night. He
had his new champions cap on, pushed back on his head, and
was heading off to look for Joan and Ed. We didn't talk again for
a week or more, after the parties and the parade. He called me—
he sounded different, so relieved and youthful that for a moment I wasn't sure who it was on the phone—and we had a long,
easy talk.

He said he'd wanted to tip me off on the news about that possible start in the Series in Game Four the moment he'd heard
it—give it to me as a little exclusive—but then Joe surprised him
by telling the media so quickly. He was sorry about that. I told
him it was O.K.—and how did he feel about the Yankees' championship?

"A tremendous relief," he said. "At least nobody can blame
me anymore."

He knew that Piazza at-bat, that lone out, wasn't quite the
late redemption or turn of fortune that his friends had been pre-
dicting for him. Stuart Hershon had been saying for weeks that
something large and fated would turn up. I had scripted a more
particular miracle, which would bring him on in the tenth or

eleventh or twelfth inning of the seventh game, to strike out Piazza, swinging, for the save.

"Not quite," he said, "but it wasn't all that insignificant. It helps in my mind a little."

He'd been looking back at his season and breaking it down. "I spent so much time at the beginning just trying to find myself," he said. "There was all the experimenting, and the rushing to catch up. I never had any pain and I kept reaching out for something I could almost touch. After that I had some bad games and some bad luck. I began to feel out of it. After I was called down to Tampa I pitched better, but the accident changed things. It was pain and consequences after that."

He wasn't complaining, but he'd fallen into the reviewing, rewinding form that I knew so well. "Plus there was something else," I said. "Times when you were heroic. I know—I was there."

"No, I'm too realistic for that," he said. "I'm a super-realist. Sometimes I think I was almost a better player back when I wasn't thinking. You know what the old scouts say—the dumbest players are the best."

He and Lynn were about to go away on vacation, down in Puerto Rico. He'd call me when they got back. "Sure," I said. "Or else you won't." We laughed, and without a connection he said that for the last day or so he'd found himself thinking about when these Yankees first got into the post-season, in 1995—the year he'd joined them in midsummer. They hadn't been going anywhere but suddenly there was that crazy dash through September. They'd qualified as the wild-card team just before the end, and got to play against the Mariners in the divisional play-off. David didn't say it, but I knew he'd gone 3–0 in his last three starts, with one of the big wins coming on three days' rest.

"It was a crazy ride," he said now, over the telephone. "That was the year after the strike and people were slow coming back to baseball, but not here in the city. The Yankees hadn't won in a long time, and the crowds at the Stadium before our first game there were the most excited we'd ever seen. When Donnie Mattingly ran out onto the field to stretch his legs before game time they made a noise I'd not heard before."

David had started that game and won it, but not before Junior Griffey had taken him deep, twice. And this was the same series that would be lost not long after he'd thrown ball four to Doug Strange.

"The beginning was the best," he went on. "I was late driving to the Stadium that day and I realized as I got closer that all the fans were getting there early. Two hours before the game and here they were, coming from everywhere. I'm driving my Range Rover, and when I come off that bridge from the F.D.R. Drive and make the turn onto the Deegan everybody is making the same move. They're with me and they begin to recognize me and blow their horns around me. They're waving and laughing and I'm waving back, and it's like we're in a parade together, heading for the game."

19

Extra Innings

David and Lynn came home to Tampa in November, where he could work out with Tony Ferreira, while he and Steve Fehr consulted by telephone about the coming season. The news was disappointing at first. The recrowned champion Yankees struck quickly at the winter meetings in Dallas, signing the free-agent starter Mike Mussina to a six-year $88.5-million contract. With the Orioles, Mussina had averaged almost fifteen wins per season over a decade, and his addition to the deepest pitching treasury in either league meant that the club didn't have to pursue a power hitter like Manny Ramirez, who went to the Red Sox, or worry unduly about the Texas Rangers, who'd won the Alex Rodriguez star wars with a contract worth $252 million over the next ten years. It included a zinger clause stipulating that he would be paid a million dollars above whatever sum his good friend and rival shortstop Derek Jeter, or anyone else, for that matter, might have contracted for by the ninth and tenth years.

The Yankees spoke with Steve Fehr of a possible slot for Cone as the fifth pitcher in the rotation, for a guaranteed five hundred thousand dollars, plus unspecified incentives for games started. There was never a clear offer from them, and when David and Steve tried to move toward something firmer there was little response. When Cone gave up on the non-deal, it wasn't because of the money—although a chance for him to earn another million or so if he pitched well would have made the Yankees' confidence more apparent.

Being the fifth pitcher on a starting staff that ran through Mussina, Clemens, Pettitte, and El Duque would have kept David at home but not always at work, since rainouts and off days would always spin the rotation back to the man who'd pitched four days ago. And if the Yankees made it into the post-season he would find himself in the bullpen once again. Pride came into this as well. Becoming a supernumerary in the Yankee clubhouse—shifting to a mere character actor—would be a hard role to play in his old surroundings. He and Steve conferred, and although no other offers were pending, he announced his departure from the Bronx on December 7th, the last day, under the rules, when a settlement would have been permitted.

He was bidding farewell after six years, with sixty-four wins and forty losses and a 3.91 earned-run-average record in the regular season, plus a 6–1 and 3.86 mark in the post-season, and four World Series rings. As much as anyone, he had set the tone for this remarkable club. "It was just a marvellous run," he said. "Nobody can take away from those years, regardless of what happens to me from here on out. I want to go somewhere where I'm needed, and there isn't a great need for me with the Yankees."

The Mets, who had lost their ferocious left-hander Mike Hampton to free agency (he signed with the Rockies, for eight years and $123 million), tried to reload by signing the veteran starters Kevin Appier and Steve Trachsel. Mets G.M. Steve Phillips expressed no more than cautious interest in Cone, and the moment passed. Al Leiter and John Franco called David in Florida to tell him he was still wanted at Shea, but he wasn't in a pleading mood. There was a feeling that someone higher up, maybe Fred Wilpon, didn't want his old star back.

Part of me was dismayed that Cone hadn't accepted a minimal Yankee tender. He'd asked for my opinion, but I hesitated to suggest that a lesser role might not be a bad idea for him, here near the end of an illustrious career. He still needed sixteen victories to get to the two-hundred-win plateau, but never mind. A moderately favorable W-L line and better E.R.A. for the 2001 season would prove enough about what had happened this horrible summer. He was a better pitcher than that—what more could he want? . . . But I was crazy. He had to contend, of course. He lived off that. He wanted to be himself—out in a hard place where another win or another inning could take this team closer to the post-season. As Jim Bouton said of him in an Op-Ed piece in the *Times*, you couldn't expect Spartacus to move along to gardening.

David didn't say much about his divorce from the Yankees (as he put it) over the next weeks, when awaited inquiries from the Giants or the Cardinals or the Athletics failed to materialize. It was a little humbling, he told me, and from day to day I could hear him talking himself into different settings and situations, while a few teams began to creep across the radar screen. The weather in Texas would be great for his arm, while the damp and cold out by the Bay (where the Athletics had backed off) wasn't good for him. The Rangers persisted—but the born-again tone of that clubhouse would be awkward for him, wouldn't it? What if he just went up to Montreal—a great city, a place he and Lynn really enjoyed—and played for the Expos? He could be a kid again, just playing for the fun of it. And Boston had been interested—how would that be, pitching for the Yankees' hated old rivals—but they'd cooled now, it seemed.

Meantime, he and Tony were long-throwing almost every day. They'd found a little diamond they could use near Tony's house. David wasn't ready to move to a mound yet, but his power was coming back. They were taping with a video camera, and interesting things about his motion were showing up. He felt great. He was riding a bike and skipping rope, and his legs were in better shape. Christmas brought a call from Joe Torre, who said that getting him into the World Series that way had been the greatest emotional moment he could remember. David was touched but thought Joe was probably glad he wouldn't have to walk through that particular fire once again.

It was his birthday, January 2nd, when he and I talked again. "Thirty-eight is old for a pitcher," he said. "Maybe I should retire and become a young man again." He said this without conviction and we let it pass. Doug Melvin, the Texas G.M., had seen him throw late in December—"come to kick the tires," as David put it. Meantime, George Brett had been calling from the Royals: he could have a job with his old club if he'd convert to a closer.

It came down to the Rangers, who'd offered a nearly firm million, with incentives for about four million more (Alex Rodriguez had been urging the club to grab him), and—suddenly again—Boston. Red Sox manager Jimy Williams and his pitching coach, Joe Kerrigan, turned up to watch David throw with Tony, and then stayed for a long talk. Kerrigan had made charts of Cone's pitching patterns this past year, and he'd noted the decay of his motion. He had been shocked that he'd tried to come back after the fall in Kansas City. He thought Cone could do much better. And when Williams and Kerrigan talked with him by phone, a few days later, they said they had a slot in mind for him in the Boston rotation, right after Pedro Martinez.

The job wasn't guaranteed—he would have to make the club in spring training—but David told me that he counted on Williams now. He'd stand behind him when the time came. On January 11th, Boston general manager Dan Duquette improved the deal. Cone would get a pittance for reporting but a guaranteed two million, with half of it in deferred payments, if he made the Opening Day roster. Incentive clauses could add another two million, for games started and innings pitched, and there was a further million-dollar payday if he was named the Comeback Player of the Year for 2001. Steve was uneasy about the indefinite status of things, with his client having to pitch himself into a job, but David's tone grew more excited and boyish from day to day as the Cone story once again turned toward melodrama. Carol took the call when the phone rang around supper-time that Thursday, and when I heard her cry, "David, that's just great!" I jumped up in the next room and yelled, too.

The news about Cone pitching for the Red Sox in 2001 got a big play in the New York media, of course. Most of the accounts were regretful and admiring in tone, but some writers and fans were upset with David for shifting over to the enemy, so to speak. A story in the *Post* called him a Benedict Arnold, and I could imagine David filing this away in his head as he started to get ready for the coming year. He'd found his edge once again. Nothing surprised me by now. I should have expected this out-come ever since July, when Cone had had that vivid dream in which he was pitching for the Red Sox at Fenway Park, with the Green Monster sitting just over his shoulder. And more recently, in December, Lynn told me that she'd had a dream in which David was pitching in a small park, with a lot of media watching. He was wearing a dark-colored warmup jacket with red letters on the back. Fate, not Fehr, had taken a hand, and when I real-ized that with the new league schedules in effect Cone could be back at Yankee Stadium ten times this summer, plus playoffs, I nodded in understanding. Thanks, Bud.

When Jimy Williams and Joe Kerrigan came south to look David over for the Red Sox, before he signed aboard, they watched him throw in the Ferreiras' leaf-strewn back yard in Clearwater—the same place where I'd seen him and Tony and Terry Leach tossing the old pill around, a year before. Who was writing this stuff? Not me.

20

Red Sox Nation

The celebrations of Cal Ripken Day in Baltimore on the last night of the 2001 season were fervent. The pale-eyed icon, retiring after twenty-one seasons, which had included that 2632-consecutive-games wonder, 3,184 lifetime base hits, and nineteen consecutive All-Star Game appearances, waved to the fans from a slowly circling convertible, out beyond where Camden Yards groundskeepers had mowed his No. 8 into the outfield grass. There were gifts and tears and "whereas"es. The mayor of Baltimore proclaimed him an Oriole for all seasons. Bill Clinton said he loved Cal, and Cal said he loved the fans. When the Orioles first ran out onto the field to begin the game, first baseman Jeff Conine tossed the infield warmup ball toward Ripken, as usual, but this time threw it over by the stands—over Cal's head, so that he had to run it down in short left field. When he turned around, there was no sign of his teammates. A different batch of Orioles—the lineup from August 12, 1981, his very first start in the majors—had magically appeared from the third-base dugout: Rick Dempsey behind the plate, Eddie Murray at first, Rich Dauer at second, and Gary Roenicke, Al Bumbry, and Ken Singleton heading toward their positions around the outfield. And here came Earl Weaver, tiny and snowy-haired, walking up to the home-plate ump with his lineup card. Sensation. The middle-aged O's were in their ancient uniforms, and wore caps displaying that long-gone grinning-bird logo. There were empty places at shortstop, where the late Mark Belanger had held forth, and at third, where Cal played back then.

Not a dry eye in the joint—except perhaps those of the visiting Red Sox' pitcher, David Cone, who had been waiting in the dugout all this time for the real, non-phantom baseball to get under way. "Those ceremonials were entirely deserved, but they went on forever," he said later. "I had a game to pitch." He'd been looking forward to the honor, in fact, and had given serious thought to his role on the festive day. Should he come at Cal with his full repertoire, or with token, batting-practice stuff in honor of the occasion? "It was a big responsibility to pitch to him in that situation," he said.

The action began at last, and Cone gave up an unearned run to the O's in the first inning, after a throwing error by the catcher, Joe Oliver. When Ripken stepped in, in the second, he slammed a whistling low drive to left that Troy O'Leary pulled in at the wall. Cal popped to short his next time up, and then, tipping his cap as he stepped in amid a final grand ovation, flied out to center in the eighth. All the pitches David threw him were fastballs. "I didn't want him to look bad, and I had too much respect for him to hand him anything easy, just for the crowd," he told me later. "We understood each other."

The odd situation reminded me once again why I liked to hang around David Cone. He never excused himself from a game or a serious performance. He had pitched much better this year, and had made himself a central figure in the Red Sox' run at a pennant or a playoff slot—an effort that ended with an August decline and then a gross free fall in the season's final weeks. For a club that had made a specialty of late-season disaster, this was the worst curtain yet. The game at hand, the Ripken farewell, meant nothing—the defending-champion Yankees had long since clinched their American League East Division, while the Sox were clinging to second place, trailing by a dozen games. The Orioles, for their part, had barely escaped the cellar occupied by the egregious Tampa Bay Devil Rays, and now wished only to avoid embarrassment for their retiring grandee. But David Cone, as his fans and teammates expected, pitched with intensity—pitched as if it were Game Three again, back in Atlanta. He stayed on for eight innings, striking out seven Orioles and shutting them down with three hits and no runs after that early unearned counter. The Red Sox won it, 5–1. "This was my best stuff of the year," Cone said afterward.

The win brought his pitching line for the year to 9–7, with a 4.31 earned-run average. The Sox had won fifteen games out of his twenty-five starts, including a heartening midseason streak of twelve straight without a loss. David had struck out a hundred and fifteen batters in a hundred and thirty-five and two-thirds innings pitched, and seventeen times held the opposing team to three runs or less. He was back.

Cone's season was slighted in the next day's stories, which centered on the Ripken farewell, but his teammates and his manager, Joe Kerrigan, who had replaced Jimy Williams at the helm, back in August, knew what he'd meant to the Red Sox this year—and not just on the mound. "He's class," Kerrigan had told the Boston writers two weeks before. "Just the way he treats other people—the players, staff members. I don't know if you can put it in wins and losses. He tries to create a good atmosphere in the clubhouse. He puts out small fires before they become large fires. He talks to everybody, not just the pitchers. He talks to young pitchers, older pitchers, young players, veteran players."

It wasn't the first time the new manager had singled out Cone in this fashion. Five days earlier, after another ugly Sox effort had left Cone on the short end against the Devil Rays, despite a measly two earned runs surrendered, Kerrigan said, "We really want him to finish on a good note, after all he's done for us this year. It's important for us to get him ten wins. That would be a hell of an achievement."

A teammate, the first-baseman Brian Daubach, said, "He's the kind of guy, from Day One, was in the dugout from the first pitch to the last, trying to pump us up. Nowadays you don't see that much. Hopefully, he'll come back here next year and be even more valuable. He loves playing in a town like this, where there is this kind of passion. I hope he comes back."

The general manager, Dan Duquette, had already approached Cone to ask about his plans for next year, but David was noncommittal. He was bitterly disappointed by the way the Sox season turned out; he felt the team's disintegration was the most depressing experience of his baseball career—even worse than the 1992 Mets. My conversations with him about the turnabout in his pitching always seemed to circle back to the story of these dismal 2001 Sox, because Cone was unwilling to detach himself from their fortunes. "What happened with me this year is very gratifying," he conceded one day. "I felt strong and I was able to stay in games longer than I had, and I'm glad I could help the club that way. I had great support at times, and the good luck to pitch in games that went the right way for us. But we didn't succeed, and I didn't achieve what I'd set out to do, which was to help us get into the post-season and play some big games at Fenway Park in October. It's a big letdown for us all."

"Achieve" is a constant in the Cone vocabulary, and overachieving is what the Sox did, often in astounding fashion, in the early going. The club appeared to thrive on bad news, including the sidelining of its vibrant shortstop, Nomar Garciaparra, a two-time defending batting champion, who had required wrist surgery. In June, Pedro Martinez, the best pitcher in baseball was lost to an inflamed right shoulder—or, just possibly, to the "Curse of the Bambino," that tedious local legend about the Sox' extensive failures to nail down a World Championship since 1918, when they last did it, after which the club's owner, Harry Frazee, sold Babe Ruth, then a star pitcher for the Bostons, to the Yankees, because, it was said, he needed cash as a backer of Broadway musicals. In May, Pedro, mouthing off a bit after beating the Yanks, 3–0, had laughingly offered, "I don't believe in damn curses. Wake up the damn Bambino and have me face him.

Maybe I'll drill him in the ass." As every New England grandmother, tavernkeeper, and six-year-old came to know, Pedro
didn't win a game for the rest of the distance, though he pitched
briefly in late August and September after a two-month hiatus
but without the accolade of another win. Doctors found that he
was suffering from a partial rotator-cuff tear—a darker fate than
any curse—and at last agreed to have him sit down.

Early on (to go back to the beginning, in mid-April) the
Bosox had grabbed the lead in their division, and they stayed up
there for the better part of three months, a bit above the cusp of
first place in the division or a bit below it, but never ahead by
more than four games. Manny Ramirez, the electrifying new
free-agent slugger, was leading the league in homers and
adulation, while the Sox sent a succession of stubborn elder non-
Pedros to the mound on his days off—the knuckleballer Tim
Wakefield, the tempo artist Frank Castillo, and the erstwhile
Dodger (and Met and Brewer and Tiger) strikeout machine Hideo
Nomo, who threw a no-hitter in his first start of the year. Cone,
who suffered an inflammation of his pitching shoulder in spring
training, missed the early stages of this grand revival while un-
dergoing extended shoulder rehabilitation at the Sox' camp in
Fort Myers.

By the time he arrived back north, in mid-May, the Sox were
the only story in town. Ramirez had shocked the Yankees' un-
beatable Mariano Rivera one day at Fenway with a killing tenth-
inning single up the middle. Hideo Nomo took another no-hit
skein into the seventh inning, in a winning effort against the
Twins. Carl Everett hit two grand slams in the same week.
Ramirez and three other Sox hitters mashed two-run homers in a
blowout against the tough Seattle Mariners. Catcher Jason
Varitek went four for four, with three home runs, in a game at
Kansas City. Back home, Manny crushed a fifth-inning four-
hundred-and-sixty-eight-foot homer over the Green Monster and
out by the Mass Pike, against the Athletics. Late the next day,
Varitek hit a walk-off dinger that curved around the right-field
foul pole in the eleventh inning. And so on.

Sox fans, hardened to spring hopes and crushing early failure—the Boston media habitually give up on the team during its ritual June fainting fit—were over the moon this time. The other local obsessions, the Bruins and the Celtics, had lately fallen from their accustomed heights, and Sox fever ran unchecked. "YANKEES SUCK" in blue block letters blossomed on T-shirts sported by Red Sox Nation kids and parents up and down the Fenway bleachers, and you heard the same message chanted there with impartial bliss during games against the Yanks and the Orioles and the Twins. Manny Ramirez was wearing the uniform pants of the fattest player on the squad, reliever Rich (El Guapo) Garces, for style's sake. Manny was living at the Ritz Carlton for a thousand dollars a day, and an urban legend had him joining a fashionable Ritz wedding when he was spotted in the lobby. Eddie Andelman, the ageless sports voice on Boston's station WEEI, announced a "Yankee Elimination" party on his show, and the call-ins went wild. The Sox had spent a hundred and ten million dollars on salaries this time, the second-highest total (second only to the Yankees) in baseball. The Red Sox had Nomar—he'd be back: just wait and see—and Pedro and now Manny. The Sox had to win.

"I'd never seen anything like it," Cone said to me from Boston. "I was used to a lot of noise in the stands at the Stadium, but the intensity of hopes at Fenway and all over the city was something new. It was thrilling and involving. You wanted to be part of it— make a contribution."

It was a different David Cone who turned up at Yankee Stadium on May 23rd, in his second game for the Sox, and took the 7–3 loss in a careful five-inning stint, after giving up a two-run homer to Bernie Williams. The New York writers, watching their old media master with detached affection, found that David was better defined on the mound, clearer in outline, than when they'd last seen him in those stressful few moments in the World Series. There was less anxiety and cogitation to his work now. I attributed the changes to his three months of extended throwing with Tony Ferreira, down in Florida in the off-season. His motion had become minimal, beginning with a modest step-back from the rubber, with his hands in close, and he was throwing more curves than sliders. A couple of his fastballs nipped up into the low nineties. "He's going to win a few for these guys with that kind of stuff," George King murmured to me in the press box.

I'd seen signs of the changeover in March, down in Fort Myers, and heard about it in conversations with the lean and furrowed Joe Kerrigan, still only the pitching coach back then. Cone told me that Kerrigan, a computer apostolic, also served the club as advance scout, once the season got under way, soaking up game tapes from around the league and disseminating them in daily printouts of pitcher proclivities and situational batting scenarios. "Everyone here hears from Joe," he said.

Kerrigan always seemed to be working harder than anyone else at City of Palms Park, and he was sweating in catcher's shinguards when we talked one morning on a back field. "David's step-back had been sort of swaying," he said. "For every action there's a reaction, so he was bending toward first base and then over toward third base before he'd come to the plate. We just tried to clean him up a little."

David had been looking at a video that Kerrigan had prepared for him, which showed him in Yankee pinstripes but framed in the middle of a triptych, with his teammate Bret Saberhagen in action on one side and the Braves' Greg Maddux on the other. The lesson flickered frame by frame through their pitching motions, from step-back to front-leg lift and the collapsing of the back leg. There were head positions to be noted, and arm slots before the release. "We wanted him to decide where he wanted to be," Kerrigan told me. "Now he could see where one guy was staying tall over the rubber, and another maybe breaking down a little. David had been pushing out over his knee, while Maddux and Saberhagen looked to have those hands in closer. If you wanted the best, you'd always go to Maddux."

Kerrigan also knew that Cone hadn't been in top condition the year before. "He admits this himself," he went on. "But with all this throwing he's in great shape now. He's given himself a better chance."

All the throwing may have taken its toll the very next afternoon when David removed himself from a spring game against the Twins before the start of the second inning—and suddenly walked off the field. I was sitting with Joan and Ed Cone once again, and as we slowly rose and prepared to go hear this latest sad news it occurred to me that each of us might have just concluded that we wouldn't go to David's games together anymore—not after this and the crash in Kansas City the previous September.

This time, there was no rush for him to get back into action, and the problem—tendinitis in his troubled pitching shoulder—took a full two months to mend. David had to wait for the soreness to go away, and then submit himself to the entire spring-training procedure all over again, from long-throwing to pitches on flat ground to the first tentative tosses from a mound. The team went north to begin the season, leaving him stranded with the rookies and with his pal Saberhagen, who was continuing his own extensive rehab. "Thank God for Sabes," David said.

I stayed in touch by telephone, and found him bored and subdued. To keep himself busy, he'd devised a routine that began with a morning physical session with a trainer, followed by a drive up Interstate 75 from Fort Myers to Tampa, where he called once again on Dr. Jiang at the little acupuncture salon on Kennedy Boulevard. He'd stay on at his house that night and, next morning, drive the hundred and twenty-five miles back to Fort Myers, and report to City of Palms Park. He executed the massive commute two or three times a week, from late March well on into April, and piled up something on the order of fifteen additional acupuncture sessions along the way. Slowly he felt his arm and shoulder coming back to normal. He and an elder Sox pitching coach at Fort Myers, Herm Starrette, were tinkering with a slightly altered grip on the ball for him. He was mad to get back north. The Sox had begun to play and win, and though manager Jimy Williams said they were holding a slot in the rotation for him, there were no guarantees. Later in the summer, Joe Kerrigan let him know that there had been serious consideration given to letting him go altogether in March, dropping him into the void. Word of his hard regimen and mental toughness kept it from happening, one could guess.

May came at last, and he was permitted two- and three-inning stretches of work, throwing to the Sox rookies in game conditions, and then a four-inning stint in a game against the Rangers' Class A team, at Port Charlotte. He was striking out batters again, and Jimy Williams, watching from Boston, said why not let him come up and do it here. Cone's one-year contract with the Red Sox, which called for a salary of just over two million dollars, had kicked in once the season started, but it felt good to know that he was needed.

There's nothing like winning to make a man feel right at home. Built on modest early increments—Cone was on a pitch count in these days—his string grew in June like a startup bullpen tomato patch. "Limiting my pitches has made me more selective and economical," he told me at one point. "I'm trying to be more aggressive—get in some quick innings for a change. On the other hand, I'm no longer in charge of my own destiny." Usefulness had supplanted brilliance for him, and even when he came out of games in the fifth or sixth or seventh with the score tied or the Sox behind they seemed to rally and win. He was giving up too many homers—a peculiar Boston press note in early July said, "Cone has surrendered home runs in 11 out of his last 10 games"—but without undue damage. Two of his wins snapped three-game Sox losing streaks. "He's been so valuable for us, with Pedro and so many others going down," infielder Lou Merloni said. "He's been exactly what we've needed."

David and Lynn loved Boston. Their suite at the Four Seasons looked out across the swan boats and shaded paths of the Public Gardens toward Beacon Hill. David enjoyed the funky in-

tensity of Fenway's old brick palazzo, to the west, where kid autograph hunters, face down on the pavement on Van Ness
Street, peered under the canvased-off chain-link fence of the
players' parking lot before game time, picking up no more than
an inch or two of the shoes of their arriving heroes or the make
of the tires on their swollen S.U.V.s. "Mr. Ramirez!" they cried,
shoving pens and pennants under the barrier. "Mr. Everett! Mr.
Everett!" David had been finding new friends on the club—
Jason Varitek and Tim Wakefield among them. He and Nomar
Garciaparra had some good talks, and Cone wanted to get closer
to Hideo Nomo—"an honorable guy, almost regal," as he put it.

Inside ancient Fenway Park, the tilting stone floors, stale
beer smells, and dingy lighting sometimes felt like F Deck
aboard the Titanic. So did the steerage-class clubhouse, with its
jammed-together plywood player cubicles, littered food tables,
inadequate furniture, and hovering swarms of media. There was
no player lounge, and Cone discovered that an idle comment to
a teammate headed for the showers could find its way promi-
nently into print the next morning. "Eavesdropping has become
a fine art around here," he said cheerfully. Despite the Sox' successes, the team atmosphere was tainted and edgy, with injuries
beginning to take a toll. A cranky dislike festered among some
of the players—Jose Offerman, Mike Lansing, and Dante
Bichette—directed at their semi-silent manager, Jimy Williams,
who rarely visited the clubhouse, posted late and mystifying
lineups, and responded to press queries with a gnomic and infuriating "Manager's decision." Irritability became a clubhouse refrain—why am I sitting out again; why in hell am I up in the
bullpen so often in no-win games? Manny Ramirez smiled
through it all, with CD earphones clamped on to block the
sounds of bickering, but clubhouse hostility was benign, a heat
rash, when compared with relations between Williams and his
boss, the stiff and cautious Dan Duquette, who had parted ways
so vividly a year ago that it had not been expected that Williams
would be back this year. David, new to all this, was glad that
he'd still been down in Florida on the day of an epochal scandal

out in Oakland, when the ill-tempered and explosive Everett had helped take over a team meeting to scream curses and imprecations at the manager.

"Interesting situation at times" was all that David would volunteer about this to each fresh cadre of visiting-team writers, and then he would point out that the wrangling hadn't seemed to damage the way the Sox were playing. Privately, he expressed concern about the club. "It's an extremely volatile mix, with Jimy as lame duck," he said one day. "We've had all those middle guys who were used to playing every day but are unsure of their roles. Each day you feel that it might spill over and hurt us, and in a way I'm surprised we've hung on for as long as this." I wanted lurid details, but David's loyalty to his teammates and the manager maintained an eloquent silence. Soon we would turn back to the games, and to his revived career.

Inevitably, the team slipped behind the Yankees early in July, but remained close for a time, still in line for a niche in October. When fortune and the interleague schedule brought up the Mets, on July 13th, Cone got his first start at Shea Stadium in nine years, and shut out his old team over five and two-thirds innings. The eventual 3–1 win brought his record to five and one, and lifted the team to within half a game of the first-place Yankees. His six strikeouts included Mike Piazza twice, swinging.

"Tremendously satisfying," he said to the thick cluster of writers afterward. "I expect to get deeper into the games from now on. The best feeling of all is to feel wanted. This is what I've hoped for—to be part of something again."

The next morning, his name was in the New York tabloid again: "CONE STAR" from the *News* and, in the *Post*, "HOUSE OF DAVID."

Grimly, the Sox hung in through July, waiting for their missing icons to get better. It all came apart in mid-August, when the consonantly challenged Jimy Williams was axed, after the team, in slow decline, slipped behind the onrushing Oakland Athletics in the wild-card sideline. His replacement, Kerrigan, was handicapped—in the minds of the media and some of the players—for having never previously managed a game, at any level. What Kerrigan most lacked was luck, arriving as he did in a stretch when each day seemed to bring another blow to the Sox' fortunes. The essential Jason Varitek, a textbook catcher and pitch-caller, broke his elbow while making a diving catch in foul territory. Carl Everett sat out too many games and swung at too many up pitches when he did play. Manny Ramirez fell into a depressing slump, and Garciaparra's return to action was cut short when his wrist blew up again, finishing him for the season. The emotional high-water mark, it turned out, had come in a 4–3 win over the White Sox at the Fens on July 29th, Nomar's first day back, when he tied the game with a homer in the sixth and won it with a single in his next at-bat.

"There was a real breakdown after that," Cone told me. "Our weaknesses began to show up when we didn't get Nomar again. We weren't well balanced. We had good pitching at first but our hitting was mostly just Manny, so we went down when he tailed off. Our defense wasn't so good, and our pen was overexposed. We all knew that Rod Beck was going to have to have the Tommy John surgery in the off-season. Near the end . . . well, you learn surprising things about people when things go bad. I think there's going to be a major turnover next year—maybe as much as a third of the roster."

His talk often reverted to the Saturday night, ten days into the Kerrigan regime, when the Sox ran into an abutment in Texas: a ghastly eighteen-inning, six-hour-and-thirty-five-minute standoff against the Rangers, played in soaking ninety-degree weather, which was lost, 8–7, at two-forty in the morning. Only a bit earlier, the schedule had twice—twice in ten days—forced the club to play a game a continent away from one completed the day before. "That did it for us, along with the nine pitchers we threw into the Texas game," Cone told me. "Those dawn arrivals and screwed-up body clocks hit us just before the biggest stretch of games of the season—the thirteen in a row against the Indians and the Yankees that we'd been looking forward to all year. But we were pretty much in free fall by then, and you know what happened."

The team, down to the Yanks by only four games at the time of the Texas debacle, was six behind when the two met at Fenway Park at the very end of August, for a last-gasp chance at redemption—and the Sox were swept, in vivid fashion. The Yankees, facing the Boston starters Frank Castillo, a damaged Martinez, and then Cone on successive days, were held scoreless though the first seven innings of each game but contrived to win them all: a unique turn of events in the annals. The numbed Red Sox lost thirteen out of fourteen games in here, and any chance at a post-season slot—the chance that had lured David to Boston in the first place—had become a vanished dream.

The season changed for every major-league player when the World Trade Center was attacked on September 11th, but not many of them were as intimately connected to New York as Cone. The Sox were in Tampa that day, and when play was suspended it took the better part of two days for them to get back to Boston. David and Lynn knew people who had been lost in the disaster. Baseball had become distant for David, but at the same time he sensed that it was almost all that he had. In his first two starts after play resumed, he pitched without a win and without luck, surrendering three earned runs over ten innings. Then he was pounded for six runs by the Devil Rays, in a game he came out of in the third inning with a tight shoulder. The Kerrigan regime, meanwhile, was finding grotesque ways to look bad, and the media, of course, were relentless. Up at the Fens, Carl Everett fell into a dispute with Joe during batting practice, and had to be restrained while he screamed obscenities and racial accusations at the manager. He was suspended and didn't return for the rest of the going. Everett would not appear again in a Red Sox uniform—at least there was agreement about that. To Cone, the season felt as if it would never end. Even before the World Trade Center disaster, he'd begun to wonder if the travel and the bottomless schedule weren't getting to him after all these years. Counting the early workouts with Tony, starting back in November, he'd put in ten straight months on the job. With the Ripken game just ahead, he went back to his friendly acupuncturist, Dr. Jiang, one more time, and the visit gave him the lift he needed for another outstanding performance.

When that game was over, very late, David hit bottom. Eight teams, including the Yankees, would begin post-season play within a couple of days, but there was no place for him to go and compete. He and Andrew Levy got into Andrew's car and drove non-stop to New York. When they came out of the Holland Tunnel, at four-thirty in the morning, they had a glimpse of the smoke and harsh lights of the disaster, just downtown. "I'd been away from New York up until then," he told me. "Now at least I was home."

Cone, at this writing, has not decided what he'll be doing next year. "Maybe it's time to stop this and go back to being a young man again," he said to me in October—exactly the same words he'd used a year earlier. When I asked about the two-hundred-wins landmark, still seven games away, he laughed and said, "In my own twisted mind I'm already there." He was adding on his eight post-season wins, he meant. This sounded valedictory, but a moment later he was telling me about a July conversation he'd had with Greg Maddux, who'd reminded him of the joys of National League ball. "It's kind of intriguing," he admitted. "That style of play and the chance to bat and run the bases again." He sounded like himself a year ago.

The season was over now—the Yankees and the Arizona Diamondbacks were locked in an amazing seven-game World Series—but this time when David and I went back to the Red Sox' exalted early hopes and late letdown, he said, "It was worth it—it really was. It was disappointing at the end but pretty fun. It's forgotten by everybody but not by me."

Not by me, either. In my mind, the best part of the regular season was still those three games against the Yankees, up at the

Fens, in the light and fever of late-August and early-September ball. Here were the battered, fabulous Boston loyalists jam-packed into their old green playpen, spraying unspeakable invective at the Yankees' infamous Roger Clemens as he warmed up in the bullpen just in front of the bleachers, and then applauding him, more or less, as he went on to whip them, 3–1, in the opening game, and lift his won-lost totals to 18–1 to that date. The next day, a blowy Saturday afternoon, produced Pedro against El Duque Hernandez, with a nice little rush of K's and mannerisms accumulating in the sunshine. The convalescent Martinez took his leave with a 1–0 lead after six innings, and the Sox unravelment built itself around an eighth-inning fly ball that was lost in the gusting breeze, and Bernie Williams's ninth-inning homer, which reached the first row of seats in center.

With no hope for the season left now—the Sox trailed by eight—the Sunday-night affair offered fans the tangy irony of David Cone versus his Yankee replacement, Mike Mussina, who had signed on with the Bombers for $88.5 million over six years. Mussina had come in with a 13–11 accounting, but a little luck along the way could have found him at Clemens's level; David, for his part, stood at 8–3. But the quality of the two pitchers quickly put such distractions to one side. Cone, twice victimized by infield errors, grimly worked free; by the end of eight innings he had given up but four scattered hits. The game—which would end up 1–0 Yankees, with the losing pitcher more or less in triumph and the winner in near-despair—went straight into the Boston family storybook. Indeed, you could already savor the bitter, flush-faced joy of future Back Bay grandpas and barflies when they came to the good part—the ninth-inning, pinch-hit, two-out, two-strike single to left center for the first and only Red Sox hit of the evening, and the ruination of Mussina's gem: "Sure, they won it, bucko—what did you expect—but oh, my!"

Watching Mussina and Cone pitching in swiftly arriving alternation, I saw that they worked with a similar leaning stillness out there while they took in the catcher's sign and began their little back step. Mussina had such stuff and command this time that he rarely threw the knuckle curve that has been his signature. He was brooding and hunched—a man who wanted no news at all this day and almost got that wish. Nine of his eventual thirteen strikeouts went into the books in the first five innings—he struck out the side in the second—with most of the victims standing immobile as the dismissing ninety-plus fastball or downflared two-seamer flicked by.

Cone's work provided greater entertainment, but he avoided the high counts, bases on balls, and crisis innings that we knew so well. As always, you waited to see his thinking almost more than a pitch's speed or slant—the wisdom of his four pitches just out of the strike zone to Tino Martinez in the fourth, say, before he fanned Posada, to end the inning. The game was going by in a rush, with the accruing edginess of the Mussina no-hitter and possible perfecto matched now by anxiety about Cone's pitch count and potential removal by attrition. Still no score.

Cone, visibly less by now, worked through an eighth inning of lowering troubles, with the speedy Soriano on first after a lead-off single. Knoblauch went down with a fly ball and Jeter on a strikeout; Derek said later that his tottering wave at Cone's sidearmer was the worst swing of his professional career. With Soriano on second now, Bernie Williams stroked a high drive that was pulled in by Trot Nixon a step in front of the center-field wall. The end—the first ending, that is—arrived in the Yankee ninth, when the fill-in Boston second baseman, Merloni, botched a double-play grounder that would have ended the inning. Enrique Wilson's swift double brought home the run at last—the first of the game for either team—and finished David for the day. At least he got the shot, having talked his manager into letting him go back out there and take what came: death by the bullet, not the bullpen.

The building no-hit, nobody-on melodrama by Mussina was buzzed about and gabbled over in the stands all evening, because it was Cone, as we know, who had last turned the trick, two years earlier, on that broiling Yogi Berra Day at the Stadium.

The coincidence added a flare of moral drama to the proceedings, and now, in the bottom of the ninth, Everett's two-out, 1-and-2 single, struck off a third successive high fastball, was greeted by pathetically savage and exulting Fenwayian cries.

Cone came through the strange experience in high spirits. At this late date in the season, his eight shutout innings against the Yankees and lone unearned run surrendered sent a considerable message about his potential value for any number of ambitious clubs next year, if he were to return. When I saw him again a few days later, in New York, it was known that Mussina was still brooding about his terrible luck, and David said he wanted to find a chance to talk to him when the two could be alone, maybe after batting practice at the Stadium.

"I was the loser in that game and I felt such an uplift, while Mike's the winner and ends up depressed." Coney said with a smile. "I was the last one to go through this, so I appreciated what he was feeling, with those thirty thousand camera flashes going off in the stands while he's trying to close things out. You need to feel good about an effort like that, no matter what comes. There's always bad news, but it's nice to be told you were part of what turned out to be the best game of the year."

David Cone:
Lifetime Record

CONE, DAVID   P   RED SOX

PERSONAL: Born January 2, 1963, in Kansas City, Mo. ... 6-1/200. ... Throws right, bats left. ... Full name: David Brian Cone.

HIGH SCHOOL: Rockhurst (Kansas City, Mo.).

TRANSACTIONS/CAREER NOTES: Selected by Kansas City Royals organization in third round of free-agent draft (June 8, 1981). ... On disabled list (April 8, 1983-entire season). ... Traded by Royals with C Chris Jelic to New York Mets for C Ed Hearn, P Rick Anderson and P Mauro Gozzo (March 27, 1987). ... On New York disabled list (May 28-August 14, 1987); included rehabilitation assignment to Tidewater (July 30-August 14). ... Traded by Mets to Toronto Blue Jays for IF Jeff Kent and a player to be named later (August 27, 1992); Mets acquired OF Ryan Thompson to complete deal (September 1, 1992). ... Granted free agency (October 30, 1992). ... Signed by Royals (December 8, 1992). ... Traded by Royals to Blue Jays for P David Sinnes, IF Chris Stynes and IF Tony Medrano (April 6, 1995). ... Traded by Blue Jays to New York Yankees for P Marty Janzen, P Jason Jarvis and P Mike Gordon (July 28, 1995). ... Granted free agency (November 3, 1995). ... Re-signed by Yankees (December 21, 1995). ... On New York disabled list (May 3-September 2, 1996); included rehabilitation assignment to Norwich (August 21-September 1). ... On disabled list (August 18-September 20, 1997). ... Granted free agency (November 5, 1998). ... Re-signed by Yankees (November 11, 1998). ... Granted free agency (November 3, 1999). ... Re-signed by Yankees (December 6, 1999). ... Granted free agency (November 7, 2000). ... Signed by Boston Red Sox (January 11, 2001).

RECORDS: Shares major league record for striking out side on nine pitches (August 30, 1991, seventh inning).

HONORS: Named righthanded pitcher on THE SPORTING NEWS A.L. All-Star team (1994). ... Named A.L. Cy Young Award winner by Baseball Writers' Association of America (1994).

STATISTICAL NOTES: Led Southern League with 27 wild pitches in 1984. ... Pitched 6-0 one-hit, complete-game victory against San Diego (August 29, 1988). ... Tied for N.L. lead with 10 balks in 1988. ... Pitched 1-0 one-hit, complete-game victory against St. Louis (September 20, 1991). ... Struck out 19 batters in one game (October 6, 1991). ... Pitched 4-0 one-hit, complete-game victory against California (May 22, 1994). ... Led A.L. with 229 1/3 innings pitched in 1995. ... Struck out 16 batters in one game (June 23, 1997). ... Tied for A.L. lead with 14 wild pitches in 1997. ... Pitched 6-0 perfect game against Montreal (July 18, 1999).

MISCELLANEOUS: Singled in only appearance as pinch hitter (1990).

Year League	W	L	Pct.	ERA	G	GS	CG	ShO	Sv.	IP	H	R	ER	BB	SO
1981— GC Royals-Blue (GCL)	6	4	.600	2.55	14	12	0	0	0	67	52	24	19	33	45
1982— Charleston, S.C. (S.Atl.)	9	2	.818	2.06	16	16	1	1	0	104⅔	84	38	24	47	87
— Fort Myers (FSL)	7	1	.875	2.12	10	9	6	1	0	72⅓	56	21	17	25	57
1983— Jacksonville (Sou.)							Did not play.								
1984— Memphis (Sou.)	8	12	.400	4.28	29	29	9	1	0	178⅔	162	103	85	114	110
1985— Omaha (A.A.)	9	15	.375	4.65	28	27	5	1	0	158⅔	157	90	82	*93	115
1986— Omaha (A.A.)	8	4	.667	2.79	39	2	2	0	14	71	60	23	22	25	63
— Kansas City (A.L.)	0	0	...	5.56	11	0	0	0	0	22⅔	29	14	14	13	21
1987— New York (N.L.)■	5	6	.455	3.71	21	13	1	0	1	99⅓	87	46	41	44	68
— Tidewater (I.L.)	0	1	.000	5.73	3	3	0	0	0	11	10	8	7	6	7
1988— New York (N.L.)	20	3	*.870	2.22	35	28	8	4	0	231⅓	178	67	57	80	213
1989— New York (N.L.)	14	8	.636	3.52	34	33	7	2	0	219⅔	183	92	86	74	190
1990— New York (N.L.)	14	10	.583	3.23	31	30	6	2	0	211⅔	177	84	76	65	*233
Year League	W	L	Pct.	ERA	G	GS	CG	ShO	Sv.	IP	H	R	ER	BB	SO
1991— New York (N.L.)	14	14	.500	3.29	34	34	5	2	0	232⅓	204	95	85	73	*241
1992— New York (N.L.)	13	7	.650	2.88	27	27	7	*5	0	196⅔	162	75	63	*82	214
— Toronto (A.L.)■	4	3	.571	2.55	8	7	0	0	0	53	39	16	15	29	47
1993— Kansas City (A.L.)■	11	14	.440	3.33	34	34	6	1	0	254	205	102	94	114	191
1994— Kansas City (A.L.)	16	5	.762	2.94	23	23	4	3	0	171⅔	130	60	56	54	132
1995— Toronto (A.L.)■	9	6	.600	3.38	17	17	5	2	0	130⅓	113	53	49	41	102
— New York (A.L.)■	9	2	.818	3.82	13	13	1	0	0	§99	82	42	42	47	89
1996— New York (A.L.)	7	2	.778	2.88	11	11	1	0	0	72	50	25	23	34	71
— Norwich (East.)	0	0	...	0.90	2	2	0	0	0	10	9	3	1	1	13
1997— New York (A.L.)	12	6	.667	2.82	29	29	1	0	0	195	155	67	61	86	222
1998— New York (A.L.)	•20	7	.741	3.55	31	31	3	0	0	207⅔	186	89	82	59	209
1999— New York (A.L.)	12	9	.571	3.44	31	31	1	1	0	193⅓	164	84	74	90	177
2000— New York (A.L.)	4	14	.222	6.91	30	29	0	0	0	155	192	124	119	82	120
2001— Boston (A.L.)	9	7	.563	4.31	25	25	0	0	0	135.2	148	74	65	57	115
Major League totals (16 years)	193	123	.611	3.44	445	415	56	22	1	2880.2	2484	1209	1102	1124	2655

DIVISION SERIES RECORD

RECORDS: Shares A.L. career record for most games started—5.

Year League	W	L	Pct.	ERA	G	GS	CG	ShO	Sv.	IP	H	R	ER	BB	SO
1995— New York (A.L.)	1	0	1.000	4.60	2	2	0	0	0	15 2/3	15	8	8	9	14
1996— New York (A.L.)	0	1	.000	9.00	1	1	0	0	0	6	8	6	6	2	8
1997— New York (A.L.)	0	0	...	16.20	1	1	0	0	0	3 1/3	7	6	6	2	2
1998— New York (A.L.)	1	0	1.000	0.00	1	1	0	0	0	5 2/3	2	0	0	1	6
1999— New York (A.L.)								Did not play.							
Division series totals (4 years)	2	1	.667	5.87	5	5	0	0	0	30 2/3	32	20	20	14	30

CHAMPIONSHIP SERIES RECORD

Year League	W	L	Pct.	ERA	G	GS	CG	ShO	Sv.	IP	H	R	ER	BB	SO
1988— New York (N.L.)	1	1	.500	4.50	3	2	1	0	0	12	10	6	6	5	9
1992— Toronto (A.L.)	1	1	.500	3.00	2	2	0	0	0	12	11	7	4	5	9
1996— New York (A.L.)	0	0	...	3.00	1	1	0	0	0	6	5	2	2	5	5
1998— New York (A.L.)	1	0	1.000	4.15	2	2	0	0	0	13	12	6	6	6	13
1999— New York (A.L.)	1	0	1.000	2.57	1	1	0	0	0	7	7	2	2	3	9
2000— New York (A.L.)	0	0	...	0.00	1	0	0	0	0	1	0	0	0	0	0
Champ. series totals (6 years)	4	2	.667	3.53	10	8	1	0	0	51	45	23	20	24	45

WORLD SERIES RECORD

NOTES: Member of World Series championship team (1992, 1996, 1998, 1999 and 2000).

Year League	W	L	Pct.	ERA	G	GS	CG	ShO	Sv.	IP	H	R	ER	BB	SO
1992— Toronto (A.L.)	0	0	...	3.48	2	2	0	0	0	10 1/3	9	5	4	8	8
1996— New York (A.L.)	1	0	1.000	1.50	1	1	0	0	0	6	4	1	1	4	3
1998— New York (A.L.)	0	0	...	3.00	1	1	0	0	0	6	2	3	2	3	4
1999— New York (A.L.)	1	0	1.000	0.00	1	1	0	0	0	7	1	0	0	5	4
2000— New York (A.L.)	0	0	...	0.00	1	0	0	0	0	1/3	0	0	0	0	0
World Series totals (5 years)	2	0	1.000	2.12	6	5	0	0	0	29 2/3	16	9	7	20	19

ALL-STAR GAME RECORD

Year League	W	L	Pct.	ERA	GS	CG	ShO	Sv.	IP	H	R	ER	BB	SO
1988— National	0	0	...	0.00	0	0	0	0	1	0	0	0	0	1
1992— National	0	0	...	0.00	0	0	0	0	1	0	0	0	0	1
1994— American	0	0	...	13.50	0	0	0	0	2	4	3	3	0	3
1997— American	0	0	...	0.00	0	0	0	0	1	0	0	0	2	0
1999— American	0	0	...	4.50	0	0	0	0	2	4	1	1	1	3
All-Star Game totals (5 years)	0	0	...	5.14	0	0	0	0	7	8	4	4	3	8

Courtesy Boston Red Sox.

Acknowledgments

My first thanks go to David Cone, who expected another sort of baseball book and unflinchingly stayed with this one when it became something different. Lynn Cone was perceptive and generous and endlessly patient. Ed Cone and Chris Cone were friendly guides to Kansas City and to Cone family history, and Joan and Christal Cone patient with an uninvited visitor into their lives.

This book could not have been written without the encouragement and counsel of two remarkable editors: David Remnick, of *The New Yorker*, and Rick Wolff, of Warner Books. My thanks go to David McCormick, who first thought I should write it, and to Amanda Urban, who saw to it that I did.

I am grateful to an old friend, manager Joe Torre, and to his pitching coaches Mel Stottlemyre and Billy Connors, and bench coach Don Zimmer, and no less so to general manager Brian Cashman and the 2000 World Champion New York Yankees. I owe especial thanks to team physician Dr. Stuart Hershon. Media-relations director Rick Cerrone was unfailingly helpful, as were Arthur Richman, Jason Zillo, and Monica Yurman.

Steven Fehr was a source of balanced judgment and essential detail, and I gained wisdom and a flood of copy from talks with Tim McCarver, Donald Fehr, Keith Hernandez, Joe McIlvaine, George Brett, Father Chris Pinné S.J., Jill Cleveland Sweazy, Andrew Levy, Joe Girardi, Ron Darling, Jack Etkin, Marianne McGettigan, Steve Doherty, and Dr. Allan Lans, among many others.

The New York baseball writers and columnists extended their trust and friendship in equal parts, but I express particular gratitude to Buster Olney and George King for willingly shared ideas and expertise. Among many others I send thanks to Murray Chass, Jack Curry, Jack O'Connell, Marty Noble, Joe Donnelly, Bob Klapisch, Ira Berkow, and Tom Boswell, and to Jim Kaat, Bobby Murcer, Michael Kay, Jon Sterling, and Suzyn Waldman. Mets media director Jay Horwitz was swift and helpful, as usual, and Phyllis Merhige and Pat Courtney, of Major League Baseball, went out of their way to extend favors.

Ann Goldstein is an irreplaceable friend and copy editor. Bill Vourvoulias and Ben McGrath were cheerful and tenacious in researching and checking. Mistakes in this book are my fault, not theirs. I also counted on Lauren Porcaro, Lauren MacIntyre, Flora Prescott, Jeffrey Frank, Gerald Marzorati, and Aaron Retica for their enthusiasm and baseball smarts.

Members of my family—most of all my wife, Carol, a demanding and essential first reader—know how much I owe to them for their encouragement this past year, and have volunteered their feelings about their good fortune in passing days and weeks in the company of a writer who never groaned or sighed or complained or cursed over the task at hand.

—R.A.